MASTER THE

2002

AP*
ENGLISH LANGUAGE
& COMPOSITION

TEST

TEACHER-TESTED STRATEGIES AND

TECHNIQUES FOR SCORING HIGH

ARCO
★
THOMSON LEARNING ™

Australia • Canada • Mexico • Singapore • Spain • United Kingdom • United States

An ARCO Book

ARCO is a registered trademark of Thomson Learning, Inc., and is used herein under license by Peterson's.

About Peterson's

Founded in 1966, Peterson's, a division of Thomson Learning, is the nation's largest and most respected provider of lifelong learning resources, both in print and online. The Education Supersite[SM] at www.petersons.com—the Internet's most heavily traveled education resource—has searchable databases and interactive tools for contacting U.S.-accredited institutions and programs. In addition, Peterson's delivers unmatched financial aid resources and test-preparation tools. Peterson's serves more than 100 million education consumers annually.

Peterson's is a division of Thomson Learning, one of the world's largest providers of lifelong learning. Thomson Learning serves the needs of individuals, learning institutions, and corporations with products and services for both traditional and distributed learning. Headquartered in Stamford, Connecticut, with offices worldwide, Thomson Learning is a division of The Thomson Corporation (www.thomson.com), one of the world's leading e-information and solutions companies in the business, professional, and education marketplaces. For more information, visit www.thomsonlearning.com.

For more information, contact Peterson's, 2000 Lenox Drive, Lawrenceville, NJ 08648; 800-338-3282; or find us on the World Wide Web at: www.petersons.com/about

ISSN: International Standard Serial Number information available upon request.
ISBN: 0-7689-0739-X

Printed in the United States of America

10 9 8 7 6 5 4 3 2 1   03 02

CONTENTS

ACKNOWLEDGMENTS

My deepest thanks to all the people who helped me with this book.

To F.L. for her unflagging support of this project and great help in seeing it to completion. Her professionalism and consideration combined to make this mammoth undertaking so much easier.

My thanks to Stephanie Hammett, who spoke to me first about revising my original AP book. Thank you, Stephanie. I hope we get a chance to work together.

Several gifted and unselfish teachers tested questions for me and guided their students to write and contribute papers. In addition, several curriculum supervisors and administrators provided support for this project. These generous and accomplished people include the following:

- Dr. Sue Kelly, English Chairperson, New Hyde Park Memorial High School
- Richard Rozakis, Assistant Principal, New Hyde Park Memorial School
- Dennis Biagi, English teacher, New Hyde Park Memorial School
- Kathleen Devine, English teacher, New Hyde Park Memorial School
- Mike Lomonico, English teacher, Farmingdale High School

And to all the generous, talented, and hard-working AP students who contributed their papers. These wonderful young scholars include the following:

Alexis Acevedo	Nicole Fulgieri	Lindsay Martin	Lindsay Sarne
Alyson Bernstein	Meredith Gran	Christine Maulion	Staci Scianablo
Merry Benner	Jessica Hacker	Alex Morales	Heather Schultz
Oleg Bitman	Kimberley Harris	Michael Nathan	Lindsay Stern
Christina Caruso	Jack Hall	Laura Orgill	Michelle Stern
Claire Casaccio	Jennifer Heller	Heather Ozgerian	Laura Suarez
Sibi Chacko	Daisy Ho	Sevan Ozcentenkaya	Matt Smith
Rita Chang	Christia Ignatiadis	Kristine Peterson	Princy Thottathil
Susan Choinski	Jonathan Kadishon	Michelle Piwowarski	Robert Trasolini
Stephen Cipot	Kenneth Ko	Karina Petoe	Helen Yeung
Kevin Cordova	Ray Kuhn	Paul Rachita	Jane Youn
Melissa Costa	Karen Kwok	Jason Rostoker	Danielle Young
Ashley Dunne	Gina Lewis	Charles Rozakis	Lisa Weickert
Brian Eilbott	Adam Lowenstein	Sammi Rozakis	Rashmi Varma
Will Fellini	Scott Lustig	Katie Rhindress	
Megan Fortunato	Ashley Klein	Vanessa Rudeman	
William Frischeisen	Ryan Mannix	Lauren Sakowich	

WORKS CITED

Overview of the AP Test in English Language and Composition

WHAT IS THE ADVANCED PLACEMENT PROGRAM?

Advanced Placement (AP) is a program of college-level courses and examinations that allows high school students to earn advanced placement and/or college credit. The Advanced Placement program is administered by the College Entrance Examination Board, a division of the Educational Testing Service (ETS).

Aside from the obvious pleasure inherent in studying more challenging material, earning advanced placement in college lets you skip work you've already done in high school and, perhaps, even participate in an internship or study abroad. You may be able to graduate from college earlier, enter graduate school sooner, or begin a career more quickly. Because of AP credit, you may also be able to take additional courses and explore areas of interest that would not otherwise fit into a busy school program.

Advanced Placement courses also represent a very significant savings in college tuition. Tuition for a full year's course can be as much as $2,500. If you save a semester's work in a private college, you can save as much as $18,000 (including tuition, fees, and room and board) at current prices. However, no college is obligated to accept your AP credit—no matter what score you earn.

The program has grown tremendously since its inception. In May 1998, more than one million students took an AP exam. These students represent more than 3,500 secondary schools; credit is accepted by more than 2,000 colleges and universities. More than 100,000 examinations a year are taken in English alone.

Currently, AP courses and exams are given in 33 different subjects, including art, biology, calculus, chemistry, Chinese, computer science,

ROAD MAP

- *What is the Advanced Placement Program?*
- *The Two Types of Advanced Placement Exams in English*
- *The Format of the AP English Language and Composition Exam*
- *Overview of the Scoring System*
- *The Multiple-Choice Questions: Should You Guess?*
- *Preparing to Take the Examination*
- *FAQS: Sure-Fire Test-Taking Strategies for Success*

economics, English literature, English language, environmental science, French, German, history (European, United States, and World), Latin, music theory, physics, psychology, Spanish, statistics, and U.S. government and politics.

THE TWO TYPES OF ADVANCED PLACEMENT EXAMS IN ENGLISH

As you read in the previous paragraph, the Advanced Placement program now offers *two* different courses and examinations in English:

- English Language and Composition
- English Literature and Composition

The two different Advanced Placement courses are designed to represent the two types of freshman English generally offered in colleges and universities.

- English *Language* and Composition takes the place of freshman *writing* classes. Take this class and exam if you have attained the reading and writing skills generally expected at the end of the freshman year of college but may not have studied literary analysis. The English Language and Composition class is the newer test. As a result, many colleges may not have set up programs to give credit for this test. *Always* check with the colleges that you would like to attend before you take the class/exam to see if they give credit and, if so, for what grade.

- English *Literature* and Composition takes the place of freshman *literature* classes. Take this class and exam if you have been trained in literary analysis. You will have read recognized literary classics and discussed their symbolism, imagery, figures of speech, and so on. The English Literature and Composition is the traditional test that most colleges are familiar with. However, never assume that credit will be automatic. *Always* check with the colleges that you would like to attend before you take the class/exam to see if they give credit and, if so, for what grade.

Each examination represents a full-year college introductory English course. Either course can substitute for a year's worth of English credit, always depending on the specific policy of the college or university. *Consequently, students may take either examination—but not both.*

Each examination is 3 hours long. One hour is devoted to multiple-choice questions; 2 hours to essays. The multiple-choice questions count as 45 percent of the grade; the essays count as 55 percent of the grade.

CAUTION
Never assume that you will automatically get credit for a good score on an AP exam, even a top score. Always contact the Director of Admissions at the colleges you are considering to ask about specific AP policies. Request this information in writing.

NOTE
Rhetoric is a writer's strategic and effective use of language.

THE FORMAT OF THE AP ENGLISH LANGUAGE AND COMPOSITION EXAM

The English Language and Composition exam tests both your writing ability and your knowledge of various rhetorical modes. You'll be required to know how a writer's choice of words, sentence length, sentence structure, and other elements affects his or her style. Unlike the AP Literature exam, the AP Language exam includes only prose passages. There will not be any poetry on this test. You will also be expected to show fluency in a variety of different writing modes yourself.

You will be tested through the 2 parts of the test: multiple-choice questions and essays.

THE MULTIPLE-CHOICE SECTION

The multiple-choice section consists of approximately 50–60 questions. The exact number varies from year to year. The questions consist of 4 prose passages.

The works will be drawn from different writers and represent a wide historical span. For example, the 1996 test included the following four passages:

- a passage from Queen Elizabeth's speech to her last Parliament in 1601;
- a passage from an essay on genius/originality, written in 1821;
- a description of mangroves, published in 1982; and
- an essay on the writer's Native American grandmother, written in 1969.

As you can tell from this list, the passages will not necessarily be arranged in chronological order.

The questions will focus on your ability to analyze a writer's *style*. For example:

- You will be expected to be able to identify the different figures of speech and understand their effect in a prose passage.
- You'll also be required to identify the different parts of a sentence (subject, verb, etc.).
- Questions on tone, mood, and style are always included.
- Most of all, you'll have to understand why the writer made the choices that he or she did. For example, why are the images placed as they are? Why did the writer open the passage with a question? Why did the writer select a specific word and not another? And so on.

As mentioned earlier, you will have 1 hour to complete this section.

THE ESSAY SECTION

The essay section consists of 3 questions. Each one will require you to analyze a different prose passage.

- The passages might be part of a novel, a biography, an autobiography, an essay, or a short story, for example. In rare cases, an entire short story will be included for analysis.
- You will also be asked to react to the passage. For example, you might have to defend, challenge, or qualify the writer's point of view.

The 1996 exam, for example, included the following 3 essay prompts:

- an excerpt from a letter Lady Mary Wortley Montague (1689–1762) wrote to her daughter to discuss the education of her granddaughter. Students were asked to analyze how Lady Montague used "rhetorical strategies and stylistic devices" to convey her opinion about the role that knowledge played in the lives of women in the early-to-mid eighteenth century.
- an excerpt from contemporary writer Gary Soto's autobiography, in which Soto describes an experience from his early childhood. Students were asked to analyze how Soto created the impression of his six-year-old self in this passage.
- an excerpt from Lewis Lapham's book *Money and Class in America*, in which Lapham discusses American attitudes toward money. Students were asked to react to Lapham's argument. Students had 3 choices: support Lapham's argument, criticize it, or qualify it.

You will have 2 hours to complete all 3 essays. This gives you about 40 minutes per essay. However, you won't be told how much time to allocate to each essay. Therefore, how you allocate your time will be left to you. Nonetheless, savvy test takers spread their time equally to give adequate time to each essay. Clearly, one of the skills necessary to do well on this part of the exam is the ability to balance your time wisely.

Examinations can be divided in a number of ways. Some typical examinations may look like the following:

NOTE
You are required to write all three essays.

Possible AP English Language and Composition Exam Format

Section I multiple-choice questions	53 questions	1 hour
passage from a sixteenth-century play	14 questions	
excerpt from a modern novel	15 questions	
passage from a Victorian essay	15 questions	
modern American autobiography	9 questions	

Section II
essay questions	3 questions	2 hours
analysis of a nineteenth-century biography		40 minutes
analysis of a contemporary essay		40 minutes
analysis of a seventeenth-century letter		40 minutes

Possible AP English Language and Composition Exam Format

Section I
multiple-choice questions	55 questions	1 hour
passage from a modern novel		15 questions
excerpt from a eighteenth-century essay		15 questions
passage from a Victorian journal		15 questions
contemporary British biography		10 questions

Section II
essay questions	3 questions	2 hours
analysis of a twentieth-century poem		40 minutes
analysis of a eighteenth-century essay		40 minutes
analysis of a modern essay		40 minutes

Possible AP English Language and Composition Exam Format

Section I
multiple-choice questions	54 questions	1 hour
passage from a nineteenth-century play	14 questions	
excerpt from an eighteenth-century essay	15 questions	
passage from a seventeenth-century speech	15 questions	
contemporary American letter	10 questions	

Section II
essay questions	3 questions	2 hours
analysis of a 17th-century essay		40 minutes
analysis of a modern essay		40 minutes
analysis of a modern essay		40 minutes

OVERVIEW OF THE SCORING SYSTEM

The AP English Language and Composition exam is graded according to the following scale:

5   extremely well qualified

4   well qualified

3   qualified

2   possibly qualified

1   no recommendation

All AP exams are graded on the same scale.

How do you get an overall grade on the AP English Language and Composition exam? The process has four steps:

1. The multiple-choice section is scored.

2. The free-response section is scored.

3. The composite score is calculated.

4. The composite score is converted to an AP grade: a 5, 4, 3, 2, or 1. This is the grade that you receive.

HOW ESSAYS ARE SCORED

The essays are scored by English teachers from around the country who gather in a central location. They spent about a week reading the essays. "Table leaders," scorers with extensive experience grading AP English Language essays, are appointed to direct the scoring.

For three days before the essay exams arrive at the scoring site, Educational Testing Service graders and "table leaders" create a grading scale. This is called a *rubric*. While each rubric is tailored to an individual question, there are general qualities that define a paper and determine its score. When the rest of the grading staff arrives on the first formal day of scoring, the first morning is spent grading sample papers so that the grades can be as accurate as possible. At this time, the rubric may be adjusted to match expectations. Every few hours during the scoring, readers pause to check their accuracy by grading sample papers and comparing their scores.

Notice that the rubric is calibrated from 9–0, even though the final score you receive is calibrated from 5–1.

General Essay Grading Rubric

"9–8" papers demonstrate   originality and imagination. They are clearly focused discussions made up of coherent arguments of exceptional clarity. These papers leave the reader convinced of the soundness of the discussion, impressed with the quality of the

	writing style, and stimulated by the intelligence and insight of the writer.
"7–6" papers demonstrate	solid, logical, and persuasive discussion, but they lack the originality or insight of the "5" papers. Further, the development lacks the grace and style of the "5" papers and may seem a bit predictable and plodding.
"5" papers demonstrate	a thorough but not totally convincing discussion of the topic, marked by the sense that the writer has not completely thought out the issue. In addition, there are some writing errors that may distract the reader from the argument and the writer's point.
"4–3" papers demonstrate	an attempt made to organize the essay, but the structure is flawed and the supporting detail is weak. There may be serious problems with the mechanics of correct written English.
"2–1" papers demonstrate	a lack of understanding; either they do not address the topic directly or fail to answer the question. They draw obscure, irrelevant, or bizarre conclusions and are seriously deficient in the conventions of standard written English.
"0" papers demonstrate	papers that barely touch on the topic or write on a topic that has nothing to do with the essay question at all.

Below is a simulated essay test question for the AP exam in English Language and Composition.

Directions: Below is an excerpt from an essay written by Francis Bacon in 1597. Read the passage. Then write a carefully reasoned essay analyzing what Bacon's advice reveals about himself and his times.

It is generally better to deal by speech than by letter, and by the mediation of a third than by a man's self. Letters are good when a man would draw an answer by letter back again, or when it may serve for a man's justification afterwards to produce his own letter, or where it may be danger to interrupt or heard by pieces. To deal in person is good when a man's face breedeth regard, as commonly with inferiors, or in tender [delicate] cases, where a man's eye upon the countenance of him with whom he speaketh may give him a direction how far to go; and generally, where a man will reserve to himself liberty either to disavow or to expound. In choice of instruments, it is better to choose men of a plainer sort, that are likely to do that that is committed to them, and to report back again faithfully to the success, than those that are cunning to contrive out of other men's business somewhat to grace themselves, and will help the matter in report for satisfaction sake.

Specific Essay Grading Rubric

"9–8" papers demonstrate	what Bacon's advice reveals about himself and his times. The writers of these essays understand how the language, style, and content combine to present a glimpse into the late sixteenth century. The writer isolates specific words, phrases, and sentences to make each point. The writer thus reveals a close textual analysis of the essay and its rhetorical strategies. These essays may contain a few minor errors, but they amply demonstrate the writer's ability to analyze a prose selection with insight and to convey ideas with clarity, sophistication, and coherence.
"7–6" papers demonstrate	insights into Bacon's personality and the times in which he lived. In addition to some minor flaws in interpretation, the analysis here is not as well supported with details and examples. As a result, the analysis is less incisive and convincing. While these essays demonstrate the writer's ability to articulate ideas clearly, they lack the mastery and control of rhetoric shown by writers in the 9–8 range. In addition, there may be minor errors in grammar, usage, and mechanics, but these do not seriously affect the argument.
"5" papers demonstrate	superficial analysis. Instead of focusing on specific examples from the text and linking them to Bacon and his times, these essays may discuss outside historical information the writer has about the sixteenth century. These essays reveal shallow thinking, focus on trivial examples, and do not contribute significantly to a greater meaning of the work or the writer's rhetorical strategies. These essays are not well planned, well organized, or coherent. However, the writing style is sufficient to convey the writer's ideas.
"4–3" papers demonstrate	a general discussion rather than the focus on specific rhetorical strategies that reveal Bacon's character and his attitude toward the times in which he lived. In addition, these papers may incorrectly identify specific rhetorical strategies or misunderstand Bacon's cunning and keen political skills. These essays may contain inadequate supporting evidence and/or plot summary rather than analysis. Any analysis may be unconvincing, irrelevant, or misguided. While the writing may

	convey the student's ideas, there are serious omissions or stylistic issues. The style is flat and dull with little sentence variation, few figures of speech, and repetitious punctuation.
"2–1" papers demonstrate	little clarity or coherence. Even though the writers may have attempted to answer the question, they choose an inappropriate rhetorical element, make only obvious points about the writer's style, or seriously misread the writer's personality and intent. In addition, these essays may be too brief to convey a point in any detail. They contain distracting errors in grammar, usage, and mechanics. Overall, the essay is empty of both insight and style.
"0" papers demonstrate	no more than a passing reference to the question and any discernible rhetorical strategy.

As you can see, the essay section stresses your skill in organizing your thoughts coherently, developing ideas fully, responding to general questions with specific evidence, and writing clearly and vividly. The Advanced Placement Grading Committee will look especially for your ability to mold language, to utilize and recognize rhetorical strategies, and to link these to meaning. But a knowledge of rhetorical and stylistic devices alone by no means guarantees success on the exam.

THE MULTIPLE-CHOICE QUESTIONS: SHOULD YOU GUESS?

Should you guess wildly? No.

Your score on the multiple-choice questions is based on the number of questions you answer correctly minus a percentage for incorrect answers. Here's the math:

What You Do...	What You Get...
a correct answer:	1 point
a blank:	0 points
an incorrect answer:	minus .25

Therefore, just running down the page and filing in answers will not help you earn a better grade. But, *do make educated guesses*—eliminate one or more choices and then guess from the remaining choices.

PREPARING TO TAKE THE EXAMINATION

January: Talk about taking the examination with your English teacher, guidance counselor, and the AP Coordinator at your school. Make sure that these people understand that you wish to take the examination.

If you need special accommodations, such as a Braille exam, speak with your school's AP Coordinator or write to the College Board.

Fees: The exam carries a fee. The College Board will reduce fees by $12–15 for qualified students who can demonstrate financial need. Do not send money to the College Board. Your school's AP Coordinator will have this information.

May: Examinations are given.

June: If you do not want all your AP grades reported to your colleges, you must notify the College Board by June 15.

July: The scores are sent to you and your designated colleges and universities. In cases of a scoring conflict, the College Board allows up to one year for the multiple-choice section to be rescored and retotaled by hand. The essay sections cannot be reread.

In 1992, the AP program introduced three awards to honor those students who have earned outstanding AP achievement.

- The Scholar Award honors students who earn grades of 3 or higher on three or more AP examinations.

- The Scholar with Honor and Scholar with Distinction awards are available for those students who go beyond these criteria.

FAQS: SURE-FIRE TEST-TAKING STRATEGIES FOR SUCCESS ON THE AP ENGLISH LANGUAGE AND COMPOSITION EXAM

BEFORE THE TEST

Q: *Do I have to take the AP English Language and Composition class in my high school to take the AP English Language exam?*

A: ETS strongly suggests that students take the year-long AP English Language and Composition class, but it's not mandated. Some students who never took an AP class have earned high scores on the test. Home-schooled students, for example, can take the test if they choose. However, students who score well without taking the formal AP class often had unusually thorough English classes or studied in depth on their own.

Q: *When should I use this book?*

A: If possible, look at the book early in the year to familiarize yourself with the test's content and format. Then as you learn specifics about writing, rhetorical strategies, and writing throughout the year, you can apply that knowledge to the test. If you have just purchased the book and the test is around the corner, you can still see marked benefits from reviewing the instruction and taking the practice tests.

Q: *How should I use this book?*

A: First, use the book to become completely familiar with the essay. Know what kinds of questions you'll be asked, how the exam is graded, how much time you'll have for each section, and so on. Knowing what you're facing also helps greatly reduce the fear factor.

As you use this book, work from beginning to end. Concentrate on the parts of the test that present the greatest challenge. For example, if you're having trouble writing essays, spend most of your time reviewing the essay section.

Be sure to learn the lingo, the technical words that writers use to analyze rhetorical strategies. For example, be sure you understand such terms as *tone, mood,* and *narrator.* You can use *Part VI: Glossary of Literary Terms* for a quick review and to pick up any terms that you might have missed in class or working on your own.

Q: *How do you get to Carnegie Hall? (Or: How do I get a high score on the AP Language test?)*

A: Practice, Practice, Practice! Do all the practice tests your teacher assigns. Do all the practice tests in this book. Go over the answer explanations. You're far better off spending half an hour every day preparing for the test than trying to cram it all into one week.

Practice writing all four modes of discourse:

narration (writing that tells a story)

argumentation (writing that tries to move readers to action or belief)

exposition (writing that explains)

description (writing that uses the five senses)

Q: *What should I do the night before the test?*

A: Stay home and relax. Lay out your clothes for the next day, gather any identification you may need to get into the test site, and get your writing implements. Get plenty of sleep.

Q: *Should I cram?*

A: If by cramming you mean staying up all night before the test frantically reading novels of recognized literary value, skimming old AP tests, and biting your nails, the answer is a clear "No!" If by cramming you mean reviewing literary terms a week before the test, I'd say "Sure." The AP English Language and Composition exam measures years of study in English, so cramming the night before will get you nothing more than a headache.

Q: *Should I eat breakfast?*

A: Chow down, even if you normally skip the morning meal. Studies have repeatedly shown that test takers who eat breakfast do appreciably better than those who do not.

And while we're on the subject of food, no coffee or cola. The last thing you want during an exam is a caffeine jolt. Even if you think you need caffeine to wake up, it will make you edgy and fidgety. Ditto on sugar: donuts, toaster pastries, etc. Stick with the basics: juice, cereal, toast, and eggs. Eating a nourishing breakfast is a simple and successful way to give yourself an edge.

Q: *What should I wear during the test?*

A: Wear comfortable clothes so you can concentrate on the test.

Q: *When should I get to the school on test day?*

A: Get to the test site with ample time to spare. Allow yourself enough time to settle in the seat, lay out your pens and pencils, and relax. This is not the day to be rushing out the door in a frenzy.

Q: *Does my seat at the test matter?*

A: Yes! Choose your seat carefully because sitting near friends during a test can be disrupting. If you see your friends handing in their papers early, you may feel pressured to do the same, even if you're not finished with the test. Therefore, try not to sit near your friends.

DURING THE TEST

Q: *Does listening to the proctor matter, or can I zone out for a minute?*

A: Pay close attention to *all* directions. Even though you'll be completely familiar with the test format, the proctor may say something very important, such as safety procedures in the event of a fire drill or an actual fire.

Q: *How should I budget my time?*

A: If you don't complete a multiple-choice question in the time you have allotted, leave it and move on. You can return to the question if you have extra time at the end of the test.

On the essay part of the exam, remember that you have to write three essays. It is recommended that you spend about 40 minutes on each essay. If you go over this time limit, you'll have to cut the time from the subsequent two essays. This won't be too crucial on the second essay (unless you went way over your time on the first essay), but it will pose a very serious problem with the third essay because you will have used far too much of your time.

Q: *Are there any special words I should watch for?*

A: On the multiple-choice questions, look for absolute words. These include ALL, NONE, NOT, and EXCEPT. Misreading one of these little—but crucial—words can trip you up, so be very careful with absolutes.

Q: *How should I mark my answers?*

A: Even the best students can tank if they mismark their answer sheets. Be especially careful if you skip a question. If you don't skip that space, you might inadvertently mark an answer in it. Then every answer that comes after will be wrong. To avoid this problem, put a mark in your test book (not on your answer sheet) when skip a question. Stop working often to make sure that the number of the question on your answer sheet corresponds to the number of the question in your exam booklet.

Q: *Should I plan my essays or just start writing?*

A: Plan your answer carefully before you start to write. Think about the major points that you want to make and the evidence you plan to include to support your assertions. Before you start writing your essay, be sure that you understand the passage that you have to analyze. This will be covered in detail in *Part IV: Strategies for Success on the Essay Questions*

Q: *How much should I write?*

A: Write enough to make your point clearly and completely. Quantity doesn't always equal quality, but brief essays rarely get top scores. Figure that each essay should be at least three paragraphs, preferably four, and 350–500 words long.

Quote from the text. Use a clear and logical method of organization.

Q: *What should I do if I have time left over?*

A: Stay focused and use time to your advantage.

- Return to questions you couldn't answer the first time and work on them now.
- Double-check your answers.
- Make sure you have marked all test bubbles correctly. You surely don't want to lose credit because you mismarked answers!
- Proofread your essay for errors in grammar, usage, and punctuation.
- Recopy messy parts of your essays.

Q: *What can I do about panic?*

A: Few test situations have as much pressure as an AP exam, especially the AP Exam in English Language and Composition, because there's no "right" answer on the essay questions. If you still have some last-minutes jitters, take a few deep breaths and focus on a pleasant scene. Try not to think about anything but the test in front of you.

Q: *What should I do if some questions seem harder than others?*

A: Don't panic if some questions seem much harder than others. They probably are. That's the way the test was designed.

Q: *What should I do if other students are writing and I'm not?*

A: Relax. They may be working on another part of the test or not have thought enough. By thinking a bit longer before you answer, you might do better than someone who plunges right in.

Q: *What if other students finish before I do?*

A: Finishing early doesn't guarantee the best grade. Usually the better papers are handed in by students who have spent more time thinking about their answers and checking their papers over.

Q: *And if I can't get an answer?*

A: Just skip the question and move on. If you have enough time, you can return to the question later. If you run out of time before you can return to it, you were still better off answering more questions correctly than wasting time on a question you didn't know.

Q: *If I freeze and just can't go on?*

A: If this happens, there are many different things that you can do. First, remind yourself that you have studied and so you are well prepared. Then remember that every question you have answered is worth points. Third, stop working and close your eyes. Take two or three deep breaths. Breath in and out to the count of five. Then go on with the test.

AFTER THE TEST

Q: *What if I decide after I take the test that I don't want a college on my application list to receive the grade from my AP English Language and Composition exam ?*

A: You can stop the grade reporting *before* and *after* you take the test.

Before the test, write the names of the college(s) you wish to receive your grades. If you don't want the college to get the score, don't write their name in. If you forget to write the name of a college in, you can contact the AP program when you get home and ask that your grades be sent to the colleges of your choice.

After the exam, you have until June 15 to contact the AP Program and ask them not to send one or more of your AP grades to a college.

FOR ADDITIONAL INFORMATION

For additional information about the AP Program and its policies, you can contact the College Board and/or ETS.

General e-mail inquiries:	www. collegeboard.org
AP questions:	apexams@info.collegeboard.org

The College Board
45 Columbus Avenue
New York, NY 10023-6992

Telephone:	212-713-8000

Educational Testing Service
Rosedale Road
Princeton, NJ 08541

Telephone:	888-CALL-4-AP (toll-free)
	609-771-7300
	609-921-9000
E-mail:	etsinfo@ets.org
Fax:	609-734-5410
	609-530-0482

DIAGNOSTIC TEST AND ANSWER KEY

GENERAL DIRECTIONS FOR THE DIAGNOSTIC TEST

This test was constructed to be representative of what you will encounter on the AP English Language and Composition exam. Take the test in a quiet room without distractions, following all directions carefully and observing all time limits. Try to get as close as possible to actual test conditions, and take the test in one sitting. The more carefully you match test conditions, the more accurate your results will be and the better able you will be to evaluate your strengths and weaknesses.

ROAD MAP

- *General Directions for the Diagnostic Test*
- *Section I: Multiple-Choice Questions*
- *Section II: Essay Questions*
- *Answers and Explanations*

ENGLISH LANGUAGE AND COMPOSITION

SECTION I: MULTIPLE-CHOICE QUESTIONS

Time—1 hour

> **Directions:** This section contains selections from four passages of prose with questions on their content, style, form, rhetorical strategies, and purpose. Read each selection closely and carefully. Then choose the best answer from the five choices.

Questions 1–14. Read the following selection carefully before you mark your answers.

Ah, but poems amount to so little when you write them too early in your life. You ought to wait and gather sense and sweetness for a whole lifetime, and a long one, if possible, and then, at the very end, you might perhaps be able to write ten good lines. For poems are not, as people think, simply emotions (one has emotions enough)—they are experiences. For the sake of a single poem, you must see many cities, many people, and things, you must understand animals, must feel how birds fly, and know the gesture which small flowers make when they open in the morning. You must be able to think back to streets in unknown neighborhoods, to unexpected encounters, and to partings you had long seen coming; to days of childhood whose mystery is still unexplained, to parents whom you had to hurt when they brought in a joy and you didn't pick it up (it was a joy meant for somebody else); to childhood illnesses that began so strangely with so many profound and difficult transformations, to days in quiet, restrained rooms and to mornings by the sea, to the sea itself, to seas, to nights of travel that rushed along high overhead and went flying with all the stars—and still not enough to be able to think to all that. And yet it is not enough to have memories. You must be able to forget them when they are many, and you must have the immense patience to wait until they return. For the memories themselves are not important. Only when they have changed into our very blood, into glance and gesture, and are nameless, no longer to be distinguished from ourselves—only then can it happen that in some very rare hour the first word of a poem arises in their midst and goes forth from them.

1. The rhetorical strategy of this passage is best described as a(n)
   - (A)   comparison and contrast of successful and unsuccessful writers.
   - (B)   catalog of natural and fantastic experiences.
   - (C)   chronological list of required experiences for poets.
   - (D)   extended metaphor.
   - (E)   reduction of the argument to its bare essentials.

2. The narrator believes that poems written early in life
   (A) are great because they present fresh experiences uncensored by adult considerations.
   (B) distill experience to its essentials.
   (C) are virtually identical to those written later in life, if the poet has genuine talent.
   (D) reflect both sense and sweetness, which counters what they lack in emotion and experience.
   (E) cannot be great because emotions must be refined through experience.

3. What figure of speech does the writer use in the second line of this essay to link related ideas?
   (A) Ambiguity
   (B) Apostrophe
   (C) Alliteration
   (D) A conceit
   (E) Dialect

4. The style of this passage is characterized by all of the following rhetorical strategies and stylistic devices EXCEPT
   (A) long sentences.
   (B) sensory images.
   (C) allusions.
   (D) parallel structure.
   (E) personification.

5. The form of the fourth sentence suggests that
   (A) sensory impressions flow together to create a river of memory.
   (B) we are bombarded by too many sensory experiences.
   (C) only poets can winnow out the important memories and experiences from the distracting ones.
   (D) everyone has basically the same experiences since they are part of the larger human experience.
   (E) you must be able to think back to days of childhood, whose mystery is still unexplained.

6. The fourth sentence is unified chiefly through the author's use of
   (A) onomatopoeia.
   (B) understatement.
   (C) irony.
   (D) parallelism.
   (E) hyperbole.

7. The rhythm of the sentence "...to days in quiet, restrained rooms and to mornings by the sea, to the sea itself, to seas, to nights of travel that rushed along high overhead and went flying with all the stars—and..." echoes

   (A) the experience of drowning in sensory overload.

   (B) the form of a poem.

   (C) the rhythm of the ocean and soaring through the skies.

   (D) the experience of extreme loneliness.

   (E) the process of composing a poem.

8. With which of the following sentences would the writer most likely agree?

   (A) Poets must have extensive formal education if they are to succeed.

   (B) Everyone can be a prolific poet with the right experiences and emotions.

   (C) Poetry is for the young.

   (D) Poets are born, not made.

   (E) Poets are made, not born.

9. What role does the narrator believe that memories play in the creation of poems?

   (A) Memories distract from the composing process if past conflicts have not been resolved.

   (B) Memories help poets craft their work, but memories are not essential to poetry.

   (C) Memories become part of poetry when they become indistinguishable from the poet's own being.

   (D) All you need to be a poet is memories of past experiences and emotions.

   (E) Poets must be able to recall their memories as a basis for their inspiration.

10. The phrase "only when they [memories] have changed into our very blood" is best understood as a metaphor for

   (A) assimilating memories.

   (B) dying for one's art.

   (C) having unpleasant memories.

   (D) becoming close to another human being.

   (E) the compulsion to write.

11. The *tone* of this essay is best described as
    (A) sad because the writer suggests it is almost impossible to write a good poem.
    (B) sad because the writer suggests poetry is written at too great a personal price.
    (C) happy because the writer posits that everyone can be a poet if they have sufficient experiences and memories.
    (D) happy because the writer enjoys being a poet.
    (E) angry because people assume that it is easy to be a poet.

12. How would the author most likely define "poem"?
    (A) A poem is an impossibility.
    (B) A poem is the process of remembering.
    (C) A poem is best created through collaboration.
    (D) A poem is the artistic representation of the writer's life experiences.
    (E) A poem is an accumulation of suffering and sorrow.

13. As used in the last sentence, "rare" most nearly means
    (A) special.
    (B) meager.
    (C) raw.
    (D) common.
    (E) early.

14. The most apparent goal of the author's rhetoric and reasoning is to
    (A) demonstrate that poetry springs from the wisdom that comes from empathy.
    (B) argue that poetry is created through anguish.
    (C) explain how to become a poet.
    (D) convince everyone to become a poet.
    (E) elicit sympathy for poets the world over.

Questions 15–28. Read the following selection carefully before you mark your answers.

Samuel Johnson wrote the following letter to Lord Chesterfield in 1755.

To the Right Honorable the Earl of Chesterfield

My Lord,

I have been lately informed, by the proprietor of the *World,* that two papers, in which my *Dictionary* is recommended to the public, were written by your Lordship. To be so distinguished is an honor, which, being very little accustomed to favors by the great, I know not well how to receive, or in what terms to acknowledge.

When, upon some slight encouragement, I first visited your Lordship, I was overpowered, like the rest of mankind, by the enchantment of your address, and could not forbear to wish that I might boast myself *le vainqueur du vainqueur de la terre* [the conqueror of the conqueror of the earth], that I might obtain that regard for which I saw the world contending; but I found my attendance so little encouraged that neither pride nor modesty would suffer me to continue it. When I had once addressed your Lordship in public, I had exhausted all the art of pleasing which a retired and uncourtly scholar can possess. I had done all that I could and no man is well pleased to have his all neglected, be it ever so little.

Seven years, my Lord, have now passed since I waited in your outward rooms, or was repulsed from your door; during which time I have been pushing on my work through difficulties of which it is useless to complain and have brought it at last to the verge of publication without one act of assistance, one word of encouragement, or one smile of favor. Such treatment I did not expect, for I never had a patron before.

The shepherd in Virgil grew at last acquainted with Love and found him a native of the rocks.[1] Is not a patron, my Lord, one who looks with unconcern on a man struggling for life in the water and, when he has reached ground, encumbers him with help? The notice which you have been pleased to take of my labors, had it been early, had been kind; but had been delayed till I am indifferent and cannot enjoy it; till I am solitary and cannot impart it; till I am known and do not want it.

I hope it is no very cynical asperity not to confess obligations where no benefit has been received or to be unwilling that the public should consider me as owing that to a patron which Providence has enabled me to do for myself.

Having carried on my work thus far with so little obligation to any favorer of learning, I shall not be disappointed though I should conclude it, if less be possible, with less; for I have been long wakened from that dream of hope in which I once boasted myself with so much exultation, my Lord,

Your Lordship's most humble, most obedient servant,

Sam. Johnson

1. This is a reference to a work by the Roman poet Virgil in which a shepherd complains that love was born among jagged rocks.

15. The *tone* of the first paragraph of this letter is best described as
    (A) offended.
    (B) cynical.
    (C) mocking.
    (D) sarcastic.
    (E) gracious.

16. What was Johnson's purpose in opening with this tone?
    (A) The contrast between this tone and the rest of the letter reinforces how badly the Earl mistreated him.
    (B) To balance his later condemnation with sincere praise
    (C) To undercut the effectiveness of the Earl's recommendations
    (D) To blunt the Earl's criticism
    (E) To curry favor with a powerful patron

17. As used in the second paragraph, "address" most nearly means
    (A) appearance of his home.
    (B) speech.
    (C) location of his home.
    (D) clothing.
    (E) wealth.

18. What function do the first two paragraphs serve?
    (A) They analyze the current political situation.
    (B) They illustrate how well the Earl treats all artists.
    (C) They reveal how badly Johnson requires the Earl's continuing support.
    (D) They establish the factual basis upon which Johnson builds his complaint.
    (E) They emphasize that Johnson's dictionary is a superior book.

19. What can you infer about Johnson's personality from his statements?
    (A) He is a loyal and true friend.
    (B) He is proud and determined.
    (C) He is unwilling to stand up for himself and his principles.
    (D) He is easily pushed around.
    (E) He is arrogant and insolent.

20. The third paragraph signals
    (A) a shift in topic.
    (B) a shift in tone.
    (C) a shift in both topic and tone.
    (D) a continuation of his argument.
    (E) a shift in tense and person.

21. What rhetorical strategy does Johnson use in the third paragraph to reinforce his bitterness and make his point?
    (A) Parody
    (B) Symbolism
    (C) Personification
    (D) Parallel structure
    (E) Colloquial language

22. What is the metaphor in the fourth paragraph?

    (A) Johnson compares himself to the famous poet Virgil.

    (B) Johnson compares Lord Chesterfield to Vigil's patron.

    (C) Johnson compares his dictionary to a rock.

    (D) Johnson compares his troubles to those of a drowning man.

    (E) Johnson compares himself to a shepherd in a poem.

23. The metaphor serves to show that

    (A) Johnson is a great writer who will enjoy lasting international fame.

    (B) Chesterfield's name will live on as a synonym for generosity.

    (C) Johnson's masterpiece is solid.

    (D) without Chesterfield's support, Johnson would sink into obscurity.

    (E) as the shepherd found love painful, so Johnson was pained in his search for support from Lord Chesterfield.

24. Why are the words *enchantment, contending, exhausted,* and *uncourtly* especially effective?

    (A) They show alliteration and thus serve to link related ideas.

    (B) They have no subtext.

    (C) They show the difference between two objects.

    (D) They all have prefixes, roots, and suffixes.

    (E) They have strong connotations and thus reinforce Johnson's point.

25. Johnson's style in this letter is characterized by all of the following stylistic elements EXCEPT

    (A) precise diction.

    (B) highly abstract metaphors.

    (C) long, balanced sentences.

    (D) parallel structure.

    (E) literary allusions.

26. What method of organization does Johnson use in the fifth paragraph?

    (A) Cause and effect

    (B) Chronological order

    (C) Spatial order

    (D) Order of importance

    (E) Extended definition

27. To what does Johnson attribute his success?
    (A) His patron's continued support
    (B) The Earl's kind reviews in the newspaper
    (C) Luck
    (D) His own hard work, perseverance, and Providence
    (E) Virgil's efforts on his behalf

28. The narrative style of this passage is best described as
    (A) straightforward and honest.
    (B) abrupt and crude.
    (C) complex and confusing.
    (D) prissy and nasty.
    (E) allusive and subtle.

Questions 29–41. Read the following selection carefully before you mark your answers.

Studies serve for delight, for ornament, and for ability. Their chief use for delight is in privateness and retiring; for ornament, is in discourse; and for ability, is in the judgment and disposition of business. For expert men can execute, and perhaps judge the particulars, one by one; but the general counsels, and the plots and marshaling of affairs, come best from those that are learned. To spend too much time in studies is sloth; to use them too much for ornament is affectation; to make judgment wholly by their rules is the humor of a scholar. They perfect nature and are perfected by experience: for natural abilities are like natural plants that need proyning by study; and studies themselves do give forth directions too much at large, except they be bounded in by experience.

Crafty men contemn studies, simple men admire them, and wise men use them; for they teach not their own use; but that is a wisdom without them and above them, won by observation. Read not to contradict and confute; nor to believe and take for granted; nor to find talk and discourse; but to weigh and consider. Some books are to be tasted, others to be swallowed, and a few to be chewed and digested; that is, some books are to be read only in parts; others to be read, but not curiously, and some few to be read wholly, and with diligence and attention. Some books also may be read by deputy, and extracts made of them by others; but that would be only in the less important arguments, and the meaner sorts of books, else distilled books are like common distilled waters, flashy things. Reading maketh a full man; conference a ready man; and writing an exact man. And therefore, if a man write little, he had need have a great memory; if he confer little, he need have a great wit; and if he read little, he need have much cunning, to seem to know that he doth not.

29. The opening sentence is unified by the author's use of
    (A) parallelism.
    (B) allusion.
    (C) imagery.
    (D) metaphor.
    (E) comparison and contrast.

30. By using the word *delight* in the first sentence and repeating it in the second sentence, the author specifically emphasizes
    (A) how studying serves only for pleasure.
    (B) his personal resolve to master as much information as possible.
    (C) his own devotion to study.
    (D) the rewards that the attainment of knowledge brings.
    (E) the sacrifices necessary to become learned.

31. According to the author, what are the three primary benefits of study?
    (A) Privateness, discourse, humor
    (B) Enjoyment, adornment, competence
    (C) Secrecy, character, self-respect
    (D) Pleasure, advancement, reputation
    (E) Self-respect, proficiency, direction

32. All of the following dangers can result from excessive study EXCEPT
    (A) accomplishment.
    (B) laziness.
    (C) simplified judgments.
    (D) an attitude of superiority.
    (E) inactivity.

33. As used in this passage, *affectation* means
    (A) fondness.
    (B) respect.
    (C) pretense.
    (D) gratification.
    (E) decoration.

34. Which of the following is evident in the following sentence?

    "...for natural abilities are like natural plants that need proyning by study; and studies themselves do give forth directions too much at large, except they be bounded in by experience."
    I.   Personification
    II. Simile
    III. Allusion
    (A) I only
    (B) II only
    (C) III only
    (D) I and II
    (E) I and III

35. The figure of speech developed in the fifth sentence suggests primarily that
    (A) studying and reading widely perfects all our abilities and enables us to grow freely.
    (B) studying gives our lives direction and allows us to branch out unhindered.
    (C) restricting what you read and study can stunt your growth permanently and irrevocably.
    (D) experience holds us back; studying and reading allows us to flourish.
    (E) just as plants must be pruned to make them grow full, so too must the intellectual abilities of people be disciplined (a type of pruning) through study.

36. What rhetorical strategy does the writer use in the following line?

    "Some books are to be tasted, others to be swallowed, and a few to be chewed and digested."
    (A) Analogy
    (B) Simile
    (C) Collecting facts to support the main point
    (D) Hyperbole
    (E) Understatement

37. According to the author, you should read to
    (A) challenge what you read.
    (B) believe the writer's main points.
    (C) think about the writer's ideas.
    (D) find things to talk about.
    (E) take the writer's ideas for granted.

38. As used in the second paragraph, *meaner* most nearly means
    (A) cruel.
    (B) inferior.
    (C) fierce.
    (D) unnatural.
    (E) cheaper.

39. The author's style in this passage is best described as
    (A) simple, with terse and concise sentences.
    (B) plain, with unadorned sentences.
    (C) colloquial, characterized by commonplace diction and vivid images.
    (D) aphoristic, packed with epigrams.
    (E) sophisticated, marked by elevated diction and long sentences.

40. The speaker's tone is best described as
     (A) diffident and modest.
     (B) precarious.
     (C) ironic.
     (D) authoritative and confident.
     (E) arrogant and overbearing.

41. In this passage, the author uses rhetorical strategies and reasoning to
     (A) establish a new method of education.
     (B) explain how poorly educated the average person is.
     (C) argue in favor of study for its own sake.
     (D) delineate different methods of reading and studying.
     (E) convince readers that they are spending too much time studying.

Questions 42–52. Read the following selection carefully before you mark your answers.

I went all the first part of the time freely about the streets, though not so freely as to run myself into apparent danger, except when they dug the great pit in the churchyard of our parish of Aldgate. A terrible pit it was, and I could not resist my curiosity to go and see it. As near as I may judge, it was about forty feet in length, and about fifteen or sixteen feet broad, and at the time I first looked at it, about nine feet deep; but it was said they dug it near twenty feet deep afterwards in one part of it; till they could go no deeper for the water; for they had, it seems, dug several pits before this. For though the plague was a-coming to our parish, yet, when it did come, there was no parish in or about London where it raged with such violence as in the two parishes of Aldgate and Whitechapel...

I got admittance into the churchyard by being acquainted with the sexton who attended; who, though he did not refuse me at all, yet earnestly persuaded me not to go, telling me very seriously, for he was a good, religious, and sensible man, that it was indeed their business and duty to venture, and to run all hazards, and that in it they might hope to be preserved but that I had no apparent call to it but my own curiosity, which, he said, he believed I would not pretend was sufficient to justify my running that hazard.

His discourse had shocked my resolution a little, and I stood wavering a good while, but just at that interval I saw two links come over from the Minories, and heard the bellman and then appeared a dead cart, as they called it, coming over the streets; so I could no longer resist my desire of seeing it, and went in. There was nobody, as I could perceive at first, in the churchyard, or going into it, but the buriers and the fellow that drove the cart; but when they came to the pit they saw a man go to and again, muffled up with a brown cloak, and making motions with his hands under his cloak, as if he was in great agony, and the buriers immediately gathered about him, supposing he was one of those poor delirious or desperate creatures that used to pretend, as I have said, to bury themselves. He said nothing as he walked about, but two or three times groaned very deeply and loud, and sighed as he would break his heart.

When the buriers came up to him they soon found he was neither a person infected and desperate but one oppressed with a dreadful weight of grief indeed, having his wife and several of his children all in the cart that was just come in with him, and he followed with an agony and excess of sorrow...

This was a mournful scene indeed, and affected me almost as much as the rest; but the other was awful and full of terror. The cart had in it sixteen or seventeen bodies; some were wrapped up in linen sheets, some in rags, some little other than naked, or so loose that what covering they had fell from them in shooting out of the cart, and they fell quite naked among the rest; but the matter was not much in them, or the indecency much to anyone else, seeing they were all dead, and were to be huddled together into the common grave of mankind, as we may call it, for here there was no difference made, but poor and rich went together; there was no other way of burials, neither was it possible there should, for coffins were not to be had for the prodigious number that fell in such a calamity as this.

42. The author likely uses so many statistics and factual details in his account to
   (A) illustrate his point about the extent of the plague.
   (B) make the situation seem real and help readers visualize its horror.
   (C) suggest the plague is the worst horror humankind can imagine.
   (D) contrast life before the plague, during it, and after it.
   (E) symbolize the plague as a living creature.

43. The phrase "[The plague] raged with such violence as in the two parishes of Aldgate and Whitechapel" is an example of
   (A) personification.
   (B) metaphor.
   (C) analogy.
   (D) hyperbole.
   (E) understatement.

44. In the third paragraph, what rhetorical strategy does the writer use to make the scene come alive for readers?
   (A) Dramatic irony
   (B) Parody
   (C) A metaphysical conceit
   (D) A subtle shift in point of view
   (E) Imagery

45. The writer introduces the cloaked man as a(n)

    (A) personification of death, the great destroyer.

    (B) antithesis of life.

    (C) symbol of people who were spared by the plague, so he can't be accused of exaggerating.

    (D) symbol of the human dimension of the tragedy, all those people whose lives were changed by the plague.

    (E) illustration for the way the plague didn't discriminate against people from different socioeconomic strata.

46. Which of the following rhetorical techniques are evident in the third paragraph?

    I. Alliteration

    II. Imagery

    III. Symbolism

    (A) I only

    (B) II only

    (C) III only

    (D) I, II, and III

    (E) I and II

47. Overall, this passage is organized according to

    (A) cause and effect.

    (B) spatial order.

    (C) chronological order.

    (D) comparison and contrast.

    (E) problem-solution.

48. The *tone* of this selection is best characterized as

    (A) grieving and sorrowful.

    (B) detached and journalistic.

    (C) overwrought and emotional.

    (D) wryly ironic.

    (E) on the edge of hysteria.

49. The phrase "the common grave of mankind" functions as a(n)

    (A) symbol of infinity.

    (B) allusion to Shakespeare.

    (C) vivid example.

    (D) personification of death.

    (E) metaphor for death.

50. The speaker uses the phrase "the common grave of mankind" to illustrate the point that

    (A) all people, not just plague victims, eventually go to their graves.

    (B) we should save land by being buried in a common grave.

    (C) burial customs differ from place to place and time to time.

    (D) no one knows what will happen to them after death.

    (E) life, not death, is what truly matters.

51. The plague was factual, but this selection is fiction. What rhetorical device does the author use to make the situation seem real?

    (A) Third-person point of view

    (B) Omniscient point of view

    (C) First-person point of view

    (D) Shifting point of view

    (E) Quotes from actual eyewitnesses to the scene

52. The author's writing style is best described as

    (A) blunt and heavy-handed.

    (B) flowery and allusive.

    (C) clear and graceful.

    (D) courtly and cultivated.

    (E) complex and dense.

SECTION II: ESSAY QUESTIONS

Time—2 hours

Question 1:

Suggested Time: 40 minutes. Your response will count for one third of your total score on the essay portion of the exam.

> **Directions: In** *A Vindication of the Rights of Women,* **Mary Wollstonecraft makes the following argument about the education of women. Read the excerpt carefully. Drawing on your own knowledge and experience, write a carefully reasoned essay defending, challenging, or qualifying Wollstonecraft's thesis.**

...The education of women has, of late, been more attended to than formerly; yet they are still reckoned the frivolous sex and ridiculed or pitied by writers who endeavor by satire or instruction to improve them. It is acknowledged that they spend many of the first years of their lives in acquiring a smattering of accomplishments; meanwhile, strength of body and mind are sacrificed to libertine notions of beauty, to the desire of establishing themselves—the only way women can rise in the world—by marriage. And this desire making mere animals of them, when they marry, they act as children may be expected to act; they dress, they paint, and nickname God's creatures. Surely these weak beings are fit only for a seraglio! [harem] Can they be expected to govern a family with judgment or take care of the poor babes whom they bring into the world?

If it can be fairly deduced from the present conduct of the sex, from the prevalent fondness for pleasure which takes place of ambition and those nobler passions that open and enlarge the soul, that the instruction which women have hitherto received has only tended, with the constitution of civil society, to render them insignificant objects of desire—mere propagators of fools!—if it can then be proved that in aiming to accomplish them, without cultivating their understanding, they are taken out of their sphere of duties and made ridiculous and useless when the short-lived bloom of beauty is over, I presume that *rational* men will excuse me for endeavoring to persuade them to become more masculine and respectable.

Question 2:

Suggested Time: 40 minutes. Your response will count for one third of your total score on the essay portion of the exam.

> **Directions: Read the following passage carefully. Then write an essay in which you analyze how the writer uses rhetorical strategies and other stylistic devices to convey his views of the role of nature in our lives.**

"Nature"

Nature is a setting that fits equally well a comic or mourning piece. In good health, the air is a cordial of incredible virtue. Crossing a bare common, in snow puddles, at twilight, under a clouded sky, without having in my thoughts any occurrence of special good fortune, I have enjoyed a perfect exhilaration. I am glad to the brink of fear. In the woods, too, a man casts off his years, as the snake his slough, and at what period soever of is always a child. In the woods is perpetual youth. Within these plantations of God, a decorum and sanctity reign, a perennial festival is dressed, and the guest sees not how he should tire of them in a thousand years. In the woods, we return to reason and faith. There I feel that nothing can befall me in life—no disgrace, no calamity (leaving me my eyes), which nature cannot repair. Standing on the bare ground—my head bathed by the blithe air and uplifted into infinite space—all mean egotism vanishes. I become a transparent eyeball; I am nothing: I see all; the currents of the Universal Being circulate through me: I am part or parcel of God. The name of the nearest friend sounds then foreign and accidental: to be brothers, to be acquaintances, master or servant, is then a trifle and a disturbance. I am the lover of uncontained and immortal beauty. In the wilderness, I find something more dear and connate than in the streets or villages. In the tranquil landscape, and especially in the distant line of the horizon, man beholds something as beautiful as his own nature.

Question 3:

Suggested Time: 40 minutes. Your response will count for one third of your total score on the essay portion of the exam.

> **Directions: The following passage is an excerpt from Sir Richard Steele's description of Sir Roger de Coverley. Read the following passage carefully. Then write an essay in which you analyze how Steele uses rhetorical devices such as details, description, and imagery to comment on the stereotype of an English squire. Then identify and explain Steele's purpose in this selection.**

Friday, March 2, 1711

The first of our society is a gentleman of Worcestershire, of ancient descent, a baronet, his name Sir Roger de Coverley. His great-grandfather was the inventor of that famous country-dance which is called after him. All who know that shire are very well acquainted with the parts and merit of Sir Roger. He is a gentleman that is very singular in his behavior, but his singularities proceed from his good sense and are contradictions to the manners of the world only as he thinks the world is in the wrong. However, this humor creates him no enemies, for he does nothing with sourness or obstinacy; and his being unconfined to modes and forms makes him but the readier and more capable to please and oblige all who know him. When he is in town, he lives in Soho Square. It is said he keeps himself a bachelor by reason he was crossed in love by a perverse, beautiful widow of the next county to him. Before this disappointment, Sir Roger was what you call a fine gentleman, had often supped with my Lord Rochester and Sir George Etherege, and fought a duel upon his first coming to town, and kicked Bully Dawson in a public coffeehouse for calling him a "youngster." But being ill-used by the above-mentioned widow, he was very serious for a year and a half; and though, his temper being naurally jovial, he at last got over it, he grew careless of himself and never dressed afterwards. He continues to wear a coat and doublet of the same cut that were in fashion at the time of his repulse, which, in his merry humors, he tells us, has been in and out of fashion twelve times since he first wore it...

QUICK-SCORE ANSWERS

1. B	14. A	27. D	40. D
2. E	15. E	28. A	41. D
3. C	16. A	29. A	42. B
4. C	17. B	30. D	43. A
5. A	18. D	31. B	44. E
6. D	19. B	32. A	45. D
7. C	20. B	33. C	46. D
8. E	21. D	34. B	47. C
9. C	22. E	35. E	48. B
10. A	23. E	36. A	49. E
11. A	24. E	37. C	50. A
12. D	25. B	38. B	51. C
13. A	26. A	39. E	52. C

COMPUTING YOUR SCORE

You can use the following worksheet to compute an approximate score on the practice test. Since it is difficult to be objective about your own writing and since you are not a trained ETS scorer or English teacher, you may wish to ask a friend who has already taken the test (and earned a high score of 4 or 5) to score your three essays.

Recognize that your score can only be an approximation (at best), as you are scoring yourself against yourself. In the actual AP English Language and Composition Exam, you will be scored against every other student who takes the test as well.

Section I: Multiple-Choice Questions

	_____	number of correct answers
-	_____	25 x number of wrong answers
=	_____	raw score
	_____	raw score
x	_____	1.25
=	_____	scaled score (out of a possible 67.5)

Section II: Essays

	_____	essay 1 (0–9)
	_____	essay 2 (0–9)
	_____	essay 3 (0–9)
x	_____	3.055
=	_____	scaled score (out of a possible 82.5)

Scaled Score

	_____	multiple-choice scaled score
+	_____	essay scaled score
=	_____	final scaled score (out of a possible 150)

AP Score Conversion Chart

Scaled Score	Likely AP Score
150–100	5
99–86	4
85–67	3
66–0	1 or 2

ANSWERS AND EXPLANATIONS

SECTION I: MULTIPLE-CHOICE QUESTIONS

1. **The correct answer is (B).** The rhetorical strategy of this passage is best described as a catalog of natural and fantastic experiences. A *catalog* is a list of people, places, or things in a literary work. Walt Whitman, for example, often uses the catalog technique in his verse to suggest the fullness, diversity, and scope of American life and the human experience. Here, the essayist is using the technique to suggest the wide variety of experiences the poet needs to understand the meaning of life. You can eliminate choice (A) because the writer nowhere touches on the commercial aspects of poetry. Choice (C) may appear correct, but the experiences are not in chronological order. Further, the writer does not suggest that each and every one these specific experiences is required; rather, the writer suggests that these are the types of experiences that poets need. Choice (D) is wrong because the poet is not making any comparison here. Finally, you can eliminate choice (E) because there is nothing "bare" about this catalog; rather, it is very complete.

2. **The correct answer is (E).** The narrator believes that poems written early in life cannot be great because emotions must be refined through experience. This is stated in the very beginning of the essay: "Ah, but poems amount to so little when you write them too early in your life. You ought to wait and gather sense and sweetness for a whole lifetime, and a long one, if possible, and then, at the very end." This is the direct opposite of choices (A) and (C). There is no support for choices (B) or (D).

3. **The correct answer is (C).** The writer uses *alliteration* in the second line of this essay to link related ideas. Recall that *alliteration* is the repetition of initial consonant sounds in several words in a sentence or line of poetry. Writers use alliteration to create musical effects, link related ideas, stress certain words, or mimic specific sounds. In this instance, you can see the alliteration in the repeated "s" in the words *sense* and *sweetness*. Choice (A) is wrong because *ambiguity* allows multiple meanings to coexist in a word or a metaphor. Choice (B) is wrong because *apostrophe* occurs when a thing is addressed directly, as though it were a person listening to the conversation. Choice (D) is wrong because a *conceit* is a long, complex metaphor. Finally, choice (E) is wrong because *dialect* is the way people speak in a certain region or area. There is no dialect in this essay.

4. **The correct answer is (C).** The style of this passage is characterized by all of the following rhetorical strategies and stylistic devices EXCEPT *allusions*. Recall that an *allusion* is a reference to a well-known place, event, person, work of art, or other work of

literature. The essay does contain long sentences, choice (A); sensory images, choice (B); parallel structure, choice (D); and personification, choice (E).

5. **The correct answer is (A).** The form of the fourth sentence suggests that sensory impressions flow together to create a river of memory. You can infer this from the flow of words, unimpeded by end punctuation. Rather, the writer uses commas where we would expect periods, semicolons, or colons. Choice (B) is wrong because the writer does not suggest that we are bombarded by too many sensory experiences. Rather, he implies just the opposite: we cannot have too many experiences. Choice (C) incorrectly implies that poets are superior to other writers. Cross out choice (D) because it is directly contradicted by the passage as well as by common sense. Last, choice (E) is wrong because it is too narrow. *Some* of our childhood experiences are unexplained, the writer claims, but certainly not all.

6. **The correct answer is (D).** The fourth sentence is unified chiefly through the author's use of *parallelism*. You can see this in the infinitive phrases: "... You must be able *to think back* to streets in unknown neighborhoods, *to unexpected encounters*, and *to partings* you had long seen coming; *to days of childhood* whose mystery is still unexplained, *to parents* whom you had to hurt when they brought in a joy and you didn't pick it up (it was a joy meant for somebody else); *to childhood illnesses* that began so strangely with so many profound and difficult transformations,..." Choice (A) is wrong because *onomatopoeia* is the use of words to imitate the sounds they describe. "Hiss" and "buzz" are examples.

7. **The correct answer is (C).** The rhythm of the sentence "...to days in quiet, restrained rooms and to mornings by the sea, to the sea itself, to seas, to nights of travel that rushed along high overhead and went flying with all the stars—and..." echoes the rhythm of the ocean and soaring through the skies. This is shown in the cadence of the sentence. There is no support for choice (A). Likewise, since poems can take many different forms from sonnets to epic, choice (B) cannot be right. There is no textual support for choice (D) or choice (E).

8. **The correct answer is (E).** The writer would most likely agree that poets are made, not born. In this passage, the author argues that people become poets when they transmute emotion and experience into art. This is the direct opposite of choice (D). Since the writer argues that poets need experiences and emotions, you can eliminate choice (A). Choice (B) is wrong because the writer argues that even with experience and emotion, it is tremendously difficult to become a poet. This is shown in the following line: "...then, at the very end, you might perhaps be able to write ten good lines." There is no support for choice (C). On the contrary, the writer argues that only older and experienced people are able to create poetry.

9. **The correct answer is (C).** The narrator believes that memories become part of poetry when they become indistinguishable from the poet's own being. This is directly stated at the end of the essay: "For the memories themselves are not important. Only when they have changed into our very blood, into glance and gesture, and are nameless, no longer to be distinguished from ourselves—only then **can it happen** that in some very rare hour the first word of a poem arises in their midst and goes forth from them."

10. **The correct answer is (A).** The phrase "only when they [memories] have changed into our very blood" is best understood as a metaphor for assimilating memories. We change the memories into art. Choice (B) is a far too literal reading of the word "blood." There is no reason to suspect that the memories are unpleasant, choice (C); indeed, some are very pleasant. Choice (D) and choice (E) are not supported in the essay.

11. **The correct answer is (A).** The tone of this essay is best described as sad because the writer suggests it is almost impossible to write a good poem. You can find this at the very beginning of the essay: "Ah, but poems amount to so little when you write them too early in your life. You ought to wait and gather sense and sweetness for a whole lifetime, and a long one, if possible, and then, at the very end, you might perhaps be able to write ten good lines." Choice (B) is wrong because the writer never considers the personal price. Choice (C) is a gross misreading. There is no support for choice (D). We don't even know if the writer is a poet! The writer is not angry, so eliminate choice (E).

12. **The correct answer is (D).** The author would most likely define "poem" as the artistic representation of the writer's life experiences. This is drawn from the writer's extensive discussion of the importance of melding experience and emotion into your soul in order to become a poet.

13. **The correct answer is (A).** As used in the last sentence, "rare" most nearly means special. The sentence reads as follows: "Only when they [experiences] have changed into our very blood, into glance and gesture, and are nameless, no longer to be distinguished from ourselves—only then can it happen that in some very rare hour the first word of a poem arises in their midst and goes forth from them." The hour is uncommon because it comes so infrequently; this makes it special. This is the direct opposite of choice (D). Choice (B) is not as accurate a synonym as special. Choice (C) is not the meaning of "rare" required by the sentence; neither is choice (E).

14. **The correct answer is (A).** The most apparent goal of the author's rhetoric and reasoning is to demonstrate that poetry springs from the wisdom that comes from empathy. He does not argue that poetry is created through anguish, choice (B), because some of the memories are pleasant ones. Neither does he explain how to become a poet,

choice (C). Do not mistake these ruminations for firm guidelines. Since becoming a poet is so difficult, he surely does not want to convince everyone to become a poet, choice (D). There is no support for choice (E).

15. **The correct answer is (E).** The tone of the first paragraph of this letter is best described as gracious. You can infer this from the second sentence: "To be so distinguished is an honor, which, being very little accustomed to favors by the great, I know not well how to receive, or in what terms to acknowledge." Since Johnson is not being ironic at this point in the letter, you can eliminate choice (B), choice (C), and choice (D). The later part of the letter is indeed cynical and sarcastic, but the opening is not. While Johnson is indeed offended, choice (A), this emotion is not present in the letter's opening.

16. **The correct answer is (A).** Johnson crafted this opening tone to set up a contrast: the gracious opening reinforces the sarcastic tone that comes later. In effect, Johnson is lulling the Earl into complacency with his courteous opening. This gives the rest of his letter an even stronger punch and reinforces how badly the Earl mistreated Johnson. Therefore, choice (E) can't be true. There is no sincere praise, so you can eliminate choice (B). He would not want to undercut the effectiveness of the Earl's recommendations, choice (C), because that would affect sales of his *Dictionary* and its reputation. Since the Earl has not criticized him, choice (E) cannot be correct.

17. **The correct answer is (B).** As used in the second paragraph, "address" most nearly means speech. Johnson was impressed with the Earl's kindness toward him, which lead him to erroneously believe that the Earl would support him in his efforts to produce his *Dictionary*. However, the Earl's kind words were not sincere. "Address" has multiple meanings, including the location of his home, choice (C). However, the location would not impress Johnson because it would not have any impact on his work. He knew the Earl was fabulously wealthy because he was an earl. The same is true of choices (A), (D), and (E).

18. **The correct answer is (D).** The first two paragraphs serve to establish the factual basis upon which Johnson builds his complaint. The Earl had encouraged Johnson and led him to believe that he would receive ample support. This is shown in the following lines: "I was overpowered, like the rest of mankind, by the enchantment of your address...that I might obtain that regard for which I saw the world contending." However, the support was not forthcoming: "but I found my attendance so little encouraged that neither pride nor modesty would suffer me to continue it." Choice (A) has nothing to do with the context. Choice (B) is the direct opposite of what has happened. Since Johnson finished his *Dictionary* without the Earl's support, choice (C) cannot be true. Finally, these lines have nothing to do with the quality of Johnson's *Dictionary*, so you can eliminate choice (E).

19. **The correct answer is (B).** You can infer from Johnson's statements that he is proud and determined. He finished his *Dictionary* without the Earl's help and does not hesitate to tell the Earl just that. This is the direct opposite of choice (C) and choice (D) Just the opposite is true, as this letter reveals. His tone is sarcastic, but it is not arrogant and insolent, so you can eliminate choice (E). Finally, he and the Earl are definitely not friends, so you can eliminate choice (A).

20. **The correct answer is (B).** The third paragraph signals a shift in tone from cordial to sarcastic. After the warm-up, Johnson is getting down to the real purpose of his letter. He stays on the same topic, so you can eliminate choice (A) and choice (C). In effect, he is continuing his argument, choice (E), but choice (B) is a more complete and accurate answer. Choice (E) would be an egregious grammar error. Always keep both verb tense (present, past, future, etc.) and person (first person, second person, third person) consistent within a passage.

21. **The correct answer is (D).** Johnson uses parallel structure in the third paragraph to reinforce his bitterness and make his point. You can see this most clearly toward the end of the passage: "... without *one act of assistance, one word of encouragement,* or *one smile of favor.*" Choice (A) is incorrect because a *parody* is a humorous imitation of a literary work that aims to point out the work's shortcomings. That is clearly not the case here. Choice (B) is wrong because *symbolism* occurs when an image stands for something other than what was expected. Choice (C) is wrong because *personification* is giving human traits to nonhuman things. Choice (E) is wrong because *colloquial language* is everyday speech.

22. **The correct answer is (E).** The metaphor in the fourth paragraph is Johnson comparing himself to a shepherd in a poem. Here is the relevant passage: "The shepherd in Virgil grew at last acquainted with Love and found him a native of the rocks. Is not a patron, my Lord, one who looks with unconcern on a man struggling for life in the water and, when he has reached ground, encumbers him with help?"

23. **The correct answer is (E).** The metaphor serves to show that as the shepherd found love painful, so Johnson was pained in his search for support from Lord Chesterfield. You can see this especially in the last part of the metaphor, when Johnson bitterly complains that the Earl helped him only when he no longer needed help, when he was "on the ground," when his *Dictionary* was published.

24. **The correct answer is (E).** The words *enchantment, contending, exhausted,* and *uncourtly* are especially effective because they have strong connotations and thus reinforce Johnson's point. Remember that every word has a *denotation,* its dictionary meaning. Some words also carry *connotations,* the generally accepted meaning of a word or its emotional overtones. Connotation adds richness to a word's mean-

ing. The two meanings work together to give the passage greater depth and to further the author's theme. There is no *alliteration* (the repetition of initial consonants), so choice (A) cannot be correct. All connotations carry a subtext, so choice (B) is incorrect. Choice (C) makes no sense. Choice (D) may be true, but it has nothing to do with the point.

25. **The correct answer is (B).** Johnson's style in this letter is characterized by all of the following stylistic elements EXCEPT highly abstract metaphors. All the metaphors are clear and obvious. The passage does include *precise diction,* choice (A); *long, balanced sentences,* choice (C); *parallel structure,* choice (D); and *literary allusions,* choice (E). The literary allusion is to Virgil.

26. **The correct answer is (A).** The fifth paragraph is organized by *cause and effect*. Chesterfield does not deserve credit: he has not helped, and Johnson has completed the project on his own. The paragraph is not organized by *chronological order,* choice (B); *spatial order,* choice (C); *order of importance,* choice (D); or *extended definition,* choice (E).

27. **The correct answer is (D).** Johnson attributes his success to his own hard work, perseverance, and Providence. This is shown in the following passage: "I hope it is no very cynical asperity not to confess obligations where no benefit has been received or to be unwilling that the public should consider me as owing that to a patron which Providence has enabled me to do for myself. Having carried on my work thus far with so little obligation to any favorer of learning, I shall not be disappointed though I should conclude it, if less be possible, with less; for I have been long wakened from that dream of hope in which I once boasted myself with so much exultation..." This clearly shows that he does not expect his patron's *continued* support, choice (A), since he did not have it in the beginning. Virgil never helped him (since he is long dead), so you can eliminate choice (E). Johnson never alludes to luck, so choice (C) cannot be true. The Earl's kind reviews in the newspaper sparked the letter and Johnson's bitterness, so choice (B) cannot be true.

28. **The correct answer is (A).** The narrative style of this passage is best described as *straightforward and honest.* Johnson says what he means without subterfuge or insinuation. *Abrupt and crude,* choice (B), is too strong a characterization. The other choices are too far off the mark.

29. **The correct answer is (A).** The opening sentence is unified by the author's use of parallelism. Recall that *parallelism* (or *parallel structure*) is the use of words, phrases, or sentences that have the same grammatical structure. In the first sentence, the author constructed parallel prepositional phrases: "Studies serve *for delight, for ornament,* and *for ability.*" Choice (B) is incorrect because *allusions* are a

reference to a well-known place, event, person, work of art, or other work of literature. Allusions enrich a story or poem by suggesting powerful and exciting comparisons. Choice (C) is wrong because *imagery* is words or phrases that appeal to the five senses. There are no sensory descriptions in this particular sentence. Choice (D) is wrong because a *metaphor* is a figure of speech that compares two unlike things. The more familiar thing helps describe the less familiar one. There is nothing being compared or contrasted here; rather, items are being listed.

30. **The correct answer is (D).** By using the word *delight* in the first sentence and repeating it in the second sentence, the author specifically emphasizes the rewards that the attainment of knowledge bring. Choice (A) cannot be correct because it directly contradicts the three purposes of study that he lists in the first sentence: "Studies serve for delight, for ornament, and for ability." Choice (B) and choice (C) are too narrow to be correct. Choice (E) has nothing to do with delight; rather, it implies just the opposite.

31. **The correct answer is (B).** According to the author, the three primary benefits of study are enjoyment, adornment, and competence. This information is directly stated in the first sentence: "Studies serve for delight, for ornament, and for ability." All the other choices are a misreading of the passage.

32. **The correct answer is (A).** All of the following dangers can result from excessive study EXCEPT *accomplishment*. The information is contained in the following sentence: "To spend too much time in studies is sloth; to use them too much for ornament, is affectation; to make judgment wholly by their rules is the humor of a scholar." Choice (B), *laziness*, is the same as "sloth," as is choice (E), *inactivity*. Choice (C), *simplified judgments*, is the same as "to make judgment wholly by their rules is the humor of a scholar." Choice (D), *an attitude of superiority*, is the same as "affectation."

33. **The correct answer is (C).** As used in this passage, *affectation* means "pretense." That is the only meaning the word can have. Do not confuse *affectation* with *affection*. This could result in choosing choice (A), *fondness*, in error.

34. **The correct answer is (B).** The sentence "...for natural abilities are like natural plants, that need proyning by study; and studies themselves do give forth directions too much at large, except they be bounded in by experience" is a simile. Recall that a *simile* is a figure of speech that compares two unlike things. Similes use the words "like" or "as" to make the comparison. In this simile, natural abilities are being compared to plants. The simile is explained fully in question 35. *Personification* is giving human traits to nonhuman things. For example, "The book begged to be read." That is clearly not the case here. Finally, an

allusion is a reference to a well-known place, event, person, work of art, or other work of literature. There is no reference being made here.

35. **The correct answer is (E).** The figure of speech developed in the fifth sentence suggests primarily that just as plants must be pruned to make them grow full, so too must the intellectual abilities of people be disciplined (a type of pruning) through study. None of the other choices expresses this meaning.

36. **The correct answer is (A).** The writer uses an *analogy* in the line: "Some books are to be tasted, others to be swallowed, and a few to be chewed and digested." An *analogy* is a comparison based on a similarity between things that are otherwise dissimilar. Recall that a *simile* is a figure of speech that compares two unlike things. Similes use the words "like" or "as" to make the comparison. Although this is a comparison, the words "like" or "as" are not used, so choice (B) is wrong. Choice (C) does not make sense in context. Choice (D) is wrong because *hyperbole* is exaggeration used for a literary effect such as emphasis, drama, or humor. There is clearly no exaggeration here. Finally, choice (E) is wrong because there is no *understatement* either.

37. **The correct answer is (C).** According to the author, you should read to think about the writer's ideas. This is directly stated in the following sentence: "Read not to contradict and confute; nor to believe and take for granted; nor to find talk and discourse; but to weigh and consider." None of the other choices shows this relationship between reading and considering the writer's ideas.

38. **The correct answer is (B).** As used in the second paragraph, *meaner* most nearly means "inferior." Here is the relevant passage: "...the meaner sorts of books" are those that do not measure up." Choice (A) is wrong because *cruel* is the wrong meaning of *meaner* in this context. The same is true for choices (C), (D), and (E).

39. **The correct answer is (E).** The author's style in this passage is best described as *sophisticated,* marked by elevated diction and long sentences. The author crafts careful, balanced, and graceful sentences, resulting in an elegant and refined style.

40. **The correct answer is (D).** The speaker's tone is best described as *authoritative and confident.* The author projects a tone of assurance, learning, and conviction. This is the direct opposite of choice (A) and choice (B). Since he is being completely straightforward, choice (C) cannot be correct. While he is self-assured, he is not *arrogant and overbearing,* choice (E).

41. **The correct answer is (D).** In this passage, the author uses rhetorical strategies and reasoning to delineate different methods of reading and studying. The author carefully explains the different uses of reading

and study. He identifies the uses and advantages of each and notes which methods are suitable for various purposes and for people with diverse characters and temperaments. None of the other choices reflects this summary.

42. **The correct answer is (B).** The author likely uses so many statistics and factual details in his account to make the situation seem real and help readers visualize its horror. Choice (A) has merit, but choice (B) is more inclusive. Choice (C) is too strong because the author does not compare the plague to other tragedies. The same is true for choice (D). Choice (E) has nothing to do with the author's use of numbers or facts.

43. **The correct answer is (A).** The phrase [The plague] "raged with such violence as in the two parishes of Aldgate and Whitechapel" is an example of *personification*. Recall that *personification* is giving human traits to nonhuman things. For example, "The trees groaned with pain." Here, the plague is raging as a person would. Choice (B) is wrong because a *metaphor* is a figure of speech that compares two unlike things. The more familiar thing helps describe the less familiar one. Choice (C) is wrong because an *analogy* is also a comparison. Choice (D) is wrong because *hyperbole* is exaggeration used for a literary effect such as emphasis, drama, or humor. There's no exaggeration here; rather, the plague raged with violence. Choice (E) is incorrect because the author is again being factual.

44. **The correct answer is (E).** In the third paragraph, the writer uses *imagery* to make the scene come alive for readers. An *image* is a word that appeals to one or more of our five senses: sight, hearing, taste, touch, or smell. Here are some examples from the passage: The phrase "I saw two links come over from the Minories" appeals to sight. The phrase "... and heard the bellman" appeals to sound. The phrase "He said nothing as he walked about, but two or three times groaned very deeply and loud, and sighed as he would break his heart" appeals to sound.

45. **The correct answer is (D).** The writer introduces the cloaked man as a symbol of the human dimension of the tragedy, all those people whose lives were changed by the plague. Writers frequently include a specific person in the midst of general statements to put a human face on an event or situation that affects many. This common rhetorical strategy is a useful way to make broad statements more specific and thus emotional. None of the other choices fits.

46. **The correct answer is (D).** The writer uses all three rhetorical techniques in the third paragraph: *alliteration, imagery,* and *symbolism.* Recall that *alliteration* is the repetition of initial consonant sounds in several words in a sentence or line of poetry. Writers use alliteration to create musical effects, link related ideas, stress certain words, or mimic specific sounds. In the third paragraph, alliteration is shown in

the repeated "*m*'s": *m*uffled up with a brown cloak, and *m*aking *m*otions and *d*elirious or *d*esperate. Imagery has already been discussed in question 44. Symbolism is evident in the author's use of the cloaked man as a symbol of the human dimension of the tragedy, as explained in question 45.

47. **The correct answer is (C).** Overall, this passage is organized according to *chronological order*. The writer relates events in time order, from the beginning of the story to the end. None of the other choices correctly defines this order.

48. **The correct answer is (B).** The *tone* of this selection is best characterized as *detached and journalistic*. The author does not focus on his own emotions to avoid having the selection sink into desolation. Therefore, choices (A), (C), and (E) cannot be correct. He is being straightforward, so choice (D) is incorrect.

49. **The correct answer is (E).** The phrase "the common grave of mankind" functions as a metaphor for death. See question 50 for additional explanation.

50. **The correct answer is (A).** The speaker uses the phrase "the common grave of mankind" to illustrate the point that all people, not just plague victims, eventually go to their graves. Therefore, the phrase becomes symbolic of the universal human condition. There is no support for any of the other answer choices.

51. **The correct answer is (C).** The plague was factual, but this selection is fiction. The author uses the first-person point of view to make the situation seem real. Recall that point of view is the position from which a story is told. In the *first-person point of view,* the narrator is one of the characters in the story. The narrator explains the events through his or her own eyes, using the pronouns *I* and *me.* In the *omniscient point of view,* the narrator is not a character in the story. Instead, the narrator looks through the eyes of all the characters. As a result, the narrator is all-knowing. The narrator uses the pronouns *he, she,* and *they.* The first-person point of view allows the closest connection between the narrator and the audience.

52. **The correct answer is (C).** The author's writing style is best described as *clear and graceful.* Choice (D) is too strong a characterization of his graceful style, however. Choices (A) and (E) are the opposite of his clear style. Choice (B) suggests writing that is overly ornamented, which is clearly not the case here.

SECTION II: ESSAY QUESTIONS

Question 1:

To earn a high score on this question:

- be sure to answer the question you are asked. Responses often earn low scores because they do not directly focus on the question being asked.

- provide background or additional information only if it directly pertains to the issue at hand. Don't parade your learning for the sake of impressing your reader. Also be sure that you have your facts right.

- focus on the writer's point about the education of women.

- cite specific examples from the text and your own knowledge to make your point.

- demonstrate a sophisticated use of language and an awareness of its power to communicate meaning.

- revise your essay to make sure that *you* have used all words correctly. After all, you don't want to misuse words when you're analyzing another writer's style.

- check your essay for errors in grammar, usage, punctuation, capitalization, and spelling.

The following model response would earn a top score because it fulfills the requirements of this question and the standards of good writing:

1   I believe Wollstonecraft's thesis holds true, even today. Modern society still holds the idea that many women are no more than foolish objects of desire, incapable of any actual accomplishment.

2   Wollstonecraft comments that women are "ridiculed or pitied by writers who endeavor by satire or instruction to improve them." Such writers have changed their medium from novels or short stories to television, but their material

3 is the same. From shows like "I Love Lucy" to more recent "7th Heaven" or "Ally McBeal," female characters are portrayed as scatterbrained eye candy with wacky plans that the male characters must step in to save them from.

    And television doesn't stop there. Advertisers will do anything they can to

4 encourage the idea of beauty being a woman's most important characteristic. "If you buy these shoes/this makeup/this perfume, then you will be very attractive and a big strong man with lots of money will want you," they trumpet.

5   Even if television wasn't propagating the image of women as incapable of true accomplishment, the image is still set in the minds of society. Young girls aren't taught to fix cars; they're taught to pluck their eyebrows. Schools steer them away from math and science and into "softer" subjects like English and history. Bankers, engineers,

1. Clear position on Wollstonecraft's thesis

2. Quotes from Wollstonecraft

3. Point 1, backed by excellent specific detail

4. Point 2, backed by excellent specific detail

5. Point 3, backed by excellent specific detail

		computer techs, and similar heavily math- and science-based careers are among the highest paid and highest valued in modern
6. Additional detail	6	society, and young women are steered away from them. As Wollstonecraft says, women are kept away from "important" tasks and encouraged to become the beautiful "trophy wife" of a man in one of these positions.
7. Quote from Wollstonecraft	7	Wollstonecraft calls for women to become more "masculine and respectable." It's time women demanded to be treated as the intelligent, accomplished people they are. It's time women rejected the impossible images of
8. Strong conclusion	8	physical perfection and the stereotype of wacky women. Women need to take their place in the world.

Question 2:

Try these suggestions as you answer these types of questions:

- Start by reading the essay (novel excerpt, short story excerpt, etc.) several times through. Each time you read, look for different rhetorical device, such as figures of speech and diction. As you read, see how all the rhetorical strategies fit together to help the writer express his or her point.

- Go with the obvious interpretation. If a passage is called "Nature," assume that it concerns nature. In general, these questions are not designed to trick you; rather, they are crafted to test what you have learned about rhetorical strategies, modes of discourse, and writing styles in class and on your own.

- Unless you're desperately stuck for an opening gambit, don't rephrase the question in your opening sentence. Remember that the scorers are reading hundreds of essays on the same topic, so they're not likely to be impressed if the opening to your essay is just like the opening of the previous fifty essays they have read. Instead, get right to your point by stating your thesis.

- If you *do* want to try crafting an interesting opening, try using a well-known quotation, anecdote (brief story), or fact. These techniques will be explained in detail in the essay *Part IV: Strategies for Success on the Essay Questions.*

- Follow with specific examples drawn from the passage under analysis. Relate each point to your main idea.

- Interweave all the elements together into a meaningful whole. In general, don't separate the rhetorical strategies, one in each paragraph, as this usually results in a choppy and redundant essay.

- Sum up by briefly reiterating your point. Don't introduce any new information, but reach for an insight or point that ties everything together in an intelligent and logical way.

- Be sure to proofread your essay for errors in grammar, usage, punctuation, capitalization, and spelling. You won't get clobbered for a few minor errors, but why not improve your chances of earning a top score by being letter-perfect?

The following model response would earn a top score because it fulfills the requirements of this question and the standards of good writing:

1 In this essay, the author shows readers the beauty he sees in nature. He uses such stylistic devices as simile, metaphor, and imagery to convey the
2 importance of nature to a fully realized human being. Human nature is inextricably linked to the natural world, he believes.

    The author claims that out in a natural setting, "a man cast off his years, as
3 the snake his slough." With this simile, he compares man to a snake, which becomes stifled and unable to grow in its old skin. Man is stifled and unable to grow in a city—he needs to return to nature and "shed his skin" in order to grow. The skin might symbolize all burdens we carry when we are not in nature. The
4 return to nature becomes a rebirth. The phrase "at what period soever of is always a child" reveals the metaphor of a person in nature always being a child.

5   The author uses another metaphor when he refers to the air as a "cordial." He compares the air to a drink, the fresh air leaving him intoxicated. But unlike alcohol, this is a "cordial of incredible virtue," which makes him "glad to the
6 brink of fear." He isn't drunk, but he is delighted with the beauty before him.

7   The author's imagery reinforces the power of the natural world to humans.

    Likely the most memorable image is this one: "I become a transparent eyeball; I am nothing: I see all." Through his beautiful language, the image of nature's beauty is impressed upon the reader. In the vastness of nature, an individual blends and becomes part of it, and all of humanity becomes one. The beauty of
8 nature is so incredible, it unites humanity to find God.

    In nature, the author finds a rebirth and ability for people to grow and be
9 reborn as something greater, more connected to each other and to the "Universal Being" that flows through each of us.

1. Main idea stated immediately
2. Focus on rhetorical strategies
3. Simile isolated
4. Simile explained
5. Metaphor isolated
6. Metaphor explained
7. Central image
8. Image linked to theme
9. Summarizes main points

Question 3:

Try these suggestions as you answer this type of essay:

- Break your discussion into two parts: treat the analysis of rhetorical modes in the first half and his comments on the stereotype of an English squire in the second half.

- Pay close attention to the items the question called out: details, description, and imagery.

- Cite examples from the text.

- Finish with a strong conclusion.

The following model response would earn a top score because it fulfills the requirements of this question and the standards of good writing:

1. Clear topic sentence

1 The author, Sir Richard Steele, suggests that Sir Roger de Coverley is an archetype rather than a real person. By saying that "All who know that shire are very well acquainted with the parts and merit of Sir Roger," Steele means that we

2. Understanding of topic

2 have all met someone who fits the stereotype of the English squire.

3. Highlights details, descriptions, and images

3 The details, descriptions, and images that Steele uses help him sketch the stereotype of an English squire. For example, Steele remarks that "Before this disappointment [in love], Sir Roger was what you call a fine gentleman, had often

4. Specific examples

4 supped with my Lord Rochester and Sir George Etherege, and fought a duel upon his first coming to town, and kicked Bully Dawson in a public coffeehouse for calling him a "youngster." "According to the stereotype, a fine gentleman dines with famous writers (Sir George Etherege) and defends his honor by fighting

5. More examples

5 duels and beating up infamous scoundrels (Bully Dawson). He has an easy-going personality and is popular with people in the area. "He does nothing with sourness or obstinacy," the author notes. Sir Roger is also genuinely helpful: "his being unconfined to modes and forms makes him but the readier and more capable to please and oblige all who know him."

6. Effective transition

6 Further, Sir Roger has what the author describes as "singularities" in his character and actions. His behavior is "unconfined to modes and forms," and he dresses in clothing that is long out of style. Indeed, Sir Roger has worn the same coat and doublet for so long that "he tells us, [they have] been in and out of fashion twelve times since he first wore it"!

7. Focus on author's purpose

7 Why would the author describe a man who has these peculiar character traits? Steele's purpose is to present a lesson in manners and proper behavior. Sir Roger's "singularities" spring from "his good sense and are contradictions to the manners of the world only as he thinks the world is in the wrong." The author implies that fashion is not always sensible. Sir Roger thinks for himself. He's not swayed by what's in and what's out.

8. Makes the point

8 Steele suggests that underneath the stereotype, there's a lot to admire in the country squire. He represents his class with "good sense" and a naturally "jovial" temperament. Where can we find this eighteenth-century country squire today? He's the well-off village mayor, the easy-going retired college professor, the millionaire

9. Adds individual insight

9 who got out before the dot.com crash. They all have a certain ease about them as they represent their friends in the business of life.

Strategies for Success on the Multiple-Choice Questions

You'll recall from Part I of this book and the sample AP English Language and Composition exams you've taken that the multiple-choice portion of this exam consists of 50–60 questions. The exact number varies from year to year. This portion of the exam contains four prose passages. (Occasionally, there will be five passages.) Every passage will be prose. There is NO poetry on this test. Each selection has approximately 10–15 questions.

- If the test pattern continues as it has in the past, the passages will be drawn from both fiction and nonfiction.
- The passages may be complete (as in the case of letters or journal entries, for example) or excerpts (as in the case of novels, short stories, and speeches, for instance).
- The passages will be drawn from different literary periods. For example, the test might contain readings that span the sixteenth century to the present.
- The passages will represent a wide variety of authors, including minorities and women as well as the traditional white male writers.
- Even if the passages were written by famous authors, the passages will almost always be taken from the writers' lesser-known works. Therefore, it's very unlikely that you will have studied these passages in class or read them on your own, since they rarely appear in anthologies or textbooks.

The multiple-choice questions are the sort that a teacher might ask in class to elicit a close analytical reading of a prose passage. You will be asked questions on the following topics:

Question Types	Explanations
Comprehension	You will have to identify or infer the *main idea* in nonfiction or the *theme* in fiction.
Vocabulary	You will have to define specific vocabulary words. These questions include unfamiliar words as well as words with multiple meanings.
Organization/structure	You will have to determine how information is arranged (chronological order, cause and effect, comparison and contrast, etc.). You will also have to judge what effect the organization has on the writer's purpose.
Rhetorical strategies/style	You will have to determine how the writer's strategies affect meaning.

To earn a high score on the multiple-choice part of the test...

You *won't* have to know...	You *will* have to know...
biographical information about the author	how to analyze prose, both fiction and nonfiction
historical information that might relate to the passage	rhetorical strategies such as *tone, purpose, figurative language, imagery, tone*, etc.
the author's other works	*modes of discourse* (narrative, expository, persuasive, descriptive) and *methods of organization* (cause and effect, chronological order, problem-solution, comparison-contrast, etc.)
	how to understand diction and syntax used in sixteenth-, seventeenth-, eighteenth-, and nineteenth-century writing

This book contains five practice exams and many simulated multiple-choice questions that you can use to practice. However, the Advanced Placement program of the College Board owns all the rights to the actual exams they've administered in the past. Therefore, if you wish to practice on actual past AP exams, you will have to order them directly from the College Board.

FAQS: THE MULTIPLE-CHOICE SECTION OF THE AP ENGLISH LANGUAGE AND COMPOSITION EXAM

Q: *Are there any trick questions on the multiple-choice part of the exam?*

A: No. Some of the questions may seem sneaky, but they're surprisingly straight-forward for a standardized test. Read carefully, stay calm and focused, and you'll find most of the answers.

Q: *What happens if I can't answer all the multiple-choice questions?*

A: You'll have plenty of company! Few students answer all the questions—and fewer still answer them all correctly. You can miss a few questions and still earn a 4 or 5 on the exam if you earn a high score on the essays.

Q: *What should I do if I skip a question?*

A: If you do skip a question and move on, be very careful to mark your answer sheet correctly.

Q: *What pattern of answers can I expect?*

A: None. Mark the answers that you think are correct, not the ones that make a pleasing pattern. Therefore, even if you have written four A's in a row and you're sure that the fifth answer is an A, write down A. (You may want to go back and check those other A's, however. You might have misread a question or mismarked an answer.)

Q: *How many multiple-choice questions do I have to answer correctly to do well on the test?*

A: Your final score depends on how well you do on the essays as well as the multiple-choice questions. Your final score also depends on how well everyone else does on the test. As a very, very rough gauge, figure that you would have to earn near-perfect scores on all three essays (8–9 on the 9-point scale) and answer about half the multiple-choice questions correctly to get a "3."

OVERALL MULTIPLE-CHOICE GUIDELINES: TOP TEN HINTS FOR SCORING HIGH ON MULTIPLE-CHOICE QUESTIONS

While every reading passage on the AP English Language and Composition exam is different, every multiple-choice question demands the same reasoning process. The following hints can help you boost your score.

1. Know what to expect on the multiple-choice part of the AP test.

   Complete all the practice exams in this book so you know what you're facing when you take the real test. That way, you won't waste precious time reading directions (since you'll already have them memorized) and trying to figure out what comes next (since you'll be thoroughly familiar with the test format).

2. Study.

   You can't win it if you're not in it. Getting college credit for freshman English by earning a high AP score can save you some serious money—thousands and thousands of dollars in most private colleges. Therefore, it's clearly in your best interests to do your very best on the AP English Language and Composition exam so you earn the credit. Set up a study schedule months before the exam and stick to it. Even if you're blessed with an exceptionally gifted and hard-working AP teacher, how well you do on the test has a lot to do with the amount of reading, writing, and studying *you* do on your own.

3. Use your time wisely.

   The multiple-choice questions are arranged in order of difficulty, from least difficult to most difficult. Most test takers get many of the easy questions correct, but few students get the most difficult questions right. Since every question is worth the same number of points, you're better off spending your time making sure you get the easier and middle questions right rather than rushing to finish the entire multiple-choice section.

4. Develop a test strategy.

   There are three ways you can approach any multiple-choice test:

   - Work from beginning to end, answering every question in order. Answer every single question, even if you have to guess.

   - Answer the easy questions first, and then go back and work on the harder questions.

   - Answer the hardest questions first, and then go back and answer the easy ones.

   None of these test-taking methods is right or wrong. However, for most people, Method 2 works best. If you decide to use this strategy, answer the easier questions first and then go back to figure out the more difficult ones.

   As you work from the beginning to the end, put a checkmark next to any question you skip. Write in pencil so you can erase the checkmarks to avoid leaving stray marks. When you get to the end of the multiple-choice questions, go back to the beginning of the section and start answering the items you skipped.

5. Slow down!

   If you work too fast, you risk making careless errors. You're better off skipping a few of the last (most difficult) questions rather than working so fast that you make costly blunders.

6. Guess.

   If you can eliminate any of the answer choices, it's always in your favor to guess. The more choices you can eliminate, the better your chances of selecting the right choice. Don't just guess willy-nilly, but if you can eliminate some choices, guessing is likely to earn you some extra points.

   NEVER just fill in blanks in an attractive, random pattern to make it appear that you've legitimately answered every question. If you do, you'll lose far more credit than you'll gain.

7. Use process of elimination.

   Multiple-choice test writers know that you're looking for the correct answer, so they include a lot of answers that *look* correct but are really wrong. Rather than looking for the right answer, start by looking for the wrong answers. Start by eliminating these ringers because each wrong answer you knock out brings you one step closer to finding to correct answer.

8. Think before you switch answers.

   Don't go back and change answers unless you're bedrock sure that your second choice is correct. Studies have shown that in nearly all cases, your first choice is more likely to be correct than subsequent choices, unless you suddenly recall some relevant information.

9. Stay calm.

   Don't get rattled. The answer to every question is somewhere in the poem or passage. All you have to do is find it or find the details that enable you to make the inference you need.

10. Deal with panic.

    Convince yourself that you can succeed by working carefully and resolutely. If you start losing control, pause for a second to calm yourself. Take a few deep breaths, imagine a pleasant scene, and then keep working.

NOTE
Currently, tuition at an elite Ivy League university runs about $35,000 per year. The average private university charges around $22,000 per year; state universities, around $10,500. Because the cost of goods and services continues to rise, college costs are projected to rise about 3–4 percent per year. Many students who count on getting financial aid often receive far less than they projected. As a result, the vast majority of college students take out loans to pay the cost of their education.

ANSWERING MULTIPLE-CHOICE AP QUESTIONS ON COMPREHENSION

Before you can begin to analyze a passage for its rhetorical strategies and stylistic elements, you must first understand what the passage means.

• In nonfiction, the meaning will be the author's *main idea.*

• In fiction, the author's main idea is called the *theme.* It is a general statement about life. The theme can be stated outright in the work, or readers will have to infer it from details about plot, characters, and setting. When you *make inferences*, you combine what you already know with details from the passage. In effect, you are "reading between the lines" to find unstated information and draw conclusions.

Always begin by figuring out what a passage means. You can do this by following these steps:

1. Read the passage through once and see how much of the author's meaning you can immediately grasp.
2. Then go back through the passage a second time and define all the unfamiliar words, concepts, ideas, and references. Decode the images and symbols, too.
3. Paraphrase the passage by restating it in your own words. If you can do this, you likely have a clear understanding of the meaning.

Questions about comprehension, main idea, or theme are phrased in different ways on the AP test. Notice the variations on the same question:

- The subject (or topic) of the passage is ... [you must know the subject or topic before you can infer the theme]
- The theme of this passage is best stated as …
- The theme of this passage can most precisely be stated as follows...
- The writer's main idea is...
- The reader may infer from this passage that ...
- The passage is an appeal for an understanding of all of the following EXCEPT ...
- Throughout the passage, the imagery suggests that ...
- What does (specific element) symbolize in paragraph 2?
- The passage as a whole introduces contrasts between all of the following EXCEPT ...
- (Specific quote from the passage) makes a suitable ending for all of the following reasons EXCEPT...
- The best title for this passage would be...
- What rhetorical strategy does the author use in this passage to convey his or her main idea? [This is a cross-over question, involving both theme and rhetorical strategies.]

TECHNIQUES FOR IDENTIFYING AN IMPLIED MAIN IDEA

When writers don't directly state the main idea of a passage, you have to make *inferences* to find the main idea. You can figure out the implied main idea by asking the following questions:

- What is this passage about?
- What does the passage describe?
- What does the passage suggest?
- What is the author trying to communicate about the subject?

Step 1: Identify the topic.

The *topic* of a passage is its subject, what the passage is all about. You should be able to state the topic of a passage in one or two words, such as *identity, leadership, freedom.*

Step 2: Think about what the passage describes.

After you find the topic, think about what the passage is all about. Isolate the details, including the examples, facts, statistics, reasons, definitions, and descriptions in the paragraph. See how all the details fit with the topic. As you read, ask yourself, "How can I use these pieces of information to find the main idea?"

Step 3: Think about what the description suggests.

Now that you have the topic and details, think about what the writer is saying about the subject. Put together the details to "read between the lines." Try to state the implied main idea in your own words. Then look at all the answer choices. Eliminate the choices that are too broad and general to be the main idea. Cross out the choices that are too narrow and specific to be the main idea. Get rid of the choices that don't seem to have anything to do with the topic of the passage. These choices will contain information not related to the details in the passage. From the remaining choices, pick the one that best summarizes the contents of the passage.

SAMPLE PASSAGES AND QUESTIONS

Read the following passages, and answer the practice AP questions that follow.

Passage 1

One of the rarest and most prized animals in the United States is the key deer. This tiny creature was once hunted without mercy. It was not uncommon for a single hunter to kill more than a dozen of these creatures in one day. Usually, hunters set grass fires to drive the creatures out of hiding, but other times, they were attacked with harpoons while they were swimming. In the 1950s, conservationists saved the key deer from extinction. The Boone and Crockett Clubs were especially influential in this matter. Today, the surviving key deer are protected by the United States government in the Key Deer National Wildlife Refuge, created in 1957.

1. The topic of this passage is
   (A) Florida.
   (B) conservationists.
   (C) hunting.
   (D) key deer.
   (E) the government's role in preserving endangered species.

2. The main idea in the passage is
   (A) stated in the first sentence.
   (B) stated in the second sentence.
   (C) stated in the middle of the passage.
   (D) stated in the last sentence.
   (E) unstated.

3. The main idea in the paragraph is best stated as follows:
   (A) Hunting key deer is bad.
   (B) Without intervention, the key deer probably would be extinct by now.
   (C) There are many different ways to hunt the key deer.
   (D) The government has many different conservation agencies.
   (E) Hunting any wild creatures should be actively discouraged.

Answers and Explanations

1. **The correct answer is (D).**

2. **The correct answer is (C).**

3. **The correct answer is (B).** This passage has a stated main idea. It's in this sentence: "In the 1950s, conservationists saved the key deer from extinction."

Passage 2

Ancient savage tribes played a primitive kind of football. About 2,500 years ago there was a ball-kicking game played by the Athenians, Spartans, and Corinthians, which the Greeks called *Episkuros*. The Romans had a somewhat similar game called *Harpastu*m. According to several historical sources, the Romans brought the game with them when they invaded the British Isles in the first century, AD. The game today known as "football" in the United States can be traced directly back to the English game of rugby, although there have been many changes to the game. Football was played informally on university fields more than a hundred years ago. In 1840, a yearly series of informal "scrimmages" started at Yale University. It took more than twenty-five years, however, for the game to become part of college life. The first formal intercollegiate football game was held between Princeton and Rutgers teams on November 6, 1869 on Rutgers's home field at New Brunswick, New Jersey, and Rutgers won.

1. The subject of this passage is
   (A) ancient Greek sports.
   (B) brutality in sports.
   (C) rugby.
   (D) sports in the United States.
   (E) the history of football.

2. The writer's main idea is best stated as follows:
   (A) The Romans, Athenians, Spartans, and Corinthians all played a game like football.
   (B) Football is a very old game; its history stretches back to ancient days.
   (C) American football comes from a British game called "rugby."
   (D) Football is a more popular game than baseball, even though baseball is called "America's pastime."
   (E) Football is a brutal sport with roots in barbarous cultures.

3. The best title for this passage would be
   (A) Play Ball!
   (B) Football in America.
   (C) The Origins of Football.
   (D) America's Pastime.
   (E) Savage Games.

Answers and Explanations

1. **The correct answer is (E)**.

2. **The correct answer is (B)**. This passage has an unstated main idea, so you have to infer it from details in the reading. Only choice (B) correctly gives the main idea of the passage. Eliminate choices (A) and (C) because they are too narrow to be the main idea. They give supporting details from the paragraph, not the main idea. Eliminate choices (D) and (E) because they contain information that is not included in the paragraph.

3. **The correct answer is (C)**.

ANSWERING MULTIPLE-CHOICE VOCABULARY QUESTIONS

Some multiple-choice AP questions require you to define a word as it is used in the passage. The questions may be on difficult words or easier words that have uncommon meanings. In either case, follow these four steps as you work through these test items:

1. Go back to the passage and find the word.
2. Fill in your own word for the word you are asked to define.
3. Eliminate the answer choices that don't match your word.
4. Choose the best answer choice.

AP vocabulary questions will be phrased like this:

- "Amorphous" is best interpreted as...
- "Seraphic" (paragraph 2) most nearly means...
- From its context, you can deduce that "wan" (paragraph 3) must mean...
- The best synonym for the word "fastidious" is ...
- What does "vain" mean as used in this context: "The supplicant pleaded in vain"?

As you're looking for the correct meaning, always use context clues.

- *Definition clue*s have the definition right in the passage. The definition is a *synony*m (word that means the same). It may come before or after the unfamiliar word. For example: *"Tsunamis*, or seismic sea-waves, are gravity waves set in motion by underwater disturbances associated with earthquakes." "Seismic sea-waves" are a synonym for the unfamiliar word *tsunami*s.

- *Contrast clues* tell you what something isn't rather than what it is. Often, you'll find contrast clues set off with *unlike, not,* or *instead o*f. For example: "Then arrange a handful of mulch, not fresh leaves, on the top." *Mulc*h must be the opposite of fresh leaves. It must mean "decayed leaves."

- *Common sense clues* encourage you to use what you already know to define the word. For example: "Airplanes make daily *ascent*s to gather data." Since airplanes go into the air, *ascent* must mean "to rise."

Read the following passage, and answer the practice AP questions that follow.

> The nation had few taxes in its early history. From 1791 to 1802, the United States government was supported by internal taxes on distilled spirits, carriages, refined sugar, tobacco, property sold at auction, corporate bonds, and slaves. The high costs of the War of 1812 brought about the nation's first

sales tax on gold, silverware, jewelry, and watches. In 1817, however, Congress expunged all internal taxes, relying on tariffs on imported goods to provide sufficient funds for running the government.

In 1862, in order to support the Civil War effort, Congress enacted the first nation's first income tax law. It was a forerunner of our modern income tax in that it was based on the principles of graduated taxation and of withholding income at the source. During the Civil War, a person earning from $600 to $10,000 per year paid tax at the rate of 3%. Those with incomes of more than $10,000 paid taxes at a higher rate. Additional sales and excise taxes were added, and an "inheritance" tax also made its debut. In 1866, internal revenue collections reached their highest point in the nation's 90-year-history—more than $310 million, an amount not reached again until around 1911.

1. In paragraph 1, the best synonym for "expunged" is
   (A) collected.
   (B) retained.
   (C) revamped.
   (D) reconsidered.
   (E) eliminated.

2. In the second paragraph, "forerunner" is used to mean
   (A) sequel.
   (B) supplement.
   (C) outcome.
   (D) precursor.
   (E) continuance.

3. From its context, you can deduce that "graduated" most nearly means
   (A) equal.
   (B) progressive.
   (C) selective.
   (D) mature.
   (E) intelligent.

Answers

1. **The correct answer is (E).**

2. **The correct answer is (D).**

3. **The correct answer is (B).**

ANSWERING QUESTIONS ON ORGANIZATION/STRUCTURE

Structure is the arrangement of details in a work of literature. Identifying the structure of a prose passage is a key AP English Language and Composition skill because it helps you determine the author's purpose (to entertain, to explain, to persuade, to describe).

ORGANIZATION OF FICTION

Fiction is arranged in *chronological order*, the order of time. Events are arranged from first to last, as on a timeline. However, passages may violate chronology by using a *flashback* (a scene that breaks into the story to show an earlier part of the action) or a *flashforward* (a scene that breaks into the story to show a later part of the action.) Flashbacks and flashforwards help fill in missing information, explain the characters' actions, and advance the plot.

Fiction writers often use dates to show the order of events. In addition, writers can use time-order words to show when events happen. These transitions include the following:

Time-order transitions

after	at length	before
currently	during	eventually
first	second	third, etc.
finally	immediately	in the future
later	meanwhile	next
now	soon	subsequently
then	today	

ORGANIZATION OF NONFICTION

Nonfiction can also be arranged in chronological order, but it can have many other methods of organization as well. The most common methods of organization for nonfiction include the following:

- cause and effect (what happened and why)
- comparison and contrast (how two people, places, things, or ideas are the same or different)
- problem and solution
- most-to-least important details
- process analysis (how-to essays); these are usually arranged in chronological order.
- spatial order (up and down, down and up, side to side, etc.)

Questions about organization and structure will often take this form:

- This essay is constructed primarily on ...
- The passage is developed principally by means of ...
- The author's thesis in the third paragraph is developed through ...
- The passage suggests contrasts between...

Sample Passages and Questions

Read the following passages, and answer the practice AP questions that follow.

Passage 1

Engineers say that the push-button factories may eventually permit a work schedule in which the weekend will be longer than the week. Educators see all this leisure promoting a scholastic renaissance in which cultural attainments will become the yardstick of social recognition for worker and boss alike. Gloomier observers fear the trend toward "inhuman production" will end by making workers obsolete.

The passage is developed principally by means of

(A) cause and effect.

(B) most-to-least important details.

(C) process analysis.

(D) chronological order.

(E) comparison and contrast.

The correct answer is (A), cause and effect, for the causes, such as "push-button factories," result in the effects, such as "the weekend will be longer than the week." Leisure will result in an cultural renaissance and "inhuman production" will result in workers becoming obsolete.

Passage 2

Often called the Congressional Medal of Honor, it is the nation's highest military award for "uncommon valor" by men and women in the armed forces. The medal is awarded for actions that are above and beyond the call of duty in combat against an armed enemy. The medal was first awarded by the Army on March 25, 1863, and then by the Navy on April 3, 1863. In April 1991, President Bush awarded posthumously the Medal of Honor to World War I veteran Army Cpl. Freddie Stowers. He was the first black soldier to receive the nation's highest honor for valor in either World War. Recipients of the medal receive $400 per month for life, a right to burial in Arlington National Cemetery, admission for them or their children to a service academy if they qualify and if quotas permit, and free travel on government aircraft to almost anywhere in the world, on a space-available basis. President Clinton awarded the last medals to date posthumously to two members of the ill-fated Delta Forces operation to capture warlord Gen. Aidid in Mogadishu on October 3, 1993. They are Master Sergeant Gary Gordon and Sgt. 1st Class Randall Shughart, who were killed trying to help wounded comrades.

This essay is constructed primarily according to

    (A)   least-to-most important details.

    (B)   cause and effect.

    (C)   chronological order.

    (D)   comparison and contrast.

    (E)   spatial order.

The correct answer is (C), chronological order, the order of time. Details about the Congressional Medal of Honor are presented from first ("The medal was first awarded by the Army on March 25, 1863, and then by the Navy on April 3, 1863.") to last ("President Clinton awarded the last medals to date posthumously to two members..."). Use the dates—1863 to 1994—as landmarks.

ANSWERING MULTIPLE-CHOICE QUESTIONS ON RHETORICAL STRATEGIES/STYLE

Rhetoric is the strategic use of language to accomplish the author's purpose. Writers create their distinctive *style*, their unique way of writing, by the rhetorical choices they make. Style is made up of elements such as

- diction
- sentence length and structure
- figures of speech
- tone and mood

An author may change his or her style for different kinds of writing and to suit different audiences. In fiction, for example, authors might use more imagery than they would use in nonfiction.

A significant number of the multiple-choice questions on the AP English Language and Composition exam concern an analysis of rhetorical language and techniques. These questions are designed not only to determine how well you know the elements of style but also to judge how well you can integrate these literary techniques with the writer's purpose and theme.

QUESTION FORMAT

Questions about rhetoric and style will often take the following forms:

- What is the rhetorical function of the first sentence of this passage?
- In the first paragraph, what rhetorical strategy does the writer use with the word ("insert word")?
- The long sentences in paragraph 2 serve to ...

TIP

The multiple-choice questions on the AP English Language and Composition exam are presented in chronological order. For example, you can find the information you need to answer question 10 between the information for questions 9 and 11. Taken together, the questions present a story map or chronological reading of the passage. Therefore, try to answer the questions in order rather than skipping around.

- The phrase "I must acknowledge" in the second paragraph does which of the following?
- The third paragraph is marked by ...
- The writer concludes the third paragraph with a series of metaphors to suggest...
- The stylistic element in the third paragraph serves to ... [rhetoric combined with main idea]
- When he quotes Shakespeare ("quote,") the author is using a(n)...
- The writer uses the simile ("simile") to covey the idea that ...
- The writer draws her imagery from all the following EXCEPT...
- The language of this essay is best described as ...
- The writer uses the word ("word") in relation to (part of the passage) to suggest ...
- The phrase ("specific phrase") is an example of ...
- The phrase ("phrase") functions here as a(n)
  - I.   simile
  - II. example
  - III. personification
- The tone of this passage is best described as ....
- The writer uses the phrase cited in item (item number) and others like it to ... [rhetoric combined with main idea]
- From the diction and syntax used in this passage, you can conclude that ... [rhetoric combined with main idea]

The following section examines rhetorical techniques in detail. There are practice AP multiple-choice questions in each section to help you see how these literary elements are tested on this portion of the test.

DICTION

*Dictio*n is a writer's word choice. Diction, part of a writer's style, can be described in many ways. Below are the most common types of diction you will encounter in all your reading and therefore on the AP passages:

Levels of Diction

abstract	concrete	colloquial	elevated
common	technical	formal	informal
general	specific	plain	ornate

Writers suit their diction to their purpose. For example, a writer will use formal, elevated diction to convey a serious purpose. Conversely, a writer might use colloquial diction to create humor and a light tone.

Denotation and Connotation

As you analyze a writer's diction, pay close attention to each word's *connotation* as well as its *denotation*.

- *Denotation* is a word's definition. When you look up a word in the dictionary to find out what it means, you are looking up its denotation. For example, the denotation of *aggressive* is "the action of a state in violating by force the rights of another state, particularly its territorial rights; an unprovoked offensive, attack, invasion, or the like." All words have a denotation.

- *Connotation* is a word's emotional overtones. Some words—but not all—have a connotation. For example, *assertive* and *aggressive* are close in denotation, but their connotations are far apart: *assertive* is positive, considered a desirable trait, while *aggressive* has a negative connotation, conveying the impression of brutality, excessive force, or hostility.

Writers select their words for their connotations as well as their denotation. The connotative meaning allows writers to suggest richer levels of significance as well as achieve the exact shade of meaning they want.

Sample Passages and Questions

Read the following passages, and answer the practice AP questions that follow.

> Nature is by the art of man, as in many other things, so in this also imitated, that it can be made an artificial animal. For seeing life is but a motion of limbs, the beginning whereof is in some principal part within, why may we not say that all automata (engines that move themselves by springs and wheels as doth a watch) have an artificial life? For what is the heart but a spring; and the nerve but so many strings; and the joints but so many wheels, giving motion to the whole body such as it was intended by the artificer? Art goes yet further, imitating the rational and most excellent work of nature, man.

1. The phrase "artificial animal" does which of the following in the opening sentence?
   - (A) Presents a judgment on the artificial man
   - (B) Introduces the writer's main idea
   - (C) Emphasizes the theoretical rather than the practical side of the argument
   - (D) Shifts the focus from generalities to individual cases
   - (E) Introduces the speaker

2. The writer uses the word "artificer" to connote
   - (A) a compassionate scientist.
   - (B) a monster who perverts nature for his own ends.
   - (C) a master builder.

    (D)   an inventor who has failed in the past but is likely to succeed in the future.

    (E)   a pompous and insolent bureaucrat.

3. The passage is most likely part of

    (A)   an argumentative speech.

    (B)   a historical essay.

    (C)   a general-audience magazine article.

    (D)   a light-hearted novel.

    (E)   a book introduction.

Answers

1. **The correct answer is (B).**

2. **The correct answer is (C).**

3. **The correct answer is (E).**

Rather than love, than money, than fame, give me truth: I sat at a table where were rich food and wine in abundance, but sincerity and truth were not; and I went away hungry from the inhospitable board. The hospitality was as cold as the ices. I thought that there was no need of ice to freeze them. They talked to me of the age of the wine and the fame of the vintage; but I thought of an older, newer, and purer wine, of a more glorious vintage, which they had not got, and could not buy. The style, the house and grounds and "entertainment" pass for nothing with me. I called on the king, but he made me wait in his hall, and conducted like a man incapacitated for hospitality. There was a man in my neighborhood who lived in a hollow tree. His manners were truly regal. I should have done better had I called on him.

1. The word "ice" is used symbolically to connote

    (A)   people with spiritually empty lives.

    (B)   rude and vulgar guests.

    (C)   curt and tasteless hosts.

    (D)   money wasted on frivolous social pretense.

    (E)   the difficulty that rich people, especially monarchs, endure.

2. Throughout the passage, the diction suggests

    (A)   the rewards of gainfully earned possessions.

    (B)   the pleasures of fine food and drink.

    (C)   the delight of being with close friends and warm hosts.

    (D)   the hollowness of materialism and the fulfillment of simplicity.

    (E)   the importance of showing consideration and good manners.

3. The passage as a whole introduces contrasts between all of the following EXCEPT

(A) wealth and poverty.

(B) integrity and pretense.

(C) intelligence and misunderstanding.

(D) graciousness and reserve.

(E) royalty and commoners.

Answers

1. **The correct answer is (A).**

2. **The correct answer is (D).**

3. **The correct answer is (C).**

SENTENCE LENGTH AND STRUCTURE

Writers also create their style and convey meaning through sentence length and structure.

Writers have four basic types of sentences to use: *simple, compound, complex,* and *compound-complex.*

1. *Simple sentence*

A simple sentence has one independent clause. That means it has one subject and one verb—although either or both can be compound. In addition, a simple sentence can have adjectives and adverbs. What a simple sentence can't have is another independent clause or any subordinate clauses. In the following excerpt from *The Sun Also Rises,* Hemingway uses simple sentences to convey powerful emotions:

The driver started up the street. I settled back. Brett moved close to me. We sat close against each other. I put my arm around her and she rested against me comfortably. It was very hot and bright, and the houses looked sharply white. We turned out onto the Gran Via.

"Oh, Jake," Brett said, "we could have had such a damned good time together."

Ahead was a mounted policeman in khaki directing traffic. He raised his baton. The car slowed suddenly pressing Brett against me.

"Yes," I said. "Isn't it pretty to think so?"

2. *Compound sentence*

A *compound sentence* consists of two or more independent clauses. As with a simple sentence, a compound sentence can't have any subordinate clauses. The independent clauses can be joined in one of two ways:

• with a coordinating conjunction: *for, and, nor, but, or, yet, so.*

- with a semicolon (;)

Here is a compound sentence from the Hemingway passage: "It was very hot and bright, *and* the houses looked sharply white."

3. *Complex sentence*

A *complex sentence* contains one independent clause and at least one dependent clause. The independent clause is called the "main clause." These sentences use *subordinating conjunctions* to link ideas. Writers select the subordinating conjunction that best helps them express a precise meaning. Subordinating conjunctions include *when, since, although, though, while, during*. We can rewrite the Hemingway sentence to create this complex sentence: *"When* the driver started up the street, I settled back."

4. *Compound-complex sentence*

A *compound-complex sentence* has at least two independent clauses and at least one dependent clause. The dependent clause can be part of the independent clause. Here's an example: *"When* the driver started up the street, I settled back *and* Brett moved close to me."

Writers craft each sentence to suit their audience and purpose. Most writers use a combination of all four sentence types to convey their meaning.

VOICE AND PARALLELISM

Writers also use *voice* and *parallelism* to convey their message and achieve specific stylistic effects.

1. *Voice*

Verbs can show whether the subject performs the action or receives the action. This is called *voice*.

- A verb is *active* when the subject performs the action.

Example: Robots in Japan pay union dues.

- A verb is *passive* when its action is performed upon the subject.

Example: Union dues are paid in Japan by robots.

2. Parallelism

Parallelism or parallel structure means putting ideas of the same rank in the same grammatical form. Writers parallel words, phrases, clauses, and even sentences. In the following examples, the parallel elements are in italics.

- Tyranny, like hell, is not easily conquered; yet we have this consolation with us, *that the harder the conflict, the more glorious the triumph*. ("The American Crisis," Thomas Paine, *1776)*

- Whether expressed in a sit-in at lunch counters, a freedom ride in Mississippi, a peaceful protest in Georgia, *a bus boycott in Montgomery, Alabama*, it is an outgrowth of Thoreau's insistence that evil must be resisted and no moral man can patiently adjust to injustice. ("A Legacy of Creative Protest" by Martin Luther King, Jr*.)*

Sample Passage and Questions

Read the following passage, and answer the practice AP questions that follow.

> With malice toward none; with charity for all; with firmness in the right, as God gives us to see the right, let us strive to finish the work we are in; to bind up the nation's wounds; to care for him who shall have borne the battle, and for his widow and his orphan—to do all which may achieve and cherish a just and lasting peace among ourselves, and with all nations.

1. The primary effect of using clauses that elaborate on one another is to
   - (A) show how much work the speaker has already accomplished.
   - (B) suggest that the road ahead is arduous, if not impossible, to travel.
   - (C) imply that the speaker feels aggrieved by the lack of support he has received.
   - (D) convey his reliance on a higher power to succeed.
   - (E) mirror the country's long struggle to arrive at the present point in its history.

2. The writer achieves balance and a sense of dignity through
   - (A) simple sentences.
   - (B) parallel structure.
   - (C) compound sentences.
   - (D) passive voice.
   - (E) commonplace diction.

3. The writer uses the word "cherish" to suggest
   - (A) the high cost of achieving peace.
   - (B) the need for national unity at this difficult time.
   - (C) the losses he has personally sustained in the long struggle.
   - (D) his deep love for his country.
   - (E) that he does not harbor any personal animosity toward his enemies.

Answers

1. **The correct answer is (E).**

2. **The correct answer is (B).**

3. **The correct answer is (D).**

FIGURES OF SPEECH

Prose writers have many different figures of speech at their disposal, including metaphors, similes, and personification. They also use symbols to convey their meaning. In fact, prose writers can use all the figures of speech that poets do to convey meaning and achieve specific effects.

- *Metaphor*s are comparisons of two unlike things. The more familiar thing helps describe the less familiar one. Usually the objects under comparison resemble each other in only one or two ways, differing in all other aspects. "My heart is a singing bird" is an example of a metaphor.

- *Simile*s are the same as metaphors except they use the "like," "as," "than," or "seems" to make the comparison. "My heart is like a singing bird" is a simile.

- *Personificatio*n is a type of implied metaphor, by speaking about something nonliving as though it were living. "The wind whistles in the trees" is an example of personification.

- A *symbo*l is a person, place, or object that represents an abstract idea. For example, a dove may symbolize peace or a rose may symbolize love.

Sample Passage and Questions

Read the following passage, and answer the practice AP questions that follow.

> Her husband was continually prying about to detect her secret hoards, and many and fierce were the conflicts that took place about what ought to have been common property. They lived in a forlorn-looking house that stood alone and had an air of starvation. A few straggling savin trees grew near it; no smoke ever curled from its chimney, no traveler stopped at its door. A miserable horse, whose ribs were as articulate as the bars of a gridiron, stalked about a field where a thin carpet of moss, scarcely covering the ragged beds of pudding stone, tantalized and balked his hunger; and sometimes he would lean his head over the fence, look piteously at the passer-by, and seem to petition deliverance from this land of famine.

1. Which figure of speech does the author employ in the sentence: "They lived in a forlorn-looking house that stood alone and had an air of starvation"?

   I.   Simile

   II. Symbol

   III. Personification

   (A) I

   (B) II

   (C) III

   (D) I and II

   (E) I and III

TIP

As you read the passages on the AP English Language and Composition exam and analyze metaphors and similes, decide what the writer's feelings are toward the subject and how many subjects of comparison are used. Ask yourself these questions:

- Is each subject compared to one thing, or is one subject compared to several things?

- Is the comparison developed at length? If it is, to what purpose?

- What point is the writer making through the metaphor or simile?

2. The savin trees can be interpreted as a symbol of
   (A) hope and salvation.
   (B) nature.
   (C) loneliness.
   (D) strife and dissension.
   (E) struggle and sterility.

3. In the context of the passage, the phrase "whose ribs were as articulate as the bars of a gridiron" is used as a metaphor for
   (A) deprivation.
   (B) eloquence.
   (C) sports.
   (D) conflict.
   (E) discord.

Answers

1. **The correct answer is (C).**

2. **The correct answer is (E).**

3. **The correct answer is (A).**

TONE AND MOOD

- *Tone* is the writer's or speaker's attitude toward his subject, audience, or himself or herself. Tone is a vital part of meaning because it brings emotional power to the language.

- *Mood* is the strong feeling we get from a literary work. The mood is created by characterization, description, images, and dialogue. Some possible moods include terror, horror, tension, calmness, and suspense. Mood is also called *atmosphere*.

The writer's tone is established through his choice of words and their placement in the passage. This, in turn, reveals his attitude toward the subject matter. To figure out the tone of a passage, analyze the writer's use of language. Look especially at figures of speech (similes, metaphors, personification, etc.), imagery, irony, and diction (language).

Questions about tone will often take this form:

- Which of the following best describes the overall tone of this passage?
- The tone of this passage is best described as...
- The passage indicates that the author experiences a feeling of...

Sample Passages and Questions

Read the following passages, and answer the practice AP questions that follow.

Passage 1

It takes no calendar to tell root and stem that the calm days of mid-summer are here. Last spring's sprouted seed comes to fruit. None of these things depends on a calendar of the days and months. They are their own calendar, marks on a span of time that reaches far back into the shadows of time. The mark is there for all to see, in every field and meadow and treetop, as it was last year and then years ago and when the centuries were young.

The time is here. This is the point in the great continuity when these things happen, and will continue to happen year after year. Any summer arrives at this point, only to lead on to the next and the next, and so to summer again. These things we can count on; these will happen again and again, so long as the earth turns.

The passage indicates that the author experiences a feeling of

- (A) frustration.
- (B) fear of the forces of nature.
- (C) pessimism.
- (D) serene confidence.
- (E) regret at the rapid passage of time.

Answer Explanation

The correct answer is (D), serene confidence, as the phrases "calm days," "great continuity," and "we can count on" reveal. The author has neither fear of nature nor any regret at the passage of time; rather, we sense, through the phrases cited above, a calm acceptance of the seasons.

Sample Passage 2

It is a melancholy object to those who walk through this great town, or travel in the country, when they see the streets, the roads, and cabin-doors crowded with beggars of the female sex, followed by three, four, or six children, all in rags, and importuning every passenger for an alms. These mothers, instead of being able to work for their honest livelihood, are forced to employ all their time in strolling, to beg sustenance for their helpless infants, who, as they grow up, either turn thieves for want of work, or leave their dear Native Country to fight for the Pretender in Spain, or sell themselves to the Barbadoes.

The mood of this passage is best described as

(A) incendiary.

(B) dispirited.

(C) reasonable.

(D) moralistic.

(E) choleric.

Answer Explanation

The correct answer is (B). This passage has a sad, dispirited mood, as shown from the word "melancholy" in the first sentence and the images of starving mothers having to beg food for their babies. The last sentences show a hopeless tone, as the situation will only get worse.

Passage 3

I can think of no objection that will possibly be raised against this proposal, unless it should be urged that the number of people will be thereby much lessened in the kingdom. This I freely own, and was indeed one principal design in offering it to the world. I desire the reader will observe, that I calculate my remedy for this one individual Kingdom of Ireland, and for no other that ever was, is, or, I think, ever can be upon earth. Therefore let no man talk to me of other expedients: Of taxing our absentees at five shillings a pound: Of using neither clothes, nor household furniture, except what is of our own growth and manufacture: Of utterly rejecting the materials and instruments that promote foreign luxury: Of curing the expansiveness of pride, vanity, idleness, and gaming in our women: Of introducing a vein of parsimony, prudence, and temperance: Of learning to love our Country, wherein we differ from laplanders, and the inhabitants of topinamboo: Of being a little cautious not to sell our country and consciences for nothing: Of teaching landlords to have at least one degree of mercy toward their tenants. Lastly, of putting a spirit of honesty, industry, and skill into our shopkeepers, who, if a resolution could now be taken to buy only our native goods, would immediately unite to cheat and exact upon us in the price, the measure, and the goodness, nor could ever yet be brought to make one fair proposal of just dealing, though often earnestly invited to it.

Overall, the author's tone in this passage can best be described as

(A) uncontrolled rage.

(B) righteous indignation.

(C) grievous distress.

(D) passionate anger.

(E) sorrowful depression.

Answer Explanation

The correct answer is (D), passionate anger, which best expresses the author's tone. Choice (A), uncontrolled rage, is too strong. Choice (B), righteous indignation, makes light of his fury.

In this section, I have isolated the various rhetorical strategies to discuss each one individually, but as you answer the multiple-choice questions on the AP English Language and Composition exam, always consider the various rhetorical strategies together, as they interact with each other to create meaning. When you first begin to read a passage, you may focus on one striking aspect, but when you reread the passage, the entire pattern should come together as the different rhetorical strategies will enter into your understanding of the passage's meaning.

PRACTICE MULTIPLE-CHOICE PASSAGES AND QUESTIONS

Read the following passages, and answer the practice AP questions that follow.

Passage 1

How many are the solitary hours I spend, ruminating upon the past, and anticipating the future, whilst you, overwhelmed with the cares of state, have but a few moments you can devote to any individual. All domestic pleasures and enjoyments are absorbed in the great and important duty you owe your country, for our country is, as it were, a secondary god, and the first and greatest parent. It is to be preferred to parents, wives, children, friends, and all things, the gods only excepted; for, if our country perishes, it is as impossible to save an individual, as to preserve one of the fingers of a mortified hand. Thus I do suppress every wish, and silence every murmur, acquiescing in a painful separation from the companion of my youth, and the friend of my heart.

I believe't near ten days since I wrote you a line. I have not felt in any humor to entertain you if I had taken up my pen. Perhaps some unbecoming invective might have fallen from it. The eyes of our rulers have been closed, and a lethargy has seized almost every member. I fear a fatal security has taken possession of them. Whilst the building is in flames, they tremble at the expense of water to quench it. In short, two months have elapsed since the evacuation of Boston, and very little has been done in that time to secure it, or the harbor, from future invasion. The people are all in a flame, and no one among us, that I have heard of, even mentions expense. They think, universally, that there has been an amazing neglect somewhere. Many have turned out as volunteers to work upon Noodle's Island, and many more would go upon Nantasket, if the business was once set on foot. "'Tis a maxim of state that power and liberty are like heat and moisture. Where they are well mixed, everything prospers; where they are single, they are destructive."

A government of more stability is much wanted in this colony, and they are ready to receive it from the hands of Congress. And since I have begun with a maxim of state, I will add another, namely, that a people may let a king fall, yet still remain a people; but if a king let his people slip from him, he is no longer a king. And as this is most certainly our case, why not proclaim to the world, in decisive terms, your own importance?

Shall we not be despised by foreign powers, for hesitating so long at a word?

1. Who can you infer from the language is the intended audience for this letter?
   - (A) A stranger to the writer, someone highly placed in public office
   - (B) A general newspaper audience
   - (C) An ambassador with great political influence
   - (D) Someone with whom the writer is intimately associated
   - (E) A friend from the writer's childhood from whom she had become estranged

2. How does the audience affect the tone and content of the passage?
   - (A) The tone is more relaxed, and the content more personal.
   - (B) The tone is more formal, and the content more ceremonial.
   - (C) The tone is more ironic, and the content more scathing.
   - (D) The tone is more sarcastic, and the content more personal.
   - (E) The tone is more fiery, and the content more specific.

3. The phrases "a secondary god" and "the first and greatest parent" function as
   - (A) a personification of America.
   - (B) metaphors for America.
   - (C) similes for America.
   - (D) a hyperbole for America.
   - (E) an ironic commentary on America's supposed greatness.

4. The writer uses the analogy between the nation and a hand to suggest that
   - (A) the hand that controls America controls the world.
   - (B) a country is only as great as its hired hands, its working men and women.
   - (C) individual parts work in unison; the part cannot survive apart from the whole.
   - (D) in the present situation, individual sacrifice is inevitable.
   - (E) America needs a helping hand from outsiders.

5. As used in the first sentence of the second paragraph, the word "humor" most nearly means

   (A) amusement.

   (B) witticism.

   (C) strain.

   (D) tone.

   (E) mood.

6. In the context of the passage, the phrase "the eyes of our rulers have been closed, and a lethargy has seized almost every member" is used as a metaphor to convey the writer's

   (A) realization that the country is in a dire position.

   (B) anger at defeat.

   (C) relief at the leaders' ability to take a break from their hard work.

   (D) preference for assertive leaders who are not afraid to be confrontational.

   (E) frustration at the leaders' inaction in the face of a serious situation.

7. In the phrase "Whilst the building is in flames," the building symbolizes

   (A) her home.

   (B) America.

   (C) Great Britain.

   (D) the state capitol.

   (E) freedom.

8. This symbol is most effective because it

   (A) conveys the writer's feeling that the situation is desperate.

   (B) communicates the writer's belief that time is on their side.

   (C) shows the country's determination to survive.

   (D) paints a strong visual image.

   (E) describes the country's terrible drought and its appalling results.

9. In the third paragraph, the writer is primarily using an appeal to

   (A) emotion

   (B) ethics.

   (C) reason.

   (D) passion.

   (E) comparison and contrast.

10. The most apparent goal of the writer's rhetoric and reasoning is to
    (A) convince readers that she alone has the right solutions to the current problems.
    (B) engender sympathy for America's beleaguered leaders.
    (C) persuade the Congress to resign so new members can be elected.
    (D) convince her reader to take action.
    (E) stir up pity for the difficulties the writer has experienced living in Massachusetts.

Quick-Score Answers

1.	D	6.	E
2.	A	7.	B
3.	B	8.	A
4.	C	9.	C
5.	E	10.	D

Answers and Explanations

1. **The correct answer is (D).** The last sentence in the first paragraph reveals that the audience for this letter is someone with whom the writer is intimately associated: "Thus I do suppress every wish, and silence every murmur, acquiescing in a painful separation from the companion of my youth, and the friend of my heart." The last phrase—"friend of my heart"—shows that the audience is a lover. It was, in fact, the writer's husband.

2. **The correct answer is (A).** The intimate audience creates a more relaxed tone and more personal content. This is the direct opposite of choice (B). While choices (C) and D could fit with a personal audience, the diction reveals that is not the case here.

3. **The correct answer is (B).** The phrases "a secondary god, and the first and greatest parent" function as metaphors for America. You can infer this because the phrase is a comparison that does not use the words "like" or "as."

4. **The correct answer is (C).** The writer uses the analogy between the nation and a hand to suggest that individual parts work in unison; the part cannot survive apart from the whole. This is revealed through a close reading of the relevant portion of the text: "...if our country perishes, it is as impossible to save an individual, as to preserve one of the fingers of a mortified hand."

5. **The correct answer is (E).** As used in the first sentence of the second paragraph, the word "humor" most nearly means *mood*. The writer has

not been in the right frame of mind to write pleasantries, so she has refrained from writing until now. As you answer vocabulary questions, remember to first come up with your own synonym for the word in question. Then look for the best match among the choices.

6. **The correct answer is (E).** In the context of the passage, the phrase "the eyes of our rulers have been closed, and a lethargy has seized almost every member" is used as a metaphor to convey the writer's frustration at the leaders' inaction in the face of a serious situation. The writer suggests that the leaders have abdicated their responsibility rather than taking action.

7. **The correct answer is (B).** In the phrase "Whilst the building is in flames," the building symbolizes America. This is shown by her references throughout the passage to Boston and other locations in the colonies.

8. **The correct answer is (A).** This symbol is most effective because it conveys the writer's feeling that the situation is desperate. The strong image of a building burning down conveys her sense of urgency.

9. **The correct answer is (C).** In the third paragraph, the writer is primarily using an appeal to reason. She presents facts and examples to make her point. Choices (A) and D are the same, so they cancel each other out. Choice (E) is not an appeal. Rather, it is a method of organization used primarily in expository passages.

10. **The correct answer is (D).** The most apparent goal of the writer's rhetoric and reasoning is to convince her reader to take action. She states this outright in the last paragraph: "A government of more stability is much wanted in this colony, and they are ready to receive it from the hands of Congress. ... And as this is most certainly our case, why not proclaim to the world, in decisive terms, your own importance?"

Passage 2

By the 1800s, several hundred medicine shows were traveling across America, giving a wide variety of shows. At one end of the scale were simple magic acts; at the other, complicated spectacles. From 1880 to 1910, one of the largest of these shows was "The King of the Road Shows," the Kickapoo Indian Medicine Company. Two experienced entertainers, Charles H. "Texas Charlie" Bigelow and John E. "Doc" Healy, had started the company more than two decades before. From their headquarters in New Haven, Connecticut, the partners sent as many as twenty-five shows at a time across America.

Texas Charlie managed the "medicine" end of the production, training the "Doctors" and "Professors" who gave the "Medical Lectures." Doc Healy was in charge of hiring the performers—from fiddlers to fire-eaters, including comedians, acrobats, singers, and jugglers. Both Indians and whites were hired. All the Indians, including Mohawks, Iroquois, Crees, Sioux, and Blackfeet, were billed as "pure-blooded Kickapoos," a completely fictional tribe.

The entertainers wore outrageous costumes. The Native Americans were covered in feathers, colored beads, and crude weapons. The "Doctors" and "Professors" were equally glittery. Some wore fringed leather coats, silver-capped boots; others, fancy silk shirts, frock coats, and high silk hats. One of the most outlandish figures was the glib "Nevada Ned, the King of Gold." Born Ned T. Oliver, this entertainer wore a fancy suit studded with buttons made of gold. On his head he sported a huge sombrero dangling 100 gold coins.

During the summer, the Kickapoo shows were presented under enormous tents. When the weather turned chilly, the troupe moved into town halls and opera houses. Most often, the show was free. Occasionally, adults were charged a dime to get in. Where did the profits come from? The sale of "medicine." According to the show's advertisements, these wonder-working Kickapoo brews were "compounded according to secret ancient Kickapoo Indian tribal formulas." Among the ingredients were "blood root, feverwort, spirit gum, wild poke berries, slippery elm, white oak bark, dock root, and other Natural Products." These "medicines" sold for fifty cents to a dollar a bottle, and were guaranteed to cure all the ills that afflict the human body.

1. As used in the second sentence, "spectacles" most nearly means
   (A) elaborate performances.
   (B) businesses.
   (C) corrective lenses.
   (D) arguments.
   (E) retinues.

2. The first paragraph is developed primarily through
   (A) cause and effect.
   (B) chronological order.
   (C) comparison and contrast.
   (D) problem-solution.
   (E) process analysis.

3. The first paragraph of this selection serves to
   (A) fully describe the character of Charles H. "Texas Charlie" Bigelow and John E. "Doc" Healy.
   (B) refute charges that the medicine shows were shoddy.
   (C) introduce the rest of the passage.
   (D) explain a crucial aspect of nineteenth-century history.
   (E) compare and contrast nineteenth-century styles of entertainment.

4. According to paragraph 2, the Kickapoo tribe was
   - (A) a group of Mohawks, Iroquois, Crees, Sioux, and Blackfeet.
   - (B) exclusively comprised of talented fiddlers, fire-eaters, comedians, acrobats, singers, and jugglers.
   - (C) pure-blooded Indians.
   - (D) a made-up tribe; there was no such tribe.
   - (E) the home tribe of Doc Healy and Texas Charlie.

5. The words "Doctors," "Professors," and "Medical Lectures" are in quotations to
   - (A) emphasize the importance of having advanced degrees to success.
   - (B) show the great lengths to which the Kickapoo directors went to hire qualified personnel.
   - (C) reveal how impressive these men were.
   - (D) disclose previously unrevealed information.
   - (E) indicate that the words are being used ironically

6. The phrase "fiddlers to fire-eaters" is an example of
   - I.   metaphor.
   - II. personification.
   - III. alliteration.
   - (A) I
   - (B) II
   - (C) III
   - (D) I and II
   - (E) II and III

7. By using the word *glib*, the author alludes to
   - (A) the show's slick deception.
   - (B) Oliver's shady past.
   - (C) the plight of the Native Americans.
   - (D) how easily people can be hoodwinked.
   - (E) the outrageous entertainment of our own day.

8. The tone of this passage is best characterized as
   - (A) rueful.
   - (B) straightforward.
   - (C) elegiac.
   - (D) sarcastic.
   - (E) tongue-in-cheek.

9. The author deliberately selected this tone to

(A) suggest that hypocrisy is as common in the past as in the present.

(B) hint that not all people are so easily deceived.

(C) reinforce the sense of a golden past now long gone.

(D) mock foolish people for their gullibility.

(E) reinforce the ironic content.

10. The audience for this selection is most likely

(A) Native Americans.

(B) faith healers.

(C) circus performers.

(D) general readers.

(E) historical scholars.

Quick-Score Answers

1.	A	6.	C
2.	B	7.	A
3.	C	8.	B
4.	D	9.	E
5.	E	10.	D

Answers and Explanations

1. **The correct answer is (A).** As used in the second sentence, "spectacles" most nearly means *elaborate performances*. Use a contrast context clue. If "simple magic acts" were at one end of the scale and "complicated spectacles" at the other end, "complicated spectacles" must be the opposite of "simple magic acts"; thus, they are intricate shows.

2. **The correct answer is (B).** The first paragraph is developed primarily through chronological order, the order of time. Use the dates in the passage as clues: The first date is "By the 1800s." Later in the passage, you can find the dates "From 1880 to 1910."

3. **The correct answer is (C).** The first paragraph of this selection serves to introduce the rest of the passage. The writer gives an overview of general medicine shows and then narrows the discussion to one specific show, Kickapoo Indian Medicine Company. This specific group of entertainers will be the focus of the rest of the essay.

4. **The correct answer is (D).** According to paragraph 2, the Kickapoo tribe was a made-up tribe; there was no such tribe. You can find the

answer in this sentence: "All the Indians, including Mohawks, Iroquois, Crees, Sioux, and Blackfeet, were billed as 'pure-blooded Kickapoos,' *a completely fictional tribe*." (italics added)

5. **The correct answer is (E)**. The words "Doctors," "Professors," and "Medical Lectures" are in quotations to indicate that the words are being used ironically. None of the so-named "Doctors" and "Professors" had any medical training at all, so their "Medical Lectures" were completely bogus.

6. **The correct answer is (C)**. The phrase "fiddlers to fire-eaters" is an example of alliteration, the repetition of initial consonant sounds in several words in a sentence or line of poetry. Here, the letter "f" is repeated. Recall that writers of both poetry and prose use alliteration to create musical effects, link related ideas, stress certain words, or mimic specific sounds.

7. **The correct answer is (A)**. By using the word *glib*, the author alludes to the show's slick deception. *Glib* means "facile," "artful," or "slick." The show is glib because it is deceiving people through cunning means.

8. **The correct answer is (B)**. The tone of this passage is best characterized as *straightforward*. The writer remains neutral. The writer does not editorialize (add his or her own viewpoints) or create a strong mood.

9. **The correct answer is (E)**. The author deliberately selected this tone to reinforce the ironic content. The neutral tone reinforces the ridiculous way people were cheated by the fictitious Indian tribe, the fake experts, and the useless "medicines."

10. **The correct answer is (D)**. The audience for this selection is most likely general readers. The diction and content is too general for such specific audiences as Native Americans, choice (A); faith healers, choice (B); circus performers, choice (C); or historical scholars, choice (E). If the passage were aimed at these audiences, it would contain jargon (technical words and phrases specific to a particular industry) and much more detailed information.

Strategies for Success on the Essay Questions

You'll recall from Part I of this book and the sample AP English Language and Composition exams you've taken that the essay section of the Advanced Placement exam in English Language and Composition consists of three questions. All three questions require you to analyze prose (non-poetry). You will NOT have to write an essay analyzing poetry on the exam.

In past exams, the following types of essay questions have appeared:

- an expository essay analyzing the rhetorical techniques in a prose passage to see how they contribute to the author's purpose or message

- an expository essay in which you compare and contrast the style of *two* passages

- a persuasive essay defending, challenging, or qualifying an author's position as stated in a brief excerpt or quotation

There is no guarantee that you will have each of these variations. Instead, you might have to write two persuasive essays and one expository essay, for example. Or, you may have to write two expository essays on passages and one persuasive essay on a brief quotation. Your test might not have a paired passage—or it may have one.

You must write all three essays.

You are given 2 hours to complete all three essays, which gives you about 40 minutes per essay. While you're free to decide how to spend your time, logic dictates that you divide your time equally among all three essays since each of them receives the same amount of credit.

OVERALL ESSAY GUIDELINES

While each of the three essays requires you to write on a different topic and focus on different elements, all three essays demand the same writing and thinking skills. The following hints can help you boost your scores.

Top Ten Hints for High-Scoring Essays

1.   Analyze the question.

Before you do anything else, make sure that you understand exactly what is required of you. Rephrase the question in your own words to make sure that you comprehend it and grasp any subtle points.

Watch especially for the words "analyze" and "evaluate." When you *analyze* a passage, you take it apart to examine each of its parts. Then you weave together all the parts to see how they contribute to the total effect. When you *evaluate* a passage, you make a judgment about it. You decide to what extent you agree or disagree with the author's opinions. Misunderstandings about *analyzing* and *evaluating* can result in a completely misdirected essay.

2.   Answer the question.

Follow the directions precisely, and do exactly what you're asked to do. Be sure to address every single part of the question. No matter how impressive your writing is, you will not receive any credit if you don't answer the question. For example, if the question calls for you to analyze rhetorical strategies but you write about the author's opinions, your essay will earn little credit. If the question calls for you to compare and contrast two passages and you ignore the second passage, you'll receive only partial credit because you've answered only part of the question.

If you grasp no other point from this book, make it this point: *directly answer the question you're given, and follow the directions exactly.*

3.   Use your time well.

If you allocate 40 minutes for each essay as I recommend, consider spending your time this way:

4 minutes planning

30–35 minutes writing/revising

3 minutes editing/proofreading

If you use an erasable pen, you can revise and edit as you draft. I strongly suggest that you correct your errors as you draft because you may not have time to return to your essay later.

4.   Lead with your strength.

There's no rule that you have to write the essays in order. Instead, work from what you perceive to be the easiest prompt to the most difficult one. Doing a good job on the first essay you write will increase your confidence for tackling the other two essays.

5.   Start writing.

It's natural to start your essay at the beginning with the introduction, but if you're stuck for an opening, don't waste time agonizing. Instead, start where you can, with the body paragraphs. While it's vital that all your essays are well organized and logical, it's equally vital that you get all three essays written in the 2 hours you have. The best essay in the world won't get you any points—if you don't get it down on paper within the time limit.

6.   Keep writing.

If you get stuck, skip some lines and keep on going. If you can't keep on writing, take a few deep breaths and gather your wits. If you're really blank and can't write, move on to the next question. Staring at the paper only wastes time. Planning carefully can help guarantee that you'll have the time to return to the essay you didn't finish, but even if you don't, at least you wrote another essay in the time you would have wasted feeling panic settling in.

7. Write neatly.

If you're writing is illegible, the scorer won't be able to read your paper. If it's merely messy, your scorer might misread a crucial point. And much as we don't like to admit it, neat papers *do* predispose scorers to smile more kindly. If you suspect that your handwriting is hard to read, print neatly and carefully.

8.   Be focused, serious, and mature.

Some students take the AP test for themselves and their future; others take it for their parents or to be with their friends. Other unfortunate students are forced into it, kicking and screaming. If you didn't want to take the class and the test in the first place, this isn't the time to throw the test to prove a point. As an AP scorer, I've read too many essays that reveal the students' determination to go down in flames to prove they never should have been forced into the class. If you are in this dreadful position, prove the other point: you *can* do it.

9.   Proofread.

This can be one of the most important steps in any paper, for no matter how valid your points, how precise your examples, if you have made a great many careless writing errors, you will lose credit. While your essay will be evaluated holistically (on the total impression it makes), errors can distract your readers and reduce the effectiveness of your arguments. After you finish drafting, try to let your essay sit for a few moments. Look over the short answers or another essay, and then go back to the essay refreshed. Always make sure that you have time to proofread, and be as careful as you can to read what is there, not what you *think* is there.

10. Deal with panic.

You can psyche yourself up or down—it's all in your head. Convince yourself that you can succeed by working carefully and resolutely. If you start to panic, pause for a second to calm yourself and then soldier on.

Always remember that scorers reward you for what you do well. They're not looking for perfection. After all, you have only 40 minutes in which to write each essay. Do the very best you can, but don't obsess about making your essay flawless.

THE BASIC EXPOSITORY QUESTION

When you first start writing practice AP expository questions, they may appear to be very different from each other. In fact, every expository question is simply a variation on the same basic form: *analyze how the writer uses rhetorical strategies and stylistic devices to reveal his or her meaning.* In some cases, you will have to compare and contrast two different passages as you analyze the author's use of rhetorical strategies. Often, "meaning" will be stated as "attitude toward the subject of the passage."

HOW TO ANALYZE

When you *analyze* a passage, you take it apart to examine each of its parts. Then you weave together all the parts to see how they contribute to the total effect. AP Composition essay prompts that focus on analysis usually contain one or more of these key words:

analyze	assess	clarify	classify
describe	determine	examine	explain
explore	explicate	interpret	probe
review	scrutinize	show	support

It's tempting to include a lot of summary in an analysis writing test because it pads the essay nicely and seems to fulfill the assignment. It doesn't, so resist the temptation to merely recall and list details when you're supposed to analyze.

REVIEW RHETORICAL STRATEGIES

Remember that "rhetorical strategies" is the author's strategic use of language. The rhetorical strategies can include

- allusions (references to well-known people, places, works of art, etc.)
- contrast (differences)
- diction (word choice)
- figures of speech (metaphors, similes, personification, hyperbole, etc.)
- imagery (words and phrases that appeal to the five senses)
- language
- narrative pace
- pacing
- point of view
- repetition
- sentence structure (simple sentences, compound sentences, complex sentences)
- structure of the passage (chronological order, order of importance, cause and effect, problem solution, comparison and contrast, etc.)
- syntax
- tone

Some of these terms are explained later in this chapter. The rest are explained in Part VI: Glossary of Literary Terms.

MODEL QUESTIONS

Study these typical expository questions:

Model Expository Question 1

The following essay is by (author). Read the passage and then write an essay analyzing the rhetorical techniques the author uses to convey his attitude toward the subject.

[You must describe how the author uses language to make his or her purpose clear. Since the specific rhetorical strategies are not identified, you can select any ones that you wish. Analyze at least three different rhetorical strategies, such as diction, imagery, and tone.]

Model Expository Question 2

Read the following autobiographical essay by (author). Then, in a well-written essay, analyze some of the ways in which the author recreates the experience of being a teenager. You might consider such rhetorical strategies as point of view, repetition, diction, and imagery.

[You must explain how the writer makes readers believe that they are reliving an adolescent's adventures and emotions. The words "you might consider" means that you do not have to focus on the elements listed in the prompt, but you would be well advised to do so. When you see the phrase "you might consider," be sure to analyze at least three of the elements listed. If only two elements are listed, select one of your own to include.]

Model Expository Question 3

The following passage comes from the 1699 journal ("journal title"). Read the excerpt carefully, paying close attention to syntax, figures of speech, and imagery. Then write a well-organized essay in which you identify the stylistic elements in the last paragraph that set it off from the rest of the passage. Show how this contrast reinforces the author's rhetorical purpose in the excerpt as a whole.

[This is a complex question because it has four parts:

1. Identify the syntax, figures of speech, and imagery in the entire passage.

2. Explain the contrast between the last paragraph and the rest of the passage.

3. Analyze how the author achieves the contrast by using these three rhetorical strategies.

4. Link the contrast to the author's purpose in the entire passage.

While you are free to include any other rhetorical strategies you wish, you *must* focus on the three listed in the prompt—syntax, figures of speech, and imagery. Unless you are totally stumped on one of these three, stick with them and don't add any others.]

WRITING AN EXPOSITORY ESSAY

Expository essays explain. You can remember that exposition is writing that explains by using this memory trick: *Exposition = explains.* Further, both words start with the same three letters: "exp."

The word *exposition* comes from the Latin word *exponere*, which means "to place out." When you write exposition, you try to place out or set forth specific information. As they explain, expository essays give information. Most of the practical writing you do in the coming years—business letters, personal letters, school reports, class tests, standardized examinations, job applications, business reports, insurance claims—is expository.

Exposition can be organized in the following ways:

- cause and effect analysis
- chronological order
- classify and divide analysis
- compare and contrast essays
- definition essays
- order of importance (news story)
- problem and solution essays
- process analysis ("how to") essays

Exposition shows and tells by giving information about a specific topic. On the AP English Language and Composition exam, the topic will be given to you in the form of a passage or a quotation. How you choose to organize your essay always depends on the following two considerations:

topic   the subject; what you are writing about

audience   who will read your writing

In many cases, you will be required to compare and contrast or show cause and effect on the AP Composition exposition essays. If not, it's likely that you will arrange the details of your analysis in order of importance. Therefore, let's look at these methods of arranging details.

USING COMPARE AND CONTRAST

When you *compare*, you show how things are alike. When you *contrast*, you show how they are different. Use comparison and contrast when you are asked to analyze two parts of the same passage or two separate passages.

Comparison-contrast essays can be organized two ways: *point-by-point* or *chunk*. In a *point-by-point* structure, you deal with each point in turn. In a *chunk* structure, you discuss one point completely before moving on to the next one. For example:

Point-by-point Structure   *Chunk Structure*

diction: Passage A, Passage B   Passage A: diction, imagery, tone

imagery: Passage A, Passage B

tone: Passage A, Passage B   Passage B: diction, imagery, tone

USING CAUSE AND EFFECT

The cause is *why* something happens; the effect is the *result, what happens* due to the cause. Therefore, cause and effect essays establish a relationship between events. Cause and effect usually (but not always) happen in time order: the *cause* comes first, creating an *effect*. The following chart shows this order of events:

cause   →   brings about   →   effect
elevated diction →   brings about   →   formal tone

But with complex relationships, you'll likely be dealing with multiple causes and effects. An effect may have more than one cause, as the following diagram shows:

Cause 1
Cause 2   →   bring about   →   effect
Cause 3

elevated diction
literary allusions →   bring about   →   formal tone
long sentences

A cause may also have more than one effect. For example:

			Effect 1
Cause	→	results in	→ Effect 2
			Effect 3
			extensive description
complex theme	→	results in	→ elevated diction
			long sentences

How can you make sure you're on target when you write cause and effect AP essays? Use this checklist:

1. I've shown a clear cause and effect relationship between events.

    Just because one event occurred before the other doesn't mean that causality exists. Don't push the envelope; if there's no causality, don't invent it.

2. The cause and effect relationship I describe is valid.

    Just because something happened once doesn't mean that true causality exists. For the relationship to be valid, it has to be repeated.

TIP
Use the following transitions to emphasize similarities: *like, likewise, similarly, in the same way, also, as, just as, both*. Use the following transitions to emphasize differences: *instead, rather than, unlike, on the other hand, in contrast with, however, but*.

NOTE
The cause *always* takes place before the effect: something happens, which leads to a result. But the cause and effect don't have to be presented in time order in the passage. The effect may be presented first, even though the cause occurred earlier.

3. I've included all relevant causes and effects.

   Look beneath the surface to find every factor that affects your analysis. When you omit one or more pertinent causes and effects, you weaken your writing. An *immediate cause* is an event that comes directly before an effect and helped bring it about. An *underlying cause* is not immediately apparent; a *remote cause* is distant from the effect.

The following list shows the transitions most often used to signal cause and effect relationships. The right transitions can help you link ideas clearly.

as a result	because	consequently
due to	for this (that) reason	for
if...then	nevertheless	since
so	so that	therefore
thus	this (that) is how	

USING ORDER OF IMPORTANCE

With this organizational plan, you draw attention to your key ideas by placing them first in your essay. By leading with your strongest points, you impress the scorers with your grasp of the writer's rhetorical strategies and purpose. You can arrange ideas from most to least important or save the second most important point for last. The following diagrams show these variations visually:

Most important points   Most important point
            ↓   ↓
Less important points   -or-   Least important points
            ↓   ↓
Least important points   Second most important point

FIVE-STEP METHOD TO A HIGH SCORE

1. Read the question completely, and restate it in your own words to make sure you clearly understand what you must write. For example, do you have to consider *all* the rhetorical devices listed or just a few from the list? Look for the key phrase "such as" so you know how many of the literary elements you must describe.

2. Read the excerpt, passage, or quote all the way through, at least twice. As you read, paraphrase the passage to make sure you understand what the speaker is saying. Use your paraphrase to get ideas for your essay.

3. Plan before you write. Create a quick jotted outline, take a few notes, or make a diagram showing the order in which you'll present your points.

frequent and specific references to the passage.
point as its specific rhetorical strategy or stylistic
use the specific term "parallelism" rather than the
ategy." Use "complex sentences" or "allusions"
al "stylistic element." Of course, quote words,
support your point.

minutes to proofread and check your essay.

ITORY QUESTIONS
SPONSES

by Queen Elizabeth I, which she delivered in 1752
t the coast to repel the anticipated invasion of the
rite a well-organized essay in which you analyze
how Queen Elizabeth's use of rhetorical devices reveals her purpose. You
may wish to consider diction, tone, syntax, and imagery in your analysis.

My loving people,

We have been persuaded by some that are careful of our safety, to take
heed how we commit our selves to armed multitudes, for fear of treachery; but
I assure you I do not desire to live in distrust of my faithful and loving people.
Let tyrants fear, I have always behaved myself that, under God, I have placed
my chiefest strength and safeguard in the loyal hearts and good-will of my
subjects; and therefore I am come amongst you, as you see, at this time, not
for my recreation and disport, but being resolved, in the midst and heat of the
battle, to live or die amongst you all; to lay down for my God, and for my
kingdom, and for my people, my honor and my blood, even in the dust. I know
I have the body but of a weak and feeble woman; but I have the heart and
stomach of a king, and of a king of England, too, and think foul scorn that
Parma or Spain, or any prince of Europe, should dare to invade the borders of
my realm, to which rather than dishonor shall grow by me, I myself will take
up arms, I myself will be your general, judge, and rewarder of every one of
your virtues in the field. I know already, for your forwardness you have
deserved rewards and crowns, and We do assure you in the word of a prince,
they shall be duly paid you. In the mean time, my lieutenant general shall be
in my stead, than whom never a prince commanded a more noble or worthy
subject; not doubting but by your obedience to my general, by your concord
in the camp, and your valor in the field, we shall shortly have a famous victory
over those enemies of God, of my kingdom, and of my people.

Response 1

In 1752, a speech was delivered by Queen Elizabeth I to the troops
assembled at the English coast to repel the anticipated invasion of the
Spanish Armada. She used much rhetorical devices such as diction, tone,
syntax, and imagery to reveal her character and leadership skills.

Queen Elizabeth states that some people are afraid that she will get hurt. "We have been persuaded by some that are careful of our safety, to take heed how we commit our selves to armed multitudes, for fear of treachery." She uses "we" to show that she always has guards around her. She will be safe, so her subjects do not have to worry about her.

When leading people, it is important to believe in the people. Queen Elizabeth has always "placed my chiefest strength and safeguard in the loyal hearts and good-will of my subjects." As a result, she comes to see the people to lay down her life. This portrays her serious tone.

She also uses a lot of syntax to make her point. She implies that she is not very strong because she is a woman. She has "the body but of a weak and feeble woman," she says. However, she has "the heart and stomach of a king." This shows that she is loyal and big-boned, so she can fight with the men. She sounds like Joan of Arc, another strong female leader.

Queen Elizabeth I overall conveys her strong character and leadership skills. The people respect her because she is strong, even though she is only a woman. Through her rhetorical strategies, we see the dog-eat-dog world of the sixteenth century.

Evaluation

Dull thesis statement

- The writer rephrases the prompt: "She used much rhetorical devices such as diction, tone, syntax, and imagery to reveal her character and leadership skills." This is an acceptable beginning, but it is uninteresting. It does not entice readers to continue. A quote, anecdote, or dialogue would be a more interesting opening.

- The writer should discuss three of the four rhetorical strategies listed in the prompt. It is very difficult to cover four within the time frame.

- The word "much" should be "many."

Misreadings of the passage

- Monarchs use "we" instead of "I" to show that they represent the state and all its people. The sentence "She uses 'we' to show that she always has guards around her" is therefore a serious misreading of the passage.

- Even more serious, the passage has nothing to do with the thesis. How does the pronoun "we" reveal Queen Elizabeth's purpose in this speech?

Never addresses the point

- The thesis statement leads readers to expect that the writer will discuss *diction, tone, syntax,* and *imagery.* The writer does not do this at all. Therefore, this essay does not fulfill the assignment.

Score

- This paper could receive a very low score, a 1, because it never addresses the thesis.

Response 2

As this speech clearly shows, Elizabeth I was a master politician. Her diction, tone, and imagery combine to reassure her people that she is firmly in control of the life-and-death situation. The Armada posed a very real threat to England's safety so it was very important that the Queen show her command of the government. She achieved her goal through the stirring rhetoric of her carefully constructed speech.

By addressing her subjects as "My loving people," Elizabeth immediately forges a bond between them and herself. She acknowledges that she is their leader, yet conveys through her choice of words that she governs with affection, not fear. By repeating the word "loving" in the second sentence, she reinforces this relationship. Adding "faithful"

subtly shows that she believes the country is united under her leadership and support her effort to repel the Spanish invaders. Her reference to ruling "under God" shrewdly reminds her people that she rules by divine right. The reference thus serves to reassure her people that she is being backed by the supreme being and so their cause is divinely blessed.

The speech has a calm and rational tone, created by long sentences and parallel structure. Short sentences would make the speech seem abrupt and create a choppy, desperate tone. The long sentences, in contrast, create a feeling of authority. Elizabeth also uses parallelism, shown in the following sentences: "I myself will take up arms, I myself will be your general, judge, and rewarder of every one of your virtues in the field." She parallels "I myself" as well as "general, judge, and rewarder." Parallelism is also evident in the conclusion, as "your concord in the camp," is paralleled to "your valor in the field." In addition, "of God, of my kingdom, and of my people" is parallel. These careful parallel constructions are often used in speeches to convey control and power, as in President Kennedy's famous speech: "Ask not what your country can do for you but what you can do for your country."

Finally, Elizabeth's imagery in this speech shows that she is a vigorous leader and very politically savvy. The image of the young queen living or dying in the "heat of the battle" paints the drama of the situation: in mortal danger, she is willing to sacrifice herself for her people. She will "lay down for my God, and for my kingdom, and for my people, my honor and my blood, even in the dust." This dramatic image stirs even the hardest heart. Finally, the image of the queen with the "body but of a weak and feeble woman... [with] the heart and stomach of a king, and of a king of England, too" serves as a rallying point for patriotic fervor.

The Spanish Armada was defeated at sea, so it never reached England. However, Elizabeth's courage in personally leading her troops with this vigorous speech was not diminished by the incident's happy ending.

Evaluation

Answers the question

- The prompt requires you to "Write a well-organized essay in which you analyze how Queen Elizabeth's use of rhetorical devices reveals her purpose." The writer answers this directly by stating: "Her diction, tone, and imagery combine to reassure her people that she is firmly in control of the life-and-death situation." Therefore, her purpose is to calm her subjects and assert her control.

- This expository analysis will consider Elizabeth's *diction, tone,* and *imagery*—three rhetorical devices.

- Remember to use the "magic three" points. Discuss only two points and you run the risk of not having enough detail. Discuss more than three points and you run the risk of not completing your essay in the 40 minutes and not supplying enough detail.

Clear organization

- The writer devotes one paragraph to each rhetorical device: diction in paragraph 1, tone in paragraph 2, and imagery in paragraph 3.

- You do not have to arrange your information this way, of course, but you *do* have to use a clear method of organization that suits your topic, purpose, and audience.

Specific details

- The writer uses many specific details drawn from the speech. These include "My loving people," "loving," "faithful," and "under God" in paragraph 2 alone.

- In paragraph 3, the specific examples of parallelism include "I myself will take up arms, I myself will be your general, judge, and rewarder of every one of your virtues in the field." She parallels "I myself" as well as "general, judge, and rewarder." Parallelism is also evident in the conclusion, as "your concord in the camp" is paralleled to "your valor in the field." In addition, "of God, of my kingdom, and of my people" are details that show parallelism.

- Further, the writer uses details to prove the thesis that Elizabeth uses rhetorical strategies to reassure her people that she is firmly in command.

Intelligent analysis

- The essay is distinguished by astute insights. For example, the writer notes that "Short sentences would make the speech seem abrupt and create a choppy, desperate tone. The long sentences, in contrast, create a feeling of authority."

Score

- This paper could receive a top score, an 8–9, because the thesis is proven through specific details and examples. In addition, the paper is error free, the sentences are graceful, and the diction is precise.

SAMPLE 2

Chief Joseph, leader of the Nez Perce Indians, delivered the following surrender speech in 1877. As you read the speech, analyze the rhetorical strategies he uses to convey his attitude toward his situation.

I Will Fight No More Forever

Tell General Howard I know his heart. What he told me before, I have in my heart. I am tired of fighting. Our chiefs are killed. Looking Glass is dead. Toohoolhoolzote is dead. The old men are all dead. It is the young men who say yes and no. He who led on the young men is dead. It is cold and we have no blankets. The little children are freezing to death. My people, some of them, have run away to the hills and have no blankets, no food: no one where they are—perhaps freezing to death. I want to have time to look for my children and see how many I can find. Maybe I shall find them among the dead. Hear me, my chiefs. I am tired; my heart is sick and sad. From where the sun now stands I will fight no more forever.

Response 1

In 1877, Chief Joseph was forced to surrender his tribe to the federal government. Chief Joseph feels much bitterness toward his situation, which is shown in this speech. He used many effective rhetorical strategies and stylistic devices to convey his anger at the federal government's betrayal.

I learned all about the Native Americans and Chief Joseph last year in American studies class. Chief Joseph was a great Native American leader, like Sitting Bull and Geranimo. Chief Joseph made a treaty with the US government but the government broke it. They broke it because the government wanted to tribe's land. It was very valuable. The tribe was moved all around from reservation to reservation but finally the Native Americans had enough and fought back. However, the government soldiers outnumbered the Native Americans and the Nez Perce were forced to retreat. They tried to run to Canada but by then too many warriors had died. The tribe's spirit was broken and Chief Joseph was forced to surrender. That's why he is so angry, which shows in this speech. This is evinced especially in the beginning of the speech, when he says: "Our chiefs are killed. Looking Glass is dead. Toohoolhoolzote is dead. The old men are all dead. It is the young men who say yes and no."

Chief Joseph's anger shows how he feels about the contrite way the federal government treated him and his people. Their land was stolen and they were forced into exile. They are freezing and dying. His style shows his great animosity toward his oppressors.

Evaluation

Misses the point

- Chief Joseph may feel very bitter about his situation, but that feeling is not shown in this speech. Rather, the tone of the speech is best described as "sorrowful resignation." Therefore, the writer misses the point and so misreads and misinterprets the speech.

Information not relevant

- The assignment calls for the writer to "analyze the rhetorical strategies he [Chief Joseph] uses to convey his attitude toward his situation." Instead, the writer gives unnecessary background about Chief Joseph and his tribe, the Nez Perce. This material is not relevant to the thesis and should therefore be deleted.

No proof

- The writer does not provide any analysis of rhetorical strategies. The information in the conclusion is also off topic and shows a misreading.

Score

- Since the writer misinterpreted the passage and did not fulfill the assignment, the essay would earn no more than a 1 on the 9-point scoring rubric.

Response 2

Chief Joseph uses short sentences, simple diction, and poignant details to convince readers of his determination to surrender. His style conveys his sorrow and heartbreak at the destruction of his tribe. His rhetorical strategy creates a deeply emotional word picture of a people destroyed by a long conflict and broken promises.

Writers often use long, complex sentences to create a sophisticated tone. In this speech, Chief Joseph takes the opposite approach by using simple, short sentences to

convey his heartache at the fate that has befallen his people. This rhetorical strategy is evident from the very first sentence: "Tell General Howard I know his heart." The short, simple sentences lend his words an elegance and integrity that allow his emotion to shine through. As a result, the simple sentences guide the audience to concentrate on the emotion behind the words. American novelist Ernest Hemingway used this same strategy in his novels and short stories to achieve the same effect.

Further, Chief Joseph uses simple, everyday diction. For example, he says: "I am *tired* of fighting." rather than saying " I am *enervated, haggard,* or *fatigued* from fighting." He says "Our chiefs are *killed*" rather than saying "Our chiefs are *annihilated, slaughtered,* or *massacred.*" By using plain, unadorned words, Chief Joseph emerges as an honest and direct person. The double negative in the last sentence echoes this. He says "I will fight no more forever" rather than "I will never fight again." This diction subtly suggests to readers that Chief Joseph understands what is really important: the lives of his people. He is a man of action, not words, and so he does not worry about grammar and usage. His goal is to state his intentions and get back to helping his people survive.

Finally, Chief Joseph uses heartfelt details to convey his sorrow. He identifies important members of his tribe who have died, Looking Glass and Toohoolhoolzote. Naming specific men is much more emotional than just saying, "Many people close to me have died." Readers feel a chill in their hearts to read the details of the tribe's suffering: "It is cold and we have no blankets. The little children are freezing to death." This conjures an image of emaciated toddlers huddled together for warmth. The last detail—"From where the sun now stands I will fight no more forever"—reinforces his sorrow and determination to stop fighting at once and try to help the survivors.

Writers can use many different rhetorical strategies to achieve their purpose. In this instance, Chief Joseph used simple sentences, everyday words, and emotional details to convey his anguish at the destruction of his relatives, friends, and way of life. His writing style effectively conveys his heartache.

Evaluation

Clearly answers the question

- The opening paragraph clearly states Chief Joseph's "attitude toward his situation." This is shown in the second sentence: "His [Chief Joseph's] style conveys his sorrow and heartbreak at the destruction of his tribe."

- To earn an acceptable score (not to mention an outstanding one), you must directly answer the question, as the writer does here.

Excellent organization

- This response is distinguished by clear organization. The writer isolates three rhetorical strategies—sentence length, diction, and details—and provides specific details about each.

- Note that each element is developed in its own paragraph. The writer explicates Chief Joseph's sentence style in paragraph 2, his diction in paragraph 3, and his use of details in paragraph 4. This organization follows the arrangement of points in the topic sentence—"Chief Joseph uses short sentences, simple diction, and poignant details to convince readers of his determination to surrender"—as it should.

Specific details

- The writer cites specific details to prove the thesis. For example, to show that Chief Joseph uses simple, short sentences to convey his heartache at the fate that has befallen his people, the writer quotes this sentence: "Tell General Howard I know his heart."

- The writer then makes the point: "The short, simple sentences lend his words an elegance and integrity that allow his emotion to shine through. As a result, the simple sentences guide the audience to concentrate on the emotion behind the words."

Original thought

- Outstanding essays are also distinguished by evidence of creative thinking. Papers that earn the best scores often "go the extra mile" by making connections that other students overlook. We see this here as the writer links Chief Joseph's style to Hemingway's: "American novelist Ernest Hemingway used this same strategy in his novels and short stories to achieve the same effect."

- *Never* just throw in extraneous information to impress the scorer, however. *Always* concentrate on answering the question with specific detail and staying on task. However, if you can add an original insight that further supports your thesis, do so. This will set your paper off from others as you demonstrate your wide reading and deep learning.

Score

- This paper could receive a top score, an 8–9, because the thesis is proven through specific details and examples. The writing is graceful and error-free.

PRACTICE EXPOSITORY ESSAY QUESTIONS

Use the following simulated test questions to practice what you learned thus far.

SAMPLE 1

Read the following 1527 journal entry by Alvar Nunez Cabeza de Vaca, which describes the Spaniard's exploration of America. Then, in a well-written essay, analyze some of the ways in which the author recreates the experience of being shipwrecked in a strange country. You might consider such rhetorical strategies as point of view, description, tone, and imagery.

Quickly clambering in and grabbing our oars, we had rowed two crossbow shots from shore when a wave inundated us. Being naked and the cold intense, we let our oars go. The next big wave capsized the barge. The Inspector and two others held fast, but that only carried them more certainly underneath, where they drowned.

A single roll of the sea tossed the rest of the men into the rushing surf and back onto shore half-drowned.

We lost only those the barge took down; but the survivors escaped as naked as they were born, with the loss of everything we had. That was not much, but valuable to us in that bitter November cold, our bodies so emaciated we could easily count every bone and looked the very picture of death. I can say for myself that from the month of May I had eaten nothing but corn, and that sometimes raw. I could never bring myself to eat any of the horse-meat at the time our beasts were slaughtered; and fish I did not taste ten times. On top of everything else, a cruel north wind commenced to complete our killing.

At sunset the Indians, not knowing we had gone, came again with food. When they saw us looking so strangely different, they turned back in alarm. I went after them calling, and they returned, though frightened. I explained to them by signs that our barge had sunk and three of our number drowned. They could see at their feet at least two of the dead men had washed ashore. They could also see that the rest of us were not far from joining these two.

The Indians, understanding our full plight, sat down and lamented for half an hour so loudly that they could be heard a long way off. It intensified my own grief at our calamity and had the same effect on the other victims.

SAMPLE 2

Read the following excerpt from a letter by Abigail Adams to her husband John Adams. Then write an essay analyzing the rhetorical techniques Abigail Adams uses to convey her attitude toward women and their role in public life.

Braintree, 7 May, 1776

...I cannot say that I think you are very generous to the ladies; for, whilst you are proclaiming peace and good-will to men, emancipating all nations, you insist upon retaining an absolute power over wives. But you must remember, that arbitrary power is like most other things which are very hard, very liable to be broken; and not withstanding all your wise laws and maxims, we have it in our power, not only to free ourselves, but to subdue our masters, and, without violence, throw both your natural and legal authority at our feet—

"Charm by accepting, by submitting sway,

Yet have our humor most when we obey."

I thank you for several letters which I have received since I wrote last; they alleviate a tedious absence, and I long earnestly for a Saturday evening, and experience a similar pleasure to that which I used to find in the return of my friend upon that day after a week's absence. The idea of a year dissolves all my philosophy.

SAMPLE 3

The Onondaga Indian leader Canassatego wrote the following letter around 1740 in response to an offer by the colonists to educate a group of Onondaga young men. Read the letter, and then write an essay analyzing the rhetorical techniques the author uses to convey his attitude toward the offer. You may wish to consider such elements as tone, point of view, and diction in your analysis.

We know you highly esteem the kind of learning taught in these colleges, and the maintenance of our young men, while with you, would be very expensive to you. We are convinced, therefore, that you mean to do us a great deal by your proposal; and we thank you heartily. But you who are so wise must know that different nations have different conceptions of things; and you will therefore not take it amiss if our ideas of this kind of education happen not to be the same as yours. We have had some experience of it. Several of our young people were formerly brought up in the colleges of the northern provinces; they were instructed in all your sciences; but when they came back to us, they were bad runners, ignorant of every means of living in the woods, unable to bear either cold or hunger, knew neither how to build a cabin, take a deer, or kill an enemy, spoke our language imperfectly, were therefore neither fit for hunters, warriors, nor counselors, they were totally good for nothing. We are not however not the less obligated for your kind offer, tho' we decline accepting it; and to show our grateful sense of it, if the gentlemen of Virginia shall send us a dozen of their sons, we will take great care of their education, instruct them in all we know, and make men of them.

THE BASIC PERSUASIVE QUESTION

As with the AP expository essay questions, the AP persuasive essay questions are very similar to each other. In all cases, you will be asked to support, dispute, or modify the author's viewpoint. The basic form looks like this:

Write a carefully reasoned essay in which you defend, challenge, or qualify an author's position as stated in the passage.

-or-

Write a carefully reasoned essay in which you explore the validity of the author's assertion.

HOW TO EVALUATE

AP English Language and Composition writing prompts that ask you to persuade require you to *evaluate*, which is giving your opinion by making a judgment call. You decide to what extent you agree or disagree with the author's opinions. Therefore, *evaluation* involves applying your own value system to the information that's germane to the topic. This means you can't sit on the fence—you have to take a stand. On the AP exam, the stand itself isn't as crucial as the support you muster to back it up.

Should you agree or disagree with the writing prompt? Will you earn a higher grade for taking the popular side on the issue? Conversely, will you get penalized for taking the less popular side of the issue? NEVER take a position that you don't understand or can't defend. The resulting essay will be muddled and weak. Instead, make the judgment that's in line with your value system and the material you have to support it.

When you argue a point in writing, you analyze a subject, topic, or issue in order to persuade your readers to think or act a certain way. In brief, construct your essay this way:

Step 1: First state the analytical position you'll be arguing.

Step 2: Summarize the points that support your analysis.

Step 3: Support your position with the following details and examples. Use the ones that best back-up the thesis:

- your observations
- your experiences
- your outside reading
- the author's rhetorical strategies

Step 4: Summarize your main points.

Later in this chapter, I'll provide detailed instruction in writing a persuasive essay.

MODEL QUESTIONS

Study these typical AP English Language and Composition persuasive writing prompts:

Model Persuasive Question 1

The following essay is by (author). Read the passage and then write an essay that defends, challenges, or qualifies the author's ideas about (the topic of the essay). Use specific evidence from your own life or reading to buttress your thesis.

[You have two tasks here:

1. Identify the author's position on the topic.
2. Agree, disagree, or modify the author's position.

Use at least three specific examples to make your point.]

Model Persuasive Question 2

In the first passage, the contemporary writer (name) argues that artists should be supported by the state so they can be free to create. The second writer, (name), argues that the state does not owe any special privileges to writers. Rather, they must follow the same rules of the marketplace that govern all products. Read the passages, considering each writer's assertion about art and the artist. Then, using your own understanding of art and society as evidence, write a carefully organized essay in which you take a side in this issue.

[Decide whether artists such as writers, painters, and sculptors deserve special support. Back up your opinion with evidence drawn from life. Since the time span is not specified, you can draw from any historical period that best supports your thesis.]

Model Persuasive Question 3

In his book (title of book), author John Smith makes the following observation about class structure in the United States. Drawing on your own experience and knowledge, write a carefully organized and well-reasoned essay defending, challenging, or qualifying the author's view of class structure in America.

[You have two tasks here:

1. Identify the author's position on the topic of class structure in America.
2. Agree, disagree, or modify the author's position.

Use at least three specific examples to make your point.]

WRITING A PERSUASIVE ESSAY

Persuasive writing moves readers to action or belief. Aristotle, credited as the father of persuasion, settled on three ways that people could convince others to adopt a certain point of view or approve a course of action. Broadly stated, he identified these three approaches as

- *logos:* the appeal to the audience's reason
- *pathos:* the appeal to the audience's emotions
- *ethos:* the degree of confidence that the speaker's character or personality inspires in readers

The goal of these three appeals is the same, although each one takes a different approach. Each appeal can be used separately, or they can be combined to increase the power of your argument. Let's start with the appeal to reason.

APPEAL TO REASON

> Whether our argument concerns public affairs or some other subject, we must know some, if not all, of the facts about the subject on which we are to argue. Otherwise, we can have no materials out of which to construct arguments.
>
> —Aristotle, *Rhetoric*

Writing that appeals specifically to reason is often called *argumentation*. Appeals based on reason rely on facts rather than on emotion. In turn, each logical argument in your essay must be supported by evidence: facts, anecdotes, descriptions, statistics, or details about the thesis. The basic organization for a persuasive essay developed on a logical argument looks like this:

Introduction   Catches the reader's attention and states your argument. Includes a concise statement of your position on the issue.

Body   States each logical argument by presenting supporting evidence. Disarms the opposition, establishes the writer's credibility, and sets an effective tone.

Conclusion   Restates your argument and summarizes your main points.

Logical arguments are often developed in two basic ways: *inductively* or *deductively*.

Inductive reasoning draws a logical conclusion from specific facts. It depends on drawing inferences from particular cases to support a generalization or claim. Many of our everyday conclusions are based on inductive reasoning.

1. Success of an essay built inductively depends on the strength of your examples.
2. You're better off presenting a handful of examples in detail than a pile of proof without much backing.
3. When in doubt, stick with the magical number three: introduction, three examples, conclusion. This gives you a balanced five paragraph essay and meets reader expectations.

Deductive reasoning moves in the opposite direction, from a general premise to particular conclusions. Sometimes, it depends on a logical structure called a *syllogism*. A *syllogism* is a pattern of logical thinking used in deductive reasoning. It has three parts: a major premise, a minor premise, and a conclusion. Here's an example:

Major premise: All dogs are mortal.

Minor premise: Fido is a dog.

Conclusion: Therefore, Fido is mortal.

If you accept the major premise that all dogs will eventually die and the minor premise that Fido is a dog, then you have to accept the conclusion. Many written arguments developed through a syllogism collapse because the major premise isn't true. The rest of the argument, built on a rickety frame, is bound to crash.

However, a *syllogism* can be valid but not true, as in this example:

Major premise: Ten chefs can cook faster than one chef.

Minor premise: One chef can make a chicken in an hour.

Conclusion: Therefore, ten chefs can make a chicken in 6 minutes.

To use deductive reasoning correctly:

1. First make sure that the major premise is true. If it isn't valid, the rest of the argument will collapse.
2. Write a minor premise that logically follows the major premise.
3. Decide if the conclusion is sound.

Rarely will a writer lay out a deductive argument this neatly, however. In most cases, for example, the first statement will be implied rather than stated.

It's not likely that you'll be using formal syllogisms in your AP essays, but you *will* be using this method of thinking when you construct an argument deductively. The following excerpt from the *Declaration of Independence* relies on a deductive pattern to make its argument. See if you can find the major premise. (Hint: It's in the very beginning.)

> When in the course of human events, it becomes necessary for one people to dissolve the political bands that have connected them with another, and to assume among the powers of the earth, the separate and equal station to which the laws of nature and of nature's God entitle them, a decent respect to the opinions of mankind requires that they should declare the causes which impel them to the separation.
>
> We hold these truths to be self-evident: that all men are created equal; that they are endowed by their Creator with certain unalienable rights; that among these are life, liberty, and the pursuit of happiness; that to secure these rights, governments are instituted among men, deriving their just powers from the consent of the governed; that whenever any form of government becomes destructive of these ends, it is the right of the people to alter or abolish it, and to institute new government, laying its foundation on such principles and organizing its powers in such form, as to them shall seem most likely to effect their safety and happiness.
>
> —Thomas Jefferson, *The Declaration of Independence* (1776)

APPEAL TO ETHICS

Ethics is your moral sense, your sense of right and wrong. The credibility and persuasiveness of your claim is in direct proportion to your reader's view of you as a person of good sense, good moral character, and good intentions—your *ethics*. The more trustworthy you appear in print, the more likely you are to have your arguments accepted.

Your trustworthiness arises from two factors:

- the quality of your proof. The better your proof = the stronger your argument.
- your ability to take the high ground and avoid insulting your opponent.

Cheap shots weaken your argument, especially if they intentionally deceive your audience. Always argue your point fairly and ethically. Avoid insulting your subject or your audience.

APPEAL TO EMOTION

An effective essay can draw its strength from facts and reasoning, but logic can carry you just so far with certain readers. Depending on your audience and topic, you're going to want to pour on some feeling.

   Below is an example of a persuasive appeal that relies on emotion. It's from Thomas Paine's pamphlet *Common Sense* (as in "It's just common sense to fight for our independence from England.") Paine's series of essays were so effective that they propelled the colonies into the Revolutionary War.

> These are the times that try men's souls. The summer soldier and the sunshine patriot will in this crisis shrink from the service of his country; but he that stands it NOW deserves the love and thanks for man and woman. Tyranny, like hell, is not easily conquered; yet we have this consolation with us, that the harder the conflict, the more glorious the triumph. What we obtain too cheap, we esteem too lightly; 'tis dearness only that gives everything its value. Heaven knows how to put a proper price upon its goods; and it would be strange indeed, if so celestial an article as FREEDOM should not be highly rated. Britain, with an army to enforce her tyranny, has declared that she has a right (*not only to TAX*) but "to BIND us in ALL CASES WHATSOEVER," and if being *bound in that manner*, is not slavery, then there is no such thing as slavery upon earth. Even the expression is impious, for so unlimited a power can belong only to God...

> —Thomas Paine, *The Crisis, Number I* (1776)

Emotion can be a powerful appeal, but never use an emotional appeal in place of solid proof or to stir up feelings that are dangerous or harmful.

   Which persuasive strategy should you use as you write your AP essays? Use reason, emotion, and ethics (or some combination of these) based on the following considerations:

- What kind of persuasion is most likely to sway your readers as you deal in an open and honest manner?
- What objections, if any, are they likely to have to your argument?
- How strong is your case? (Use more examples, facts, statistics, and other "hard" proof if your argument is weak.)

In general, when you're writing an AP essay, rely more heavily on reason and ethics than emotion.

ACKNOWLEDGING THE OPPOSITION

As much as you might like to, you can't ignore the arguments against your opinion. You must *always* consider the arguments that will arise. You deal with the opposition by

- identifying the main arguments against your side
- acknowledging the arguments in your writing
- countering the opposition

Of course, don't give the same space to the opposition as you do to your points. Devote more space to *your* argument or place it last in your essay so readers will understand that it's crucial.

There are three main ways that you can deal with the opposition to decrease its force. These methods are as follows:

1. Show the opposition is wrong.
2. Show the opposition has some merit, but give a point of your own that is just as convincing.
3. Show the opposition has merit, but your point is stronger.

LOGICAL FALLACIES

Faulty logic can demolish the most carefully constructed persuasive essay. It's one of the surest ways to lose points. Below are the most common *logical fallacies,* errors in reasoning. They are arranged in alphabetical order.

TIP

When you're addressing an audience that doesn't agree with your argument, search for *common ground*, or areas of agreement. If you can get readers to agree with you on one point, they're more likely to be persuaded by your other points.

Error in Logic	Definition
Ambiguity	Using expressions that are confusing because they have more than one meaning
Argument to the Person	Attacking the person rather than the topic
Begging the Question	Using circular reasoning that offers the argument itself as proof
Bogus Claims	Promising more than you can deliver
Card Stacking	Ignoring evidence on the other side of the issue
Either-or Fallacy	Offering only two choices when other valid ones exist
False Analogies	Making misleading comparisons
Guilt by Association	Attacking a person's beliefs because of the person's associations
Jumping on the Bandwagon	Suggesting that something is right because everyone else does it
Hasty Generalization	Generalizing from inadequate evidence, such as stereotyping
Irrelevant argument	Drawing a conclusion that does not relate to the premise
Loaded Terms	Using slanted or biased terms, especially those with strong connotations
Misrepresentation	Using outright lies or other deliberate misrepresentation
Oversimplifying the Issue	Twisting the truth by presenting too narrow a range of possibilities
Post hoc ergo propter hoc	Confusing *after* with *because.* (Latin for "After this, therefore because of this")
Red Herring	Diverting the issue with an unrelated topic
Self-contradiction	Arguing two premises that cannot both be true
Taking the Issue out of Context	Distorting the issue by taking it out of context

FIVE-STEP METHOD TO A HIGH SCORE

1. As you did with the expository prompt, restate the persuasive prompt in your own words to make sure you clearly understand what you must write.

2. Read the quote or excerpt all the way through, at least twice. Each time you read, focus on one specific element. Always begin with meaning. Summarize the passage so you know that you got the gist. Then select one point at a time to argue. Jot down supporting details and evidence that will help you prove your point.

3. Plan before you write. While you don't want to waste your time pondering small points, it's important to know where you're going before you begin. Otherwise, your essay will sprawl. Create a quick jotted outline, take a few notes, or make a diagram showing the order in which you'll present your points.

4. As you write, make frequent and specific references to the excerpt. Quote words, phrases, and lines to support your point. NEVER include a detail that's off the point just to prove that you know it. Unnecessary details will cost you points, not win you any.

5. Be sure to proofread your essay. You'll be surprised how many errors you can catch on rereading.

SAMPLE PERSUASIVE PASSAGE ESSAY QUESTIONS AND MODEL RESPONSES

SAMPLE 1

The philosopher Socrates once asserted: "The unexamined life is not worth living." Take some time to think about the implications of this quotation. Then write a carefully reasoned essay that explores the validity of the assertion, using examples from your reading, observation, or experience to develop your position.

Response 1

Socrates once said that "the unexamined life is not worth living." There is validity to this bold statement. Since we can all examine our own lives, there should be a pressing need to do so. I have personal experience in reference to this quote. I also relate well with certain literature that deals with this assertion.

Much more, in recent days, have I given myself an examination. I live a conscious life where I analyze myself and what I'm up to, just so I can keep myself in check. I can validate this quote with my own experiences because I usually find some hope when I do this. By analyzing life, I can make my life worth living. For example, I see that I have goals awaiting to be accomplished, things and places not yet experienced and facets of life I have not discerned yet. The pursuit of these goals that come from my examination make my life worth living. Knowing that there is more to come is very important.

Catcher in the Rye by J.D. Salinger provides more evidence that there is truth to Socrates' saying. Holden's adventures in New York City for those three days can be seen as his examination of his own life with the help of all the other characters in the book. The most significant parts would be with his former teachers, Mr. Spencer and Mr. Antolini. By examining himself through the help of these people, Holden finds a way to accept life and make it worth living. Before all this examination and thinking, Holden had many recurring thoughts of suicide. After his examination of his life, he realizes that he has a strong love for children and this devotion to helping children makes his life worth living.

There are ways to disagree with this assertion, but its validity is certainly acceptable. By examining one's life, one can definitely see what he/she should live for. Without an examination, life becomes aimless and therefore wouldn't be worth living.

Evaluation

A problem with facts

- This essay may sound good on a quick reading, but a second reading reveals that the writer's statements are both empty and false. Take the third sentence, for example: "Since we can all examine our own lives, there should be a pressing need to do so." Not everyone is equipped to examine their own lives, for a variety of different reasons. In addition, why should there be a "pressing need" just because "we can all" do it?

Statements too general

- The last two sentences in the first paragraph are far too general to be persuasive. The sentences read: "I have personal experience in reference to this quote. I also relate well with certain literature that deal with this assertion." What "personal experience"? What literature? At the very least, the writer should name the book, author, and specific point(s) that will be discussed in the essay.

Empty rhetoric

- The second paragraph is nearly totally devoid of meaning. What meaning exists is garbled and unintentionally humorous. For example, the first sentence—"Much more, in recent days, have I given myself an examination"—implies a physical rather than mental scrutiny. It conjures up an image of the writer searching for bug bites or dandruff.
- Now look at the rest of this paragraph. Why does the writer have to "keep himself in check"? Is the writer a homicidal maniac? "By analyzing life, I can make my life worth living." How? Why?
- The next sentence is equally vague and has several misused words: "For example, I see that I have goals awaiting to be accomplished, things and

places not yet experienced and facets of life I have not discerned yet." What goals? What "things" and "places"? The phrases "facets of life" and the word "discerned" appear to be thrown in to impress the reader, because they are imprecise in context and too elevated for what has come before.

Incorrect statements

- Paragraph three is equally empty. However, it also contains incorrect statements and conclusions. For example, Holden does not "accept life and make it worth living." Rather, he has a nervous breakdown at the end of the novel and ends up in a sanitarium.

- His examination is not at all conscious; rather, what introspection occurs is an accidental benefit of his mad dash through New York City as he attempts to deal with life's "phoniness" and his inability to fit in with his peers.

- The statement "Before all this examination and thinking, Holden had many recurring thoughts of suicide" is also incorrect. Holden broke his hand by smashing the car windows after the death of his brother Allie. This is one incident and thus not the same as repeated thoughts of suicide. If there were such repeated incidents, they must be documented with specific details and examples from the book.

- Finally, the last statement is incorrect. The statement reads, "He realizes that he has a strong love for children and this devotion to helping children makes his life worth living." Holden wants to save the children from the pain of growing up, the pain he experienced. The writer's statement makes it appear as though Holden has decided to become an elementary school teacher. Holden is saved largely by his sister Phoebe's unselfish love, but the novel's ending is ambiguous: it is by no means certain that he is ready to assume a mature role in the world.

Conclusion makes no sense

- The first sentence is totally devoid of meaning, and the second assumes that all introspection is successful. Just the opposite is true: many people spend years plumbing their psyches and emerge with little to show for their efforts.

- Notice that the writer does neither considers the opposition in the essay nor provides any specific examples. As a result, this essay would receive a very low score, in the 1–2 range.

Response 2

Many times, life can get way too hectic. Sometimes, we just don't want to face the truth about ourselves and our problems. As a result, we tend to go about our daily lives without giving much thought to how we feel. Routine takes the place of introspection. It may seem impossible to find the time or courage to look inward, but it is essential. As Socrates said, "An unexamined life is not worth living." This is true in real life as well as in fiction, as shown by the experiences of NFL hockey player Ken Daneyko and those of the fictional character Holden Caufield from J.D. Salinger's novel *The Catcher in the Rye*.

On the surface, everything seemed great in Ken Daneyko's life. The New Jersey Devils were finally at the top of the NHL. Just a few seasons ago, they had won the Stanley Cup for the first time in their history. They were creating a dynasty atop the Atlantic Division and Ken Daneyko was making it happen. He was one of the original Devils, having played every game for the team since they moved to New Jersey in 1982. Daneyko was on top of the world. He had recently been honored for playing 1,000 games in the NHL, all with the same team, a feat rarely accomplished. On the side, Daneyko owned a flourishing restaurant in Caldwell, New Jersey, called "Mezzanottes." However, something was wrong below the surface—deeply wrong. Daneyko realized that he had a problem he had been ignoring for too long. He was an alcoholic. Finally, Daneyko looked into his soul and realized that it was time he got off the treadmill and started to examine his life. When he did, he checked himself into a rehab center for six weeks. During this time, he examined his life so he could fix what was wrong and get ready to approach his problems alcohol-free. This time when the Devils won the Stanley Cup again, Daneyko was able to understand what mattered in his life...and what didn't. He realized that the victory now had meaning because he was able to enjoy it with his family and friends, sober. Holden Caufield had a similar awakening when he examined his life closely.

Holden Caufield had been labeled a problem child. When the novel opens, he had been expelled from four private schools and was headed for expulsion from the fifth school. He thought that everyone was a hypocrite, a "phony" who put on airs. Holden was so lost that it seemed like he was headed for the same fate as his former classmate James Castle, who had committed suicide by jumping out a window. When he knew that he was going to be expelled, Holden took a three-day trip to New York City to put off having to tell his parents what had happened to him. In New York, Holden begins to examine his life to find his place in it. Holden wants to stay a child forever but through his interactions with his teacher Mr. Antolini and the support of his younger sister Phoebe, Holden realizes that he must grow up. Through his experiences in New York, Holden realized that he couldn't save the helpless creatures in the world. He could not help the ducks freezing in the Central Park lake during the winter or the little children who were not understood by their peers or parents. Holden had a nervous breakdown as a result of his introspection, but it paved the way for his eventual recovery.

Perhaps you don't realize that anything is wrong with your life so you go along without looking too deeply into your feelings. Or maybe you face the opposite situation: things seem so very wrong that it's too painful to examine why your life has derailed. In either case, it's vital to probe your life to gain clarity and meaning as both NHL player Ken Daneyko and fictional character Holden Caufield realized.

Evaluation

Excellent opening

- The opening paragraph weaves the two examples—the real-life hockey player Ken Daneyko and the fictional character Holden Caufield—into the thesis.

- The writer clearly states the argument: people must examine their lives in order to create meaning and solve life-threatening problems. This thesis directly responds to the prompt and so is an excellent opening.

Superb specific examples and details

- The example of Ken Daneyko's experiences in the second paragraph not only unequivocally supports the writer's argument but also engages the reader's interest. It's an interesting example because it's unusual, on the task but not something scorers will be reading over and over.

- Using fresh examples engage your readers because they are different from what they have been reading all afternoon.

- Second, this is also a superb example because of the specific details, such as "New Jersey Devils," "top of the NHL," "creating a dynasty atop the Atlantic Division," "since they moved to New Jersey in 1982, " "recently been honored for playing 1,000 games in the NHL," "Daneyko owned a flourishing restaurant in Caldwell, New Jersey, called "Mezzanottes."

Point made

- Notice how well the writer makes the point in the end of the second paragraph, through sentences such as "During this time, he examined his life so he could fix what was wrong and get ready to approach his problems alcohol-free."

- The last sentence in this paragraph functions as a smooth transition to the third paragraph.

More great details prove the point

- The third paragraph is distinguished by equally specific details. Notice especially the names—James Castle, Mr. Antolini, and Phoebe.

- The writer also includes descriptions that directly answer the question, including the following sentence: "He could not help the ducks freezing in the Central Park lake during the winter or the little children who were not understood by their peers or parents."

Thesis proven

- The conclusion shows a clear understanding of the novel's seemingly paradoxical ending: "Holden had a nervous breakdown as a result of his introspection, but it paved the way for his eventual recovery."

- The final paragraph sums up the thesis and makes the writer's point clear.

Score

- This essay would clearly earn a top score, in the 8–9 range.

SAMPLE 2

Read the following excerpt from Hector St. John de Crevecoeur's essay "What is an American?" Drawing on your own knowledge and experience, write a carefully reasoned essay in which you defend, challenge, or qualify Crevecoeur's view of an "American."

What, then, is the American, this new man? He is neither a European nor the descendent of a European; hence that strange mixture of blood, which you will find in no other country. I could point out to you a family whose grandfather was an Englishman, whose wife was Dutch, whose son married a French woman, and whose present four sons now have four wives of different nations. *He* is an American who, leaving behind all his ancient prejudices and manners, received new ones from the new mode of life he has embraced, the new government he obeys, and the new ranks he holds. He becomes and American by being received in the broad lap of our great Alma Mater. Here individuals of all nations are melted into a new race of men, whose labors and posterity will one day cause great changes in the world. Americans are the western pilgrims who are carrying along with them that great mass of arts, sciences, vigor, and industry which began long since in the East; they will finish the great circle. The Americans were once scattered all over Europe; here they are incorporated into one of the finest systems of population which has ever appeared, and which thereafter become distinct by the power of different climates they inhabit. The American ought therefore to love this country much better than that wherein he or his forefathers were born. Here the rewards of his industry follow with equal steps the progress of his labor; his labor is founded on the basis of nature, self-interest; can it want a stronger allurement? ...The American is a new man, who acts upon new principles; he must therefore entertain new ideas and form new opinions.

Response 1

An American is a rainbow of various customs, knowledge of numerous backgrounds; he is a "strange mixture of blood" who coexists with society. His genes can no longer be distinguished, but instead incorporate different cells varying from any other human. Is he immortal? American society defines a threshold of uniqueness; it has created an uncanny orb of a new race. As Crevecoeur stated, this "new man" defines the genuine future and progress of the coming day and age.

I am an American. My viewpoints, my customs, my religion, my appearance define a true American. Yet, I am still innocently asked, "What are you?" Unlike most people, I am left in a state of confusion. What is meant by asking, "What are you?" Well, I am a human, I am a woman, I am an American. Of course if I were to respond in that manner, I would receive a confused look and would probably be perceived to be insane. Society today is still trying to fester the true meaning of American. A skin tone, a belief, a mere manner in no way represents the aspects of American life. Minorities born in the States tend to place significant emphasis of past history. Ethnic parades seem to bring out more of a response than Labor Day. In tenth grade, my history teacher went around the classroom and asked us individually "What are you?" Whether the person was born in the United States or a citizen, neither responded, "I am an American."

At this point in my life, I have come to the conclusion what I am is an American. The fact that Americans are "different" cannot be debated. You may ask, why? Or why not? Each individual has been placed in a new world.

Evaluation

Sacrifices sense for sound

- *Always write simple and plainly. This writer didn't. As a result, the essay doesn't make sense.* Here we have an essay in which the writer fell in love with the sound of the words and didn't realize that they don't make sense.

- For example, how can someone be "a rainbow of various customs," as the first sentence claims? The metaphor doesn't make sense.

- The genetic metaphor in the following sentence is equally muddy and nonsensical.

- The sentence "Is he immortal?" has absolutely nothing to do with the thesis; the sentence "American society defines a threshold of uniqueness" is both totally incorrect and absurd.

- What is an "uncanny orb of a new race"? Again, we have another statement that doesn't make sense.

- Be VERY careful that everything you write makes sense. Look past the words to make sure that you're actually saying something that is intelligible and intelligent.

Lack of organization

- Since there is no method of organization, the ideas are jumbled together. As a result, the argument does not develop.

Continued lack of logic

- Look closely at each statement. For example, the sentence "My viewpoints, my customs, my religion, my appearance define a true American" cannot be correct. What are "American" viewpoints? What are "American" customs? America does not have a state religion, nor a set appearance. As a result, this sentence makes no sense.

- Further, since the writer clearly states that she is an American, why should she be "left in a state of confusion" when she is asked questions about her nationality? It's highly unlikely that anyone would think that she was "insane" if she answered the question by saying: "I am a human, I am a woman, I am an American."

Words misused

- The word "fester" is misused; it is reserved for decaying sores or wounds. The rest of the paragraph is equally illogical, even nonsensical.

Score

- This essay would receive a 1, the lowest grade, as it makes little sense.

Response 2

Is anyone purely American? The Native Americans were the first to come to America, but they weren't American. Rather, they were Asian in origin, crossing the Bering Strait over a land bridge and coming down from the North, becoming the first known immigrants to set foot in North America. Next came the Spanish, the British, and the French, carrying their foreign flags from far away, calling themselves "settlers" or "conquistadors," but being nothing more than glorified immigrants. In present times, citizens of almost every nationality and ethnicity populate our monumental cities and ever-growing suburbs. However, the question remains: Who is "more" American? Is it the Native Americans with their unspoken "We got here first" claim, or the more prosperous European immigrants who have made great fortunes? Perhaps it's the newest immigrants, who make up today's blue-collar work force.

Contrary to Crevecoeur's claim, the American is not a "new man" but an old man in new clothes. Americans are less a fusing of cultures and peoples and more an amalgamation. Therefore, Crevecoeur is wrong when he claims that Americans are "individuals of all nations melted into a new race of men." Instead, most Americans cling to their cultural past, for it is a source of identity. Most Americans feel that if they combine their culture with another or relinquish it completely, they are becoming some form of "ethnic communist." Americans are all different types of people, U-Hauling their culture from another land and hiding it inside their three-piece business suits. Although we are all equal in spirit and law, there is an unspoken segregation because we still fear the unfamiliar changes that acculturation brings.

We cannot define the American, as Crevecoeur attempted, because our Democracy decrees that no one's ideas have to be the same. Further, Americans rejoice in their differences and make them part of their identity. This makes us who we are—unique.

Evaluation

Thesis clearly stated

- The thesis is stated directly in the first sentence: "Is anyone purely American?"

Vivid language

- The thesis is backed up with specific details expressed in vivid language. For example: "The Native Americans were the first to come to America, but they weren't American. Rather, they were Asian in origin, crossing the Bering Strait over a land bridge and coming down from the North, becoming the first known immigrants to set foot in North America. Next came the Spanish, the British, and the French, carrying their foreign flags from far away, calling themselves 'settlers' or 'conquistadors,' but being nothing more than glorified immigrants."

Original thesis

- The writer has clearly thought deeply about this topic, as shown by the conclusion: "Contrary to Crevecoeur's claim, the American is not a "new man" but an old man in new clothes. Americans are less a fusing of cultures and peoples and more an amalgamation."

Score

- This is a superb essay, distinguished by clear a thesis, vivid language, and original thinking. As a result, this essay would receive a top score, in the 8–9 range.

Response 3

What about an American makes him or her different from a European or any other group of people? Are an American's values different from those of people in his ancestral homeland? For the first part of this nation's history, there was no difference between an American and an Englishman. In New England, the Puritans' values and religion dominated society. This was not some new belief system created in America but rather a continuation of what the original settlers believed in England. When this country was settled in the seventeenth century, there was nothing uniquely American about "Americans." The same is still true today, as Americans are not a group of "new men" that Crevecoeur describes. Rather they are a continuation of their ancestry, the values and beliefs of their non-American ancestors.

   Crevecoeur's example of American uniqueness demonstrated by a "strange mixture of blood" is not entirely correct. For much of American history, different immigrant groups remained separate and distinct. For example, early immigrants settled in small groups with their fellow countrymen from the "Old Side." We can see this in the proliferation of Chinatowns, Germantowns, and Little Italys. Immigrants didn't blend in even when they wanted to. This can be seen in the Irish, who experienced great prejudice because of their religious beliefs when they came to American at the end of the nineteenth century and beginning of the twentieth century. Their Catholicism conflicted with the Anglican beliefs of the English descendants. As a result, the Irish were held back from many professional careers and settled into blue-collar jobs. Many Irish immigrant women became maids; the men, police officers. Even today, immigrant groups tend to stay with their "own kind" and experience prejudice for their beliefs. This is seen in many Mexican, Hispanic, and Latino immigrants, who are being shunned, cheated, and even beaten when they try to get work as day laborers.

The original Americans did not "leave behind" their old ideals and embrace the "new ranks he holds," as Crevecoeur claims. In America, Southern settlers created a new aristocracy of landowners based on the systems they knew from Europe. Even the delegates to our Continental Congress, the exalted body that gave us the Declaration of Independence, were no different from the aristocrats of Europe. They were not the product of some new American idealism but rather a manifestation of the old ways. In fact, even the republican ideals so cherished in America were not unique or American when they were used on our shores. The ideas were European and almost a century old.

Crevecoeur is incorrect when he claims that in America, "individuals of all nations melted into a new race." Rather, they clumped together. Most of the interactions Crevecoeur considers unique to America are simply the result of old ideals creating the same actions in a new setting. The American does not love this country more than the place of his ancestry. Often times just the opposite is true: he feels more connected to his heritage. There is no new race of Americans; simply a conglomeration of the old.

Evaluation

While this essay may lack the eloquence of the previous example, its thesis is more clearly stated. The examples are very well stated and show a clear organization. Notice how well the writer isolates specific points from Crevecoeur's essay to refute. This is a fine essay, in the 8–9 range, and serves to illustrate how clear organization and examples combine to prove a point with skill and success.

SAMPLE 3

Read the following excerpt from Roger Ascham's The Schoolmaster. Then write a carefully reasoned essay in which you agree or disagree with Lady Jane Grey's view of using love or fear to educate children. To support your opinion, use details drawn from your experiences or reading.

And one example, whether love or fear doth work more in a child for virtue and learning, I will gladly report; which may be heard with some pleasure and followed with more profit. Before I went into Germany, I came to Broadgate to take my leave of that noble Lady Jane Grey...

"And how came you, madame," quoth I, "to this deep knowledge of pleasure, and what did chiefly allure you unto it, seeing not many women, but very few men, have attained thereunto?"

"I will tell you," quoth she, "and tell you a truth which perchance ye will marvel at. One of the great benefits that ever God gave me is that he sent me so sharp and severe parents and so gentle a schoolmaster. For when I am in presence either of father or mother, whether I speak, keep silence, sit, stand, or go, eat, drink, be merry or sad, be sewing, playing, dancing, or doing anything else, I must do it, as it were, in such weight, measure, and number, even so perfectly as God made the world, or else I am so sharply taunted, so cruelly threatened, yea, presently sometimes, with pinches, nips, and bobs, and other ways which I will not name for the honor I bear them, so without measure disordered, that I think myself in hell till time come that I must go to Master Aylmer, who teacheth me so gently, so pleasantly, with such fair allurements to learning, that I think all the time nothing whilst I am with him. And when I am called from him, I fall on weeping because whatsoever I do else but learning is full of grief, trouble, fear, and whole misliking unto me. And thus my book hath been so much pleasure, and bringeth daily to me more pleasure and more, that in respect of it all other pleasures in very deed be but trifles and troubles unto me."

I remember this talk gladly, both because it is so worthy of memory and because also it was the last talk I ever had, and the last time that I ever so that noble and worthy lady.

Response 1

Fear allows the victim to be cognizant of his/her weaknesses, thus playing an insuperable role in the education of children. Children can easily lose their conscience and remain trapped within their comfort zone if they are manifested with an abundance of love, rather than strict conditions. Fear detaches oneself from his/her sea of security, hence allowing him/herself to strive further beyond his/her limits.

Lady Jane Grey explicitly tells of her great boon of her "God-sent" parents and schoolmaster. With her parents who were callously severe and a schoolmaster who was ever-so gentle, Grey sustained the balance between love and fear in her journey of education. I believe that this preserved balance indubitably holds much potent in educating children. Take an example of a young girl whose parents trained her to do nothing else but study. With fear warily hidden in her heart, her mental conscience is mitigated in sharp contrast with her classmate who was nurtured with love alone, and now is too scared to face reality. Either way, fear is inevitable. If one does not experience fear in the early years of his/her childhood, it WILL come back to haunt him/her later. Though the word "fear" may seem like a burden to carry, it is, in fact, a substantial learning process where an individual can grow from the experience. It builds an individual's personae, reflected spirit and resolve.

Fear—it brings an individual to his/her knees, allowing him/herself to be wary of his/her true reflection. Though burdensome, it is certainly essential to complete the character.

Evaluation

Thesis not proven

- The writer has a controversial thesis—"[fear] it is certainly essential to complete the character." While any persuasive thesis must be supported by appeals to reason, ethics, or emotion, the more controversial a thesis, the more proof is needed. Unfortunately, there is no proof here at all. As a result, the paper fails to persuade.

Words misused

The writer misuses far too many words. These include

- *insuperable* means "overwhelming." The writer wants a word such as *invaluable*.
- *manifested* means "shown" but not as used in this context. The word "shown" is much clearer and more direct and thus a far better choice here.
- *potent* means "powerful." The writer wants the word "potential" here.
- *personae* means the voice the speaker adopts. In this context, the writer wants the word "character."

Awkward pronouns

- The writer is to be applauded for trying to use nonbiased language, but the attempt comes off as awkward. Instead of using singular pronouns, make the pronouns plural.
- For example: "Fear—it brings an individual to *his/her* knees, allowing *him/herself* to be wary of *his/her* true reflection" can become "Fear—it brings people to *their* knees, allowing people to be wary of *their* true reflection."

Score

- This paper could receive no more than a 1 on the 9 point scale. The thesis is not proven, many words are misused, and the paper fails to make sense.

Response 2

"It is better to rule in fear than in love," Machiavelli once stated. He was wrong. Children all over the world today live in fear of their parents, their teachers, and their peers. This fear hinders both imagination and creativity. From my own brush with the pain of being taught by fear, I can truly relate to Lady Jane Grey's experiences. As a result, I can unequivocally conclude that children should be motivated to learn through love and kindness rather than fear and cruelty.

When I was seven years old, my soccer coach used terror to motivate us to master the game. It was a dismal failure because his methods served only to make me hate him and soccer. Every Sunday afternoon, he belittled me and my abilities. When I didn't understand his directions, he screamed: "You're such a loser." When I missed a goal, he bellowed: "Any fool could have gotten that kick, wimp. Get the %#@! off the field!" Every game, I cried. My parents could not be at the games because they worked at our store on the weekends so there was no one to protect me. As a result of the coach's fear tactics, I dropped out of soccer and became very timid about trying new things. As my self-esteem plummeted, I began to think that I was a loser, as pitiful as my soccer coach claimed I was.

Lady Jane Grey had a similar reaction to her parents, who motivated her with fear: "For when I am in presence either of father or mother …I must do it [assigned tasks], as it were, in such weight, measure, and number, even so perfectly as God made the world, or else I am so sharply taunted, so cruelly threatened, yea, presently sometimes, with pinches, nips, and bobs, and other ways which I will not name for the honor I bear them, so without measure disordered, that I think myself in hell."

Fortunately, my parents lavished love on me. They reassured me that there was no crime in failing, as long as I tried. My father told me how he tried to learn to swim. Even though some of the other boys made fun of him, they grew to respect him for his determination. My father never became a top swimmer (or even a very good one) but he respected himself for sticking in there. Lady Jane Grey had a kind schoolmaster who gave her the same confidence in learning as my parents gave me. Master Aylmer taught Lady Jane Grey "so gently, so pleasantly, with such fair allurements to learning" that she derived great pleasure from her books. His gentleness sparked a true love of learning in her: "And thus my book hath been so much pleasure, and bringeth daily to me more pleasure and more, that in respect of it all other pleasures in very deed be but trifles and troubles unto me."

The people you fear and the people you love both leave their mark on your soul.

Teaching with fear might motivate some children to succeed, but it is much more likely to leave terrible scars. Lady Jane Grey speaks of weeping with "grief, trouble, [and] fear" when her parents taught her with cruelty. Teaching with love and kindness helps children succeed. It worked for me.

Evaluation

Excellent opening

- Use an apt quotation to open an essay because it simultaneously grabs the reader's attention and suggests the topic of the paper. This quotation is especially good because it reverses our expectations.

- You can also use an anecdote (brief story), dialogue, or statistic, as well as a restatement of the prompt. Since you're always working with reader interest, you will want to make your opening as intriguing as possible.

Clear thesis

- The writer clearly states the thesis: "…I can unequivocally conclude that children should be motivated to learn through love and kindness rather than fear and cruelty."

- In a persuasive paper, always state your thesis clearly so your reader can understand the point you are arguing.

Excellent examples

- The anecdote that describes the cruel soccer coach fulfills the assignment to "support your opinion [by using] details drawn from your experiences or reading."
- These details are very effective because they are especially vivid, as shown by the dialogue ("You're such a loser." and "Any fool could have gotten that kick, wimp. Get the %#@! off the field!")
- Notice that the writer uses the details to prove the thesis by showing the negative results of using fear as a teacher: "As a result of the coach's fear tactics, I dropped out of soccer and became very timid about trying new things. As my self-esteem plummeted, I began to think that I was a loser, as pitiful as my soccer coach claimed I was."

Examples related to passage

- The writer links the examples to Lady Jane Grey's experience with her parents. This further helps the writer argue the point and prove the thesis that love is a better motivator than fear.

Conclusion sums up main points

- The final statement clearly proves the point: "Teaching with love and kindness helps children succeed. It worked for me." As a result, there's no doubt where the writer stands on the issue.

Score

- This paper could receive a top score, a 9, because the thesis is proven through specific details and examples.

PRACTICE PERSUASIVE ESSAY QUESTIONS

Use the following simulated test questions to practice what you learned in this lesson.

SAMPLE 1

English novelist E.M. Forster once said "If I had to choose between betraying my country and betraying my friend, I hope I should have the guts to betray my country." Consider the implications of this statement. Then write a carefully reasoned essay in which you defend, challenge, or qualify Forster's statement. Use specific evidence from your own life, history, current events, or reading to back up your claims.

SAMPLE 2

Read the following excerpt from an essay by contemporary writer Joan Didion. Then write a carefully reasoned essay evaluating Didion's argument that young people today do not feel the same sense of place as their parents do.

Sometimes I think that those of us who are now in our thirties were born into the last generation to carry the burden of "home," to find in family the source of all tension and drama. I had by all objective accounts a "normal" and a "happy" family situation, and yet I was almost thirty years old before I could talk to my family on the telephone without crying after I had hung up. We did not fight. Nothing was wrong. And yet some nameless anxiety colored the emotional charge between me and the place I came from. The question of whether or not you could go home again was a very real part of the sentimental and largely literary baggage with which we left home in the fifties: I suspect that it is irrelevant to the children born of the fragmentation after World War II.

ADDITIONAL PRACTICE TESTS

GENERAL DIRECTIONS FOR THE PRACTICE TESTS

These tests were constructed to be representative of what you will encounter on the AP English Language and Composition exam. Take the test in a quiet room without distractions, following all directions carefully and observing all time limits. Try to get as close as possible to actual test conditions, and take the test in one sitting. The more carefully you match test conditions, the more accurate your results will be and the better able you will be to evaluate your strengths and weaknesses.

ROAD MAP

- *Practice Test 1*
- *Practice Test 2*
- *Practice Test 3*
- *Practice Test 4*

PRACTICE TEST 1

ENGLISH LANGUAGE AND COMPOSITION

SECTION 1

Time—1 hour

> **Directions: This section contains selections from two passages of prose and two poems with questions on their style, content, form, and purpose. Read each selection closely and carefully. Then choose the best answer from the five choices.**

Questions 1–12. Read the following selection carefully before you mark your answers.

...On the 18th of April at eleven at night, about eight hundred Grenadiers and light infantry were ferried across the Bay to Cambridge, from whence they marched to Concord, about twenty miles. The Congress had been lately assembled at that place, and it was imagined that the General had intelligence of a magazine being formed there and that they were going to destroy it.

The people in the country (who are all furnished with arms and have what they call Minute Companies in every town ready to march on any alarm) had a signal, it is supposed, by a light from one of the steeples in town. Upon the troops' embarking, the alarm spread through the country, so that before daybreak the people in general were in arms and on their march to Concord.

About daybreak a number of people appeared before the troops near Lexington. When they [the American colonists] were told to disperse, they fired on the troops and ran off, upon which the Light Infantry pursued them and brought down about fifteen of them. The troops went on to Concord and executed the business they were sent on, and on their return found two or three of their people lying in the agonies of death, scalped, with their noses and ears cut off and eyes bored out—which exasperated the soldiers exceedingly. A prodigious number of people now occupied the hills, woods, and stone walls along the road. The Light Troops drove some parties from the hills, but all the roads being enclosed with store walls served as a cover to the rebels, from whence they fired on the troops....In this manner were the troops harassed in their return for seven or eight miles.

1. What story does the writer tell of the confrontation on Lexington Common?

   (A) When the British told the colonists to disperse, the British fired first and the colonists pursued them. The Native Americans joined the battle on the American side.

   (B) The British attacked the colonists, who fought back with great bravery and zeal.

   (C) When the British told the colonists to disperse, the colonists fired first but the British pursued them.

   (D) An unknown person fired, then a British solider fired on an unarmed American. Finally, all the British soldiers started firing.

   (E) The Americans gathered to fight off the invading British, who greatly outnumbered the rebels.

2. As used in the first paragraph, a *magazine* is most likely

   (A) a periodical publication featuring nonfiction articles, commentary, and light fiction.

   (B) a building in which ammunition and explosives are stored for military use.

   (C) an ammunition gunbelt.

   (D) a preacher advocating rebellion.

   (E) a mutinous newspaper determined to bring down the government.

3. The writer's tone in the second paragraph is best described as

   (A) carefully impartial.

   (B) horrified and dismayed.

   (C) astonished and amazed.

   (D) disdainful and condescending.

   (E) admiring and worshipful.

4. The rhetorical strategy employed in the second paragraph is best described as

   (A) recounting facts and details to persuade readers of the writer's point of view.

   (B) highly ironic.

   (C) using an extended metaphor to relate a narrative.

   (D) making an abstraction concrete through the use of an analogy.

   (E) inductive reasoning.

5. The word "exasperated" in the phrase "exasperated the soldiers exceedingly" is an example of
   (A) onomatopoeia.
   (B) understatement.
   (C) foreshadowing.
   (D) hyperbole or exaggeration.
   (E) personification.

6. In the last paragraph, the writer is primarily using an appeal to
   (A) reason.
   (B) ethics.
   (C) logic.
   (D) emotion.
   (E) patriotism.

7. The writer refers to the American colonists as *rebels* to
   (A) show her sympathy for the British.
   (B) reveal her secret support for the colonists.
   (C) further the cause of American independence.
   (D) address her audience with respect.
   (E) indicate that the colonists were justified in their actions in this instance.

8. The writer is most likely
   (A) a British soldier.
   (B) an American colonist loyal to England.
   (C) an American rebel.
   (D) a visitor to America from Europe.
   (E) someone considering moving to America to join the colonists.

9. The most apparent goal of the writer's rhetoric and reasoning is to
   (A) convince readers in England to come to America to fight for the Loyalists.
   (B) engender sympathy for the British troops.
   (C) persuade the rebels to side with the British.
   (D) alert people of the dangerous situation in America.
   (E) stir up pity for the difficulties the writer has experienced living in Massachusetts.

10. As used in this passage, *prodigious* most nearly means
    - (A) accomplished.
    - (B) unusual.
    - (C) huge.
    - (D) meager.
    - (E) few.

11. The author includes the description "lying in the agonies of death, scalped, with their noses and ears cut off and eyes bored out" to
    - (A) convince readers that the difficulties between the British and Americans must be settled as soon as possible and without any further violence.
    - (B) make her narrative more compelling reading.
    - (C) elicit pity for the rebel soldiers, oppressed by the British.
    - (D) evoke sympathy for the British troops.
    - (E) portray the Native Americans as brutal savages and justify their mass relocation and slaughter.

12. This document is most likely a(n)
    - (A) letter to the editor of a Massachusetts newspaper.
    - (B) plea for peace and moderation.
    - (C) editorial for a colonial newspaper.
    - (D) diary entry.
    - (E) letter to a friend.

Questions 13–28. Read the following selection carefully before you mark your answers.

It does no good to write autobiographical fiction cause the minute the book hits the stands here comes your mama screamin how could you and sighin death where is thy sting and she snatches you up out your bed to grill you about what was going down back there in Brooklyn when she was working three jobs and trying to improve the quality of your life and come to find on page 42 that you were messin around with that nasty boy up the block and breaks into sobs and quite naturally your family strolls in all sleepy-eyed to catch the floor show at 5:00 AM but as far as your mama is concerned, it is nineteen-forty-and-something and you ain't too grown to have your ass whipped.

And it's no use using bits and snatches even or real events and real people, even if you do cover, guise, switch-around and change-up cause next thing you know your best friend's laundry cart is squeaking past but your bell ain't ringing so you trot down the block after her and there's this drafty cold pressure front the weatherman surely did not predict and your friend says in this chilly way that it's really something when your own friend stabs you in the back with a pen and for the next two blocks you try to explain that the character is not her at all but just happens to be speaking one of her lines and right about that time you hit the Laundromat and you're ready to just give it up and take the weight, she turns to you and says that seeing as how you have plundered her soul and walked off with a piece of her flesh, the least you can do is spin off half the royalties her way.

So I deal in straight-up fiction myself, cause I value my family and friends, and mostly cause I lie a lot anyway.

13. The topic of this essay is
    (A) the difficulties that arise when writers weave incidents from their own lives into their writing.
    (B) the strife that can result in poor families when one family member unexpectedly becomes rich.
    (C) dealing with an overbearing mother who does not understand the wellsprings of artistic talent.
    (D) the writer's powerlessness to deal with the legacy of child-hood abuse and how that abuse shapes fiction.
    (E) the importance of disguising incidents from real life when writing nonfiction as well as fiction.

14. The author uses only one sentence in the first paragraph to
    (A) generate reader interest.
    (B) mimic a popular style of writing.
    (C) show that the speaker's mama is not well educated.
    (D) capture the breathless drama and emotion of the scene.
    (E) distinguish between the past and the present.

15. The statement "death where is thy sting" is an example of
    (A) personification.
    (B) a metaphor.
    (C) an allusion.
    (D) an analogy.
    (E) meter.

16. This essay is told from which point of view?
    (A) First person
    (B) Second person
    (C) Third-person limited
    (D) Omniscient
    (E) All-knowing

17. In context, the phrase "floor show" refers to
    (A) a show held in an open space, such as a living room or kitchen.
    (B) any late-night entertainment.
    (C) a solo nightclub singer.
    (D) a musical revue.
    (E) the argument between the narrator and her mother.

18. Which of the following phrases is an example of slang?
    (A) Quite naturally your family strolls in
    (B) Messin around
    (C) The quality of your life
    (D) Sleepy-eyed
    (E) Bits and snatches

19. To capture the flavor of her family's typical discourse, the author uses all of the following rhetorical strategies EXCEPT
    (A) colloquialism.
    (B) dialect.
    (C) lack of punctuation.
    (D) idioms.
    (E) humor.

20. In context, what does *guise* mean?
    (A) Appearance
    (B) Disguise
    (C) Aspect
    (D) Shape
    (E) Guile

21. What does the author mean when she says "...the next thing you know your best friend's laundry cart is squeaking past but your bell ain't ringing"?
    (A) The family is very poor, and their doorbell is broken.
    (B) The phrase is metaphorical; the writer is not excited to see her friend.
    (C) Furious at what she perceives as a betrayal, the writer's best friend is trying to sever the friendship.
    (D) The family is going to assault her friend for trying to extort money.
    (E) If we are going to keep our friends, we must treat them with respect.

22. The speaker characterizes autobiography as an art form that is
    - (A) basically honest.
    - (B) fundamentally duplicitous.
    - (C) tremendously difficult to write.
    - (D) easy to sell.
    - (E) not worth the trouble it engenders.

23. The speaker uses the incident with her girlfriend in the second paragraph to illustrate the idea that
    - (A) even the people you trust the most can be self-serving and thus try to profit from your success.
    - (B) it is virtually impossible for writers to maintain close friendships because they must remain true to their craft.
    - (C) writers should not use any details from the lives of their friends.
    - (D) writers should prepare legal releases before they draw incidents from someone else's life.
    - (E) her friend's sense of betrayal is justified.

24. In essence, this essay is
    - (A) highly ironic, since the author is doing that which she directly inveighs against.
    - (B) very serious, as the author regrets her choices.
    - (C) forgiving of those who have wronged her.
    - (D) an extended metaphor.
    - (E) symbolic.

25. Which of the following choices best describes the tone of this essay?
    - (A) Self-pitying
    - (B) Sarcastic
    - (C) Despairing
    - (D) Tongue-in-cheek
    - (E) Vicious

26. The speaker's primary rhetorical strategy in this passage can best be described as
    - (A) developing an argument against autobiographies by using incidents from her own life.
    - (B) providing specific examples to illustrate a highly abstract concept.
    - (C) debating the advantages and disadvantages of writing an autobiography.
    - (D) discrediting autobiography as an art form.
    - (E) using humor to make a serious point about life and art.

27. By reading between the lines, you can infer that
    (A) the author's family feels a deep sense of pride in the author's talent and accomplishments.
    (B) the author's family is deeply embarrassed by her revelations in print.
    (C) the author's family is indifferent to her literary accomplishments as long as she does not discuss personal matters.
    (D) the author deeply regrets drawing incidents from her own life to use in her writing, no matter how minor the details may be.
    (E) the author and her mother have become estranged as a result of the author's writing.

28. This essay was most likely published
    (A) as an apology for the embarrassment she caused people.
    (B) as a preface to the author's autobiography.
    (C) in a newspaper.
    (D) on the back cover of her next book.
    (E) in an advertisement for her writing.

Questions 29–42. Read the poem carefully before you mark your answers.

(1)   In May, when the sea winds pierced our solitudes,
       I found the fresh Rhodora in the woods
       Spreading its leafless blooms in the damp nook,
       To please the desert and the sluggish brook.
(5)   The purple petals, fallen in the pool,
       Made the black water with their beauty gay;
       Here might the red-bird come his plumes to cool,
       And court the flower that cheapens his array.
       Rhodora! If the sages ask thee why
(10) This charm is wasted on the earth and sky,
       Tell, then, dear, that if eyes were made for seeing,
       Then Beauty is its own excuse for being;
       Why thou wert, O rival of the rose!
(14) I never thought to ask. I never knew;
       But, in my simple ignorance, I suppose
       The self-same Power that brought me there brought you.

29. The Rhodora is a(n)
    (A) person.
    (B) bird.
    (C) tree.
    (D) flower.
    (E) abstract concept rather than a concrete object.

30. What rhetorical device does the poet use in lines 9 and 11?
    (A) Apostrophe
    (B) Metaphor
    (C) Alliteration
    (D) Personification
    (E) Simile

31. In line 1, the speaker uses personification to
    (A) make the ocean seem to come alive.
    (B) describe the ocean's transcendent power of humankind.
    (C) emphasize the importance of beauty.
    (D) suggest the power of nature to affect humankind.
    (E) provide a context for the analysis of nature that follows.

32. The poem's rhyme scheme is best described as
    (A) a sonnet.
    (B) three sets of interlocking quatrains.
    (C) two couplets followed by a quatrain and another two couplets followed by a quatrain.
    (D) ottava rima.
    (E) free verse.

33. The meter is basically
    (A) dactyls.
    (B) spondaic.
    (C) accented.
    (D) iambic pentameter.
    (E) unaccented.

34. Which of the following ideas can be inferred from lines 9–12?
    (A) The sages seem to expect a purpose, while the speaker trusts some superior power to have its reasons.
    (B) The Rhodora's purpose must be related to human needs.
    (C) The poet despairs of his inability to understand the Rhodora's purpose for being.
    (D) The sages are as wise as their name suggests.
    (E) There is a historical context that illuminates the Rhodora's presence in the forest.

35. The author uses the rhetorical strategy of alliteration in line 5 to
    - (A) compare two unlike things; the more familiar thing helping to describe the less familiar one.
    - (B) create musical effects and link related ideas.
    - (C) refer to a well-known place, event, person, work of art, or other work of literature.
    - (D) capture the natural rhythm of speech.
    - (E) help readers form pictures in their minds.

36. The tone of this poem is best described as
    - (A) deeply spiritual and optimistic.
    - (B) somber and restrained.
    - (C) elegiac.
    - (D) thrilled.
    - (E) despairing.

37. The speaker uses the Rhodora as an example to illustrate the concepts of
    - (A) life and death.
    - (B) love and hate.
    - (C) common sense.
    - (D) deep spirituality.
    - (E) nature and beauty.

38. The poem includes all the following rhetorical strategies EXCEPT
    - (A) alliteration.
    - (B) rhyme.
    - (C) meter.
    - (D) parallelism.
    - (E) personification.

39. As the poem builds, the speaker's focus shifts from
    - (A) an analysis of causes to an analysis of effects.
    - (B) objective reporting to personal experience.
    - (C) a general discussion to a specific example.
    - (D) a specific discussion to a generality.
    - (E) a defense of nature to an attack on those who defile it.

40. The author's style in this poem is best described as
    - (A) experimental.
    - (B) radical.
    - (C) traditional.
    - (D) loose and relaxed.
    - (E) highly allusive and symbolic.

41. The final line expresses the
    (A) speaker's determination to preserve the Rhodora.
    (B) speaker's determination to spend more time enjoying nature and less time working.
    (C) speaker's subjugation to a higher power.
    (D) speaker's independence.
    (E) speaker's belief in a spiritual unity among all living things.

42. The most apparent goal of the poet's rhetoric and description is to
    (A) argue that people should spend more time in nature.
    (B) express his philosophy of life.
    (C) convince the audience that nature must be preserved.
    (D) elicit an emotional response to the fate of the vanishing wilderness.
    (E) describe a sight that gives him pleasure.

Questions 43–52. Read the following speech carefully before you mark your answers.

I Will Fight No More Forever

Chief Joseph

Tell General Howard I know his heart. What he told me before I have in my heart. I am tired of fighting. Our chiefs are killed. Looking Glass is dead. Toohoolhoolzote is dead. The old men are all dead. It is the young men who say yes or no. He who led the young men is dead. It is cold and we have no blankets. The little children are freezing to death. My people, some of them, have run away to the hills and have no blankets, no food; no one knows where they are, perhaps freezing to death. I want time to look for my children and see how many of them I can find. Maybe I shall find them among the dead. Hear me, my chiefs, I am tired; my heart is sick and sad. From where the sun now stands, I will fight no more forever.

43. Chief Joseph's reasons for deciding to "fight no more forever" include all of the following EXCEPT
    (A) the chiefs have been killed.
    (B) he is dying.
    (C) it is cold and his people have no shelter.
    (D) his people are starving.
    (E) the leader of the young warriors has died.

44. Rather than fighting, Chief Joseph wants time to
    (A) negotiate honorable surrender terms with the federal govern-ment.
    (B) escape to Canada from the tribe's home in Oregon.
    (C) fight one last battle and then never fight again.
    (D) meet with General Howard, with whom he has an under-standing.
    (E) look for his scattered children.

45. Who are Looking Glass and Toohoolhoolzote?
    (A) Young men in the tribe
    (B) Other Native Americans who are helping the tribe negotiate with the federal government
    (C) Chief Joseph's favorite children
    (D) Great chiefs of his tribe
    (E) Historical leaders, long dead before the time of this speech

46. As used in context, the phrase "It is the young men who say yes and no" is best understood to mean that
    (A) even the young men cannot save them now.
    (B) Chief Joseph laments the necessity of having the tribe led by inexperienced men.
    (C) young men are better leaders than older men.
    (D) Chief Joseph has been forced from power by the young men.
    (E) young men cannot be trusted as older men can.

47. The writer's rhetorical style can best be described as
    (A) the repeated use of short, simple sentences and simple diction.
    (B) extending a metaphor to prove a point.
    (C) making an abstract concept specific through the use of first-person narrative.
    (D) alternating comparisons and contrasts.
    (E) simple language masking symbolism and elaborate figures of speech.

48. The writer's style contributes to the impact of his speech by
    (A) decreasing the emotional appeal of his words.
    (B) downplaying his main points with arrogance.
    (C) emphasizing his main points with dignity.
    (D) revealing his reliance on literary allusions.
    (E) emphasizing the difference between appearance and reality.

49. His language reinforces the effect of his rhetoric by
    - (A) making the speech easy to read.
    - (B) allowing the facts to tell the story without any literary contrivances.
    - (C) masking his true sorrow.
    - (D) relying on symbolism to convey his emotion.
    - (E) excoriating the federal government for betraying his people.

50. The tone of this speech is best described as
    - (A) ironic.
    - (B) somber and despairing.
    - (C) resigned and thoughtful.
    - (D) hopeful.
    - (E) combative.

51. The tone is revealed through Chief Joseph's
    - (A) complex imagery.
    - (B) vivid sensory images.
    - (C) insight and metaphor.
    - (D) direct statements about his feelings and stark descriptions of the sufferings of his people.
    - (E) hyperbole.

52. Chief Joseph delivered his speech to notify federal troops of his tribe's surrender. What other purpose could his speech have had?
    - (A) To ensure a favorable peace treaty for his people
    - (B) To burnish his reputation in the tribe
    - (C) To escape charges of incompetence
    - (D) To blame the federal government for broken promises
    - (E) To point out the plight of the Native Americans

ENGLISH LANGUAGE AND COMPOSITION

SECTION II

Time—2 hours

Question 1:

Suggested Time: 40 minutes. Your response will count for one third of your total score on the essay portion of the exam.

In the following passage, English essayist William Hazlitt (1778–1830) discusses the capacity of a great work of art to evoke a wide range of emotional or sensory responses.

Directions: Read the following essay carefully. Then write an essay in which you analyze how Hazlitt uses rhetorical strategies and other stylistic devices to convey his views of the role of "gusto" in literature.

Gusto in art is power or passion defining any object. It is not so difficult to explain this term in what relates to expression (of which it may be said to be the highest degree) as in what relates to things without expression, to the natural appearances of objects, as mere color or form. In one sense, however, there is hardly any object entirely devoid of expression, without some character of power belonging to it, some precise association with pleasure or pain, and it is in giving this truth of character from the truth of feeling, whether in the highest or lowest degree of which the subject is capable, that gusto consists.

There is gusto in the coloring of Titian [sixteenth-century Venetian painter]. Not only his heads seem to think—his bodies seem to feel. This is what the Italians mean by the *morbidezza* [softness] of his flesh color. It seems sensitive and alive all over; not merely to have the look and texture of flesh but the feeling in itself. For example, the limbs of his female figures have a luxurious softness and delicacy, which appears conscious of the pleasure of the beholder. As the objects themselves in nature would produce an impression on the sense, distinct from every other object, and having something divine in it, which the heart owns and the imagination consecrates, the objects in the picture preserve the same impression, absolute, unimpaired, stamped with all the truth of passion, the pride of the eye, and the charm of beauty. Rubens made his flesh color like flowers; Albano's is like ivory; Titian's is like flesh, and nothing else. The blood circulates here and there, the blue veins just appear; the rest is distinguished throughout only by that sort of tingling sensation to the eye, which the body feels within itself. This is gusto.

Question 2:

Suggested Time: 40 minutes. Your response will count for one third of your total score on the essay portion of the exam.

In the following passage, English essayist Thomas De Quincey (1785-1859) discusses the literature of knowledge and the literature of power.

Directions: Read the following essay carefully. Then write an essay in which you defend, challenge, or qualify De Quincey's distinctions.

What is it that we mean by *literature*? Popularly, and amongst the thoughtless, it is held to include everything that is printed in a book. Little logic is required to disturb *that* definition. The most thoughtless person is easily made aware that in the idea of *literature* one essential element is some relation to a general and common interest of man—so that what applies only to a local, or professional, or merely personal interest, even though presenting itself in the shape of a book will not belong to Literature. So far the definition is easily narrowed; and it is easily expanded. For not only is much that takes a station in books is not literature; but inversely, much that really *is* literature never reaches a station in books. The weekly sermons of Christendom, that vast pulpit literature which acts so extensively upon the popular mind—to warn, to uphold, to renew, to comfort, to alarm—does not attain the sanctuary of libraries in the ten-thousandth part of its extent. The Drama again—as, for instance, the finest of Shakespeare's plays in England, and all leading Athenian plays in the noontide of the Attic stage—operated as literature on the public mind, and were (according to the strictest letter of that term) *published* through the audiences that witnessed their representation some time before they were published as things to be read; and they were published in this scenic mode of publication with much more effect than they could have had as books during ages of costly copying or of costly printing...

But a far more important correction, applicable to the common vague idea of literature, is to be sought not so much in a better definition of literature as in a sharper distinction of the two functions which it fulfills. In that great social organ which, collectively, we call literature, there may be distinguished two separate offices ...There is, first, the literature of *knowledge;* and secondly, the literature of *power*. The function of the first is—to *teach;* the function of the second is—to *move:* the first is a rudder; the second, a sail. The first speaks to the *mere* discursive [ordered in a logical way] understanding; the second speaks ultimately, to the higher understanding or reason, but always *through* affections of pleasure and sympathy.

Question 3:

Suggested Time: 40 minutes. Your response will count for one third of your total score on the essay portion of the exam.

Directions: Read the following excerpt from an essay by contemporary writer Joan Didion. Then write a carefully reasoned essay evaluating Didion's argument that young people today do not feel the same sense of place as their parents do.

Sometimes I think that those of us who are now in our thirties were born into the last generation to carry the burden of "home," to find in family the source of all tension and drama. I had by all objective accounts a "normal" and a "happy" family situation, and yet I was almost thirty years old before I could talk to my family on the telephone without crying after I had hung up. We did not fight. Nothing was wrong. And yet some nameless anxiety colored the emotional charge between me and the place I came from. The question of whether or not you could go home again was a very real part of the sentimental and largely literary baggage with which we left home in the fifties: I suspect that it is irrelevant to the children born of the fragmentation after World War II.

Quick-Score Answers

1. C	14. D	27. A	40. C
2. B	15. C	28. B	41. E
3. D	16. A	29. D	42. B
4. A	17. E	30. A	43. B
5. B	18. B	31. D	44. E
6. D	19. D	32. C	45. D
7. A	20. B	33. D	46. B
8. B	21. C	34. A	47. A
9. B	22. B	35. B	48. C
10. C	23. A	36. A	49. B
11. D	24. A	37. E	50. B
12. E	25. D	38. D	51. D
13. A	26. E	39. D	52. E

Computing Your Score

You can use the following worksheet to compute an approximate score on the practice test. Since it is difficult to be objective about your own writing and since you are not a trained ETS scorer or English teacher, you may wish to ask a friend who has already taken the test (and earned a score of 4 or 5) to score your three essays.

Recognize that your score can only be an approximation (at best), as you are scoring yourself against yourself. In the actual AP English Language and Composition Exam, you will be scored against every other student who takes the test as well.

Section I: Multiple-Choice Questions

	_____	number of correct answers
-	_____	.25 x number of wrong answers
=	_____	raw score
	_____	raw score
x	_____	1.25
=	_____	scaled score (out of a possible 67.5)

Section II: Essays

	_____	essay 1 (0–9)
	_____	essay 2 (0–9)
	_____	essay 3 (0–9)
x	_____	3.055
=	_____	scaled score (out of a possible 82.5)

Scaled Score

	_____	multiple-choice scaled score
+	_____	essay scaled score
=	_____	final scaled score (out of a possible 150)

AP Score Conversion Chart

Scaled Score	Likely AP Score
150–100	5
99–86	4
85–67	3
66–0	1 or 2

Answers and Explanations

1. **The correct answer is (C).** The writer says, "When they [the American colonists] were told to disperse, they fired on the troops and ran off, upon which the Light Infantry pursued them." There are no Native Americans in the account at all, so choice (A) cannot possibly be correct.

2. **The correct answer is (B).** The soldiers would be gathering to eliminate a military depot, which only choice (B) explains. It would not be logical to gather 800 soldiers to destroy a publication, no matter how seditious, so choices (A) and (E) cannot be correct. The same is true for choices (C) and (D).

3. **The correct answer is (D).** The writer's tone in the second paragraph is best described as *disdainful and condescending*. This is shown especially in the phrases "and *have what they call* Minute Companies" and "it is supposed." This directly contradicts choice (A), as the author is clearly biased toward the British. The writer is not "horrified and dismayed" or "astonished and amazed" until the brutality in paragraph 3, eliminating choices (B) and (C). Overall she admires the British, choice (E), but she is not worshipful toward them and certainly not in this paragraph.

4. **The correct answer is (A).** The writer clearly sets forth the events on that fateful day to convince readers that the colonial rebels are barbarians and the British soldiers were justified in their actions. There is no *metaphor*, choice (C), or *analogy*, choice (D). On the contrary, the writer's style is plain rather than figurative. The writer is not at all *ironic,* so choice (B) cannot be correct.

5. **The correct answer is (B).** The contrast between the rebels' bloody brutality and the word "exasperated" creates *understatement*, choice (B). The British soldiers must have been furious at the barbarity, which is the opposite of choice (B). *Onomatopoeia* is the use of words to imitate the sounds they describe, such as *crack, hiss,* and *buzz*. Therefore, choice (A) cannot be correct. *Personification* is giving human traits to nonhuman things. For example: "The book begged to be read." This is not the case in this passage, so choice (E) is wrong. *Foreshadowing* are clues that hint at what will happen later on in the story. Since this incident does not hint at future brutality, choice (C) is not correct.

6. **The correct answer is (D).** The writer appeals to emotion with details of the massacre. These details serve to marshal support for the colonists. The writer does not try to convince us that the British are justified through *reason*, choice (A); *ethics,* choice (B); or *logic*, choice (C). A close reading reveals that the writer does not explain the British reasons for trying to retain the American colonies; on the

contrary, the writer assumes the reader agrees with the British position so it does not need to be justified.

7. **The correct answer is (A).** By using the term *rebels,* the writer reveals that she sides with the British against the Americans. If she sided with the Americans, choice (B), she would have used a term that showed her sympathy, such as *freedom fighters.* Therefore, choices (B), (C), and (E) cannot be correct. Choice (D) does not make sense: the term *rebels* does not indicate respect in this context.

8. **The correct answer is (B).** The writer's sympathetic account of the problems the British soldiers faced at the hands of American rebels and her familiarity with the situation suggests that she is a colonist loyal to the British. This directly contradicts choice (C). A British soldier would most likely use the first-person point of view, so choice (A) cannot be correct. Choice (D) would not be as familiar with the situation. The same is true of Choice E.

9. **The correct answer is (B).** The writer's goal is to engender sympathy for the British troops, which she does by portraying the American rebels as barbarians. She is not trying to muster more soldiers, choice (A). She is convinced that the rebels are too barbaric to understand the error of their ways, so choice (C) cannot be correct. Likewise, she is not warning people of the dangerous situation in America, choice (D). The letter she writes does not stir up pity for the difficulties the writer has experienced living in Massachusetts, choice (E). Rather, she is trying to show the difficulties the British have in subduing the American rebels.

10. **The correct answer is (C).** The answer can be derived from context: Since the Light Troops were "harassed in their return for seven or eight miles," there must be many, many people gathered on the road. Otherwise, they would not be able to cover so much distance. This is the direct opposite of choice (E), *few,* and choice (D), *meager.* The other choices have nothing to do with context.

11. **The correct answer is (D).** Since the American rebels attacked the British and left them "lying in the agonies of death, scalped, with their noses and ears cut off and eyes bored out," this description serves to evoke sympathy for the British troops, choice (D). This is the direct opposite of choice (C); therefore, choice (C) cannot be correct. The description does make her narrative more compelling reading, choice (B), but it is more than mere gratuitous violence. There are no Native Americans mentioned in the article, so choice (E) cannot be correct. Finally, while the writer may indeed want the difficulties between the British and Americans settled as soon as possible, there is no indication that she wishes to convince her readers of this, nor that she believes that further violence must be avoided. Therefore, choice (A) cannot be correct.

12. **The correct answer is (E).** The informal tone suggests the document is a letter to a friend, choice (E). The next best choice is (D), *a diary entry*, but the tone suggests the document was intended for a specific audience. The writer would not be foolish enough to publish these sentiments in an *editorial for a colonial newspaper*, choice (C), or *a letter to the editor of a Massachusetts newspaper*, choice (A) with emotions running this high and such bloodshed going on. Since the document has such a marked bias toward the British, it cannot be *a plea for peace and moderation*, choice (B).

13. **The correct answer is (A).** The author traces the difficulties that arise when writers weave incidents from their own lives into their writing. These difficulties include conflict with her mother over long-ago teen sexual experimentation and jealously from close friends. There is no mention of her family even reacting to the writer's good fortune, so choice (B) is incorrect. This is a misreading: the writer's close friend envies her friend's good fortune and wants her cut. The writer's mother is clearly a strong woman, but since the writer treats her mother's anger with humor, you can eliminate choice (C). There is no indication that the writer was abused as a child; rather, the writer's mother suggests that this might be the time to give her a smack: "as far as your mama is concerned, it is nineteen-forty-and-something and you ain't too grown to have your ass whipped." Thus, you can eliminate choice (D). Finally, the writer deals only with autobiography, so choice (E) is wrong.

14. **The correct answer is (D).** While choice (A) is correct—*the writer does use only one sentence in the first paragraph to generate reader interest*—choice (D) is a better response because it is more precise: *capture the breathless drama and emotion of the scene*. That the writer chose to capture her mother's anger in one sentence does not show that the woman is not well educated. Don't confuse the writer's craft and rhetorical strategies with the characters themselves. As a result, choice (C) is incorrect. Choice (B) has no basis in fact; choice (E) makes no sense in context.

15. **The correct answer is (C).** An *allusion* is a reference to a well-known place, event, person, work of art, or other work of literature. Allusions enrich a story or poem by suggesting powerful and exciting comparisons. This allusion to Shakespeare provides an ironic counterpoint to the author's use of slang and dialect. Choice (B) is incorrect because a *metaphor* is a figure of speech that compares two unlike things. The more familiar thing helps describe the less familiar one. Choice (D) is wrong because an *analogy* is a comparison and nothing is being compared here. Choice (E), *meter*, is incorrect because *meter* is the beat or rhythm in a poem. It is created by a pattern of stressed and unstressed syllables. This is not a poem.

16. **The correct answer is (A).** *Point of view* is the position from which a story is told. In the *first-person point of view*, the narrator is one of

the characters in the story. As a result, the narrator explains the events through his or her own eyes, using the pronouns *I* and *me*. The last line clearly shows the first-person point of view: "So I deal in straight-up fiction myself, cause I value my family and friends, and mostly cause I lie a lot anyway." In the *third-person limited point of view,* the narrator tells the story through the eyes of only one character, using the pronouns *he, she,* and *they.* In the *omniscient point of view,* the narrator is not a character in the story. Instead, the narrator looks through the eyes of all the characters. As a result, the narrator is all-knowing. Therefore, choices (D) and (E) are the same, and both can be eliminated.

17. **The correct answer is (E).** The term "floor show" usually refers to a musical revue, choice (D), but in context, the writer is using it to refer to the disagreement she is having with her mother. You can infer this from the following passage: "...and breaks into sobs and quite naturally your family strolls in all sleepy-eyed to catch the floor show at 5:00 AM."

18. **The correct answer is (B).** Only the phrase "messin around" is slang; all the other choices are standard written English.

19. **The correct answer is (D).** The writer does not use *idioms,* words and phrases that cannot be taken literally. On the contrary, her writing is quite literal and specific. She uses *colloquialism* in phrases such as "grill you," choice (A), and *slang and dialect* in phrases such as "messin around with that nasty boy" and "you're ready to just give it up and take the weight," choice (B). There is a conspicuous *lack of punctuation,* choice (C), and a great deal of *humor,* choice (E), as shown in phrases such as "there's this drafty cold pressure front the weatherman surely did not predict" and "stabs you in the back with a pen."

20. **The correct answer is (B).** *Guise* is a shorted form of "disguise." This is an example of colloquial English, which the narrator uses to create the flavor of her family's speech.

21. **The correct answer is (C).** Furious at what she perceives as a betrayal, the writer's best friend is trying to sever the friendship. As a result, she walks by her friend's house without asking her to come to the laundromat. The phrase is literal, not metaphorical, so choice (B) is incorrect. There is no proof for choice (D) or choice (E).

22. **The correct answer is (B).** The speaker characterizes autobiography as an art form that is fundamentally duplicitous. This is shown in the final paragraph: "So I deal in straight-up fiction myself, cause I value my family and friends, and mostly cause I lie a lot anyway."

23. **The correct answer is (A).** The speaker uses the incident with her girlfriend in the second paragraph to illustrate the idea that even the people you least expect can be self-serving and thus try to profit from

the success of others. The girlfriend acts highly indignant at being included in the autobiography but states that her ire can be assuaged for money. Choice (B) is mythic nonsense. Many writers have close, enduring friendships. The writer does not abjure her act, so choice (C) is incorrect. The same is true for choice (D) and choice (E). Just the opposite is true for choice (E): her friend emerges as selfish and self-serving as she tries to extort money.

24. **The correct answer is (A).** In essence, this essay is highly ironic, since the author is doing that which she directly inveighs against. She describes the trouble she caused by drawing incidents from her own life, and then she does just that to make her point. The evident humor means that choice (B) cannot be true. Nowhere does she forgive those who have wronged her, so choice (C) is wrong. There is no comparison being made here, so the passage cannot be an extended metaphor, choice (D). She is being quite literal, so the passage is not symbolic, choice (E).

25. **The correct answer is (D).** The author adopts a tongue-in-cheek tone to mock the situation. She is not *self-pitying*, choice (A), nor is she *sarcastic*, choice (B). The tone is happy rather than despairing, so choice (C) cannot be correct. Finally, the tone is humorously gentle, not at all vicious, choice (E).

26. **The correct answer is (E).** The speaker's primary rhetorical strategy in this passage can best be described as using humor to make a serious point. While the essay is very amusing, she has a serious point: to explore the dilemmas a writer faces when drawing incidents from real life. Do not be misled by the last line—"So I deal in straight-up fiction myself." It does not mean that she is developing an argument against autobiography by using incidents from her own life, choice (A). Choice (D) makes the similar incorrect point. Her concept is specific, not abstract, so choice (B) is incorrect. There is no debate here; she clearly states her point. Therefore, eliminate choice (C).

27. **The correct answer is (A).** By reading between the lines, you can infer that the author's family feels a deep sense of pride in the author's talent and accomplishments. You can infer this because the author's mother has read her daughter's book several times and very closely, as shown in the detail: "find on page 42 that..." Further, if they did not care about her writing, choice (C), the author's family would not bother reading it or discussing it. If the family were so deeply embarrassed by her revelations, choice (B), the author would not have shown their reaction with tongue-in-cheek humor. Rather, she would have used a much more serious tone. The same is true of choice (D). If she was repentant, she would not be using humor. Finally, there is no proof at all that the author and her mother have become estranged as a result of the author's writing, choice (E). If anything, they seem close and loving, as their humorous quarrel indicates.

28. **The correct answer is (B).** This essay was most likely published as a preface to the author's autobiography. The preface would serve to announce the author's literary intentions: to transmute life into art. You can see this in the last paragraph: "So I deal in straight-up fiction myself, cause I value my family and friends, and mostly cause I lie a lot anyway. " The tone is at odds with an apology, so choice (A) is wrong. Choice (C) and choice (D) are too general to be meaningful. There is no reason to publish such a long essay in an advertisement for her writing, so you can eliminate choice (E).

29. **The correct answer is (D).** You can infer that the Rhodora is a flower from these lines: "Spreading its leafless blooms in the damp nook,/ ...And court the flower that cheapens his array."

30. **The correct answer is (A).** The poet uses *apostrophe*, directly addressing an inanimate object. This is clearly shown when he says in line 9: "Rhodora! If the sages ask thee why." In a sense, the poet is personifying the flower, choice (D), by addressing it, but choice (A) is more precise. There is no comparison being made here, so choice (B) and choice (E) are incorrect.

31. **The correct answer is (D).** While the poet does indeed use personification to make the ocean seem to come alive, choice (A), choice (D) provides a more inclusive reading of the poet's purpose. Choice (B) is not correct because the line focuses on the sea's *winds,* not the sea itself. The poet does not emphasize the importance of beauty, choice (C), but rather links beauty to a richer context. The poem is not an analysis of nature, so choice (E) cannot be correct.

32. **The correct answer is (C).** The poem has 16 lines: lines 1 and 2 do not rhyme, while lines 3 and 4 rhyme (*nook, brook*). This is followed by four lines that rhyme ababa (*pool, gay, cool, array*). Next comes another couplet that rhymes (*why, sky*) and another couplet (*seeing, being*). The final four lines follow the alternating rhyme (*rose, knew, suppose, you*). Choice (A) cannot be correct because a sonnet has 14 lines. The rhyme scheme means that choice (E) cannot be correct, because free verse does not rhyme. Three sets of interlocking quatrains cannot be correct because that would add up to 12 lines, not 16 lines. An *ottava rima*, choice (D), is an eight-line stanza rhyming abababcc. This is clearly not the rhyme scheme here.

33. **The correct answer is (D).** Remember that *meter* is the beat or rhythm in a poem created by a pattern of stressed and unstressed syllables. The most common meter in English poetry is *iambic pentameter,* a pattern of five *feet* (groups of syllables), each having one unstressed syllable and one stressed one. That is the case here. *Dactyls,* choice (A), is one stressed syllable followed by two unstressed, as in this example: *take her up tenderly.* Spondaic, choice (B), is two stressed syllables, as in this example: *Smart lad, to slip betimes away.* Neither *accented,*

choice (C), or *unaccented*, choice (E), are types of meter. Both refer to stress placed on syllables.

34. **The correct answer is (A).** The lines "If the sages ask thee why/This charm is wasted on the earth and sky," suggests the sages seem to expect a purpose. Lines 11–12 "Tell, then, dear, that if eyes were made for seeing,/Then Beauty is its own excuse for being" suggests that the speaker trusts some superior power to have its reasons.

35. **The correct answer is (B).** Only *alliteration* creates musical effects and links related ideas. It also stresses certain words or mimics specific sounds. Choice (A) is wrong because *metaphors* compare two unlike things, the more familiar thing helping describe the less familiar one. Choice (C) is wrong because *allusions* refer to a well-known place, event, person, work of art, or other work of literature. Blank verse, not alliteration, captures the natural rhythm of speech. Therefore, choice (D) is wrong. *Description* and *images* help readers form pictures in their minds, eliminating choice (E).

36. **The correct answer is (A).** The final couplet most clearly shows the poem's deeply spiritual and optimist tone. Lines such as "Here might the red-bird come his plumes to cool,/And court the flower that cheapens his array" show that the tone is not somber and restrained, eliminating choice (B). If choice (A) is correct, choice (E) must be wrong. The speaker does not mourn a deceased person or time past, so choice (C) is wrong. The poet is happy but not overly so, choice (D).

37. **The correct answer is (E).** The line "Then Beauty is its own excuse for being" shows the flower represents beauty. The flower comes from nature and so represents it. Do not be misled by the last lines—"The self-same Power that brought me there brought you"—the poem has a deep spirituality, but the flower does not symbolize it. None of the other choices makes any sense in context.

38. **The correct answer is (D).** The poet uses *alliteration* in line 5: "The purple petals." As established in question 32, the poem has a set rhyme scheme. Therefore, choice (B) is incorrect. As established in question 33, the poem is written in iambic pentameter. Therefore, choice (C) is incorrect. The sea is personified in line 1 ("when the sea winds pierced our solitudes"). Therefore, choice (E) is incorrect.

39. **The correct answer is (D).** The poem moves from a specific discussion of the flower to a generality by linking the flower's beauty to the spiritual being that links all of nature. Perceptive students will recognize this philosophy as the cornerstone of transcendentalism.

40. **The correct answer is (C).** The author's style in this poem is best described as *traditional* because the poem uses traditional rhyme, rhythm (meter), and images (flowers, nature). This is the opposite of

experimental, choice (A), and *radical,* choice (B). Since the style is so tight, it cannot be *loose and relaxed,* choice (D). Finally, the flower is symbolic, but the overall style is not *allusive.* Therefore, choice (E) cannot be correct.

41. **The correct answer is (E).** The final line expresses the speaker's belief in a spiritual unity among all living things. The line reads: "The self-same Power that brought me there brought you." The key word is "Power," which refers to a spirituality. The speaker does not indicate that he is in any way oppressed by his awareness of a universal spirituality, so choice (C) cannot be correct.

42. **The correct answer is (B).** The most apparent goal of the poet's rhetoric and description is to express his philosophy of life. This can be inferred by a close reading of the second half of the poem.

43. **The correct answer is (B).** Chief Joseph's reasons for deciding to "fight no more forever" include all of the following *except* he is dying. Chief Joseph says: "I am tired; my heart is sick and sad." You cannot infer from this that he is dying, however. All the other choices are directly stated in the speech.

44. **The correct answer is (E).** Rather than fighting, Chief Joseph wants time to look for his scattered children. This is directly stated in the following line: "I want time to look for my children and see how many of them I can find." Choice (B) is partly correct—his Nez Perce tribe did try to escape to Canada from their home in Oregon—this cannot be inferred from Chief Joseph's words. Choice (A) is again historically correct, since the tribe had negotiated honorable surrender terms with the federal government, but these terms were ignored. This question illustrates the importance of reading a text closely and not bringing in outside information, which may be factually or historically correct, but neither correct nor relevant in context.

45. **The correct answer is (D).** Looking Glass and Toohoolhoolzote are great chiefs of his tribe from the time the speech was written. This comes from the line "Our chiefs are killed. Looking Glass is dead. Toohoolhoolzote is dead."

46. **The correct answer is (B).** As used in context, the phrase "It is the young men who say yes and no" is best understood to mean that Chief Joseph laments the necessity of having the tribe led by inexperienced men. You can neither assume that he does not trust these leaders, choice (E), nor assume that Chief Joseph has been forced from power by the young men, choice (D). In fact, just the opposite must be true if he has been charged with surrendering to the federal government. Since you can infer from the passage that older leaders are more valued that younger ones, choice (A) is not valid.

47. **The correct answer is (A).** The writer's rhetorical style can best be described as the repeated use of short, simple sentences and simple diction. It is not until half-way through the speech that Chief Joseph uses a compound sentence. The speech is not based on a *metaphor,* so choice (B) is incorrect. In the same way, choice (E) cannot be correct. His point is very specific (the tribe is starving and falling apart) so choice (C) is wrong. There are no comparisons and contrasts, so you can eliminate choice (E).

48. **The correct answer is (C).** The writer's style contributes to the impact of his speech by emphasizing his main points. Chief Joseph's simple style focuses the reader's attention on the meaning of his words. This is the direct opposite of choices (A) and (B). The speech does not have any literary allusions, so you can eliminate choice (D). He stresses his people's plight in specific, concrete language, so choice (E) is illogical.

49. **The correct answer is (B).** The simplicity of his language reinforces the effect of his rhetoric by allowing the facts to tell the story without any literary contrivances. Therefore, choice (D) cannot be true. The speech is easy to read, choice (A), but this has nothing to do with the effect of his rhetoric. Rather than masking his true sorrow, choice (C), the speech reveals it. His tone is sorrowful, not violent, so choice (E) is false.

50. **The correct answer is (B).** The tone of this speech is best described as somber and despairing. The next closest choice, choice (C), is not quite as accurate a description. The other choices are far off the mark.

51. **The correct answer is (D).** The tone is revealed through Chief Joseph's direct statements about his feelings and stark descriptions of the sufferings of his people. There is no *complex imagery*, choice (A); *metaphor*, choice (C); or *hyperbole,* choice (E), since the speech does not exaggerate his tribe's sufferings. The speech does have vivid sensory images, but choice (D) is a more complete description of Chief Joseph's rhetorical strategies.

52. **The correct answer is (E).** Chief Joseph delivered his speech to notify federal troops of his tribe's surrender. He also wanted to point out the plight of the Native Americans. His words could not ensure a favorable peace treaty for his people, choice (A), because he does not refer to any requests or demands. He is not seeking to escape charges of incompetence, choice (C), as his dignity reveals. In addition, there is no one left in his tribe to assign blame. He does not seem to care at all for his reputation in the tribe, choice (B); rather, he seems far more concerned with protecting the remaining people under his care. He does not assign blame, choice (D).

Question 1:

A well-written essay will demonstrate how Hazlitt uses rhetorical strategies and other stylistic devices to convey his views of the role of "gusto" in literature. Students should focus on the author's use of the following elements:

- diction, as in this lush description: "luxurious softness and delicacy"
- similes and other figures of speech that illustrate the writer's point
- the movement from a general statement to specific examples
- sensory images
- sentence length and complexity
- appositives
- punctuation, especially his use of dashes for emphasis

Question 2:

A well-written essay must defend, challenge, or qualify De Quincey's distinctions. As a result, the essay must take a stance. Essays that waffle between opinions will not earn high credit. In addition, the essay must contain

- an opening that clearly states the students' opinion on the topic.
- specific examples that illustrate the writer's opinion. The examples should be drawn from the essay and can also be drawn from the writer's own experience.
- evidence of original thought.
- a conclusion that sums up what has been said and provides an intriguing and perhaps original insight.

Question 3:

A well-written essay should evaluate Didion's argument that young people today do not feel the same sense of place as their parents do. Students should draw examples from their own experience, the media, and perhaps the experiences of their friends.

In addition, the essay must contain

- an opening that clearly states the students' opinion on the topic.
- specific examples that illustrate the writer's opinion.
- evidence of careful analysis.
- logic and coherence.
- a conclusion that sums up what has been said and provides an intriguing and perhaps even original insight.

PRACTICE TEST 2

ENGLISH LANGUAGE AND COMPOSITION

SECTION 1

Time—1 hour

> **Directions:** This section contains selections from two passages of prose and two poems with questions on their style, content, form, and purpose. Read each selection closely and carefully. Then choose the best answer from the five choices.

Questions 1–14. Read the poem carefully before you mark your answers.

To His Excellency, George Washington

(1)   Celestial choir! enthron'd in realms of light,
      Columbia's scenes of glorious toils I write.
      While freedom's cause her anxious breast alarms.
      She flashes dreadful in refulgent arms,
(5)   See mother earth her offspring's fate bemoan,
      And nations gaze at scenes before unknown!
      See the bright beams of heaven's revolving light
      Involved in sorrows and the veil of night!
    The goddess comes, she moves divinely fair.
(10) Olive and laurel binds her golden hair:
      Wherever shines this native of the skies,
      Unnumber'd charms and recent graces rise.
      Muse! bow propitious while my pen relates
      How pour her armies through a thousand gates,
(15) As when Eolus heaven's fair face deforms,
      Unwrapp'd in tempest and a night of storms;
      Astonish'd ocean feels the wild uproar,
      The refulgent surges beat the sounding shore;
      Or thick as leaves in Autumn's golden reign.
(20) Such, and so many, moves the warrior's train.
      In bright array they seek the work of war,
      Where high unfurl'd the ensign waves in air.
      Shall I to Washington their praise recite?
      Enough thou know'st them in the fields of fight.
(25) Thee, first in peace and honors, —we demand
      The grace and glory of thy martial band.
      Fam'd for thy valor, for thy virtues more,
      Hear every tongue thy guardian aid implore!

One century scarce perform'd its destined round,
(30) When Gallic powers Columbia's fury found;
And so may you, whoever dares disgrace
The land of freedom's heaven-defended race!
Fix'd are the eyes of nations on the scales,
For in their hopes Columbia' arm prevails.
(35) Anon Britannia droops the pensive head,
While round increase the rising hills of dead.
Ah! cruel blindness to Columbia's state!
Lament thy thirst of boundless power too late.
Proceed, great chief, with virtue on thy side,
(40) Thy ev'ry action let the goddess guide.
A crown, a mansion, and a throne that shine,
With gold unfading, WASHINGTON! be thine.

1. In line 2, the poet personifies America as

   (A) as a hard-working but under-appreciated drudge.

   (B) a celestial choir, heavenly and sweet-sounding.

   (C) Columbia, a noted Ivy-league university.

   (D) Columbia, a powerful and resplended goddess.

   (E) Columbia, a strategically placed South American nation.

2. The personification in line 2 serves to imply that

   (A) nothing omnipotent can last.

   (B) America is beautiful and powerful.

   (C) music is a key component to a fully-realized life.

   (D) music has the power to make thought come alive.

   (E) work assumes a life of its own.

3. What causes Columbia's "anxious breast" alarm?

   (A) Something dreadful has happened.

   (B) Refulgent arms

   (C) A conflict with mother earth

   (D) The prospect of an undiscovered future

   (E) The cause of freedom

4. As used in line 4, "refulgent" most nearly means

   (A) radiant and glowing.

   (B) flowing back.

   (C) hostile and vicious.

   (D) rejecting.

   (E) unrestricted.

5. In context, what do the olive branch and laurel symbolize (line 10)?

   (A)   The olive is a symbol of abundance; the laurel, a symbol of fertility.

   (B)   The olive is a symbol of victory; the laurel, a symbol of peace.

   (C)   The olive is a symbol of peace; the laurel, a symbol of victory.

   (D)   The olive is a symbol of food; the laurel, a symbol of harvests.

   (E)   The olive is a symbol of tradition; the laurel, a symbol of innovation

6. What does the god Eolus personify?

   (A)   Tempests and other wild storms

   (B)   The fierce British warriors

   (C)   Autumn

   (D)   The unbeatable American forces

   (E)   Aspects of the natural world

7. The poet uses the metaphors in lines 13–20 to suggest that

   (A)   America's forces are at the whims of nature.

   (B)   America's forces are poorly organized and commanded.

   (C)   America's forces are as mighty, powerful, and valiant as the forces of nature.

   (D)   George Washington is as powerful as unrestrained nature.

   (E)   the Muse guides the poet's hand in creating this poem.

8. The personification developed in the poem is best understood to suggest that

   (A)   since the Americans are fighting for a worthy cause, they have God on their side.

   (B)   since George Washington is a valiant leader, he will live on in history.

   (C)   since nature is in an uproar, there is something wrong with America's government.

   (D)   when the gods are satisfied, good things happen to mortals like George Washington.

   (E)   if America was an older and more dignified country, she would get more respect on the world stage.

9. What are the scales that the poet refers to in line 33?

   (A)   The scales of a snake, a traitor to the cause

   (B)   A scale that measures weight

   (C)   A climb up a seemingly insurmountable peak

   (D)   The scales that fall from the eyes of disbelievers

   (E)   The scales of justice

10. Why are the eyes fixed on the scales in line 33?
    (A) Disgraced people the world over are hoping for vindication.
    (B) Everyone wants to come to America, where people are treated fairly.
    (C) The world believes that America is fighting for the cause of freedom and justice.
    (D) No one believes that the obstacle can be overcome.
    (E) People anxiously await the revelation of the truth.

11. The poet uses elevated diction to
    (A) mock the pretensions of colonial American to grandeur.
    (B) convey the solemn cause Americans are fighting against the British.
    (C) subtly support tradition, the British side of the conflict.
    (D) satirize heroic war poems.
    (E) suggest that George Washington is the greatest leader the world has ever known.

12. What do the last two lines suggest about the influence of British social and political systems on American thinking?
    (A) The British political system has corrupted American values of democracy and individuality.
    (B) The British social system is fatally flawed, and Americans are intelligent enough to recognize this and strike out on their own.
    (C) The British political system has shown that elected governments are doomed to failure, and so we should appoint Washington to be our king.
    (D) The British social structure correctly identifies natural rulers, men such as the heroic and glorious George Washington.
    (E) The British monarchy has been so influential that the poet suggests that Washington be crowned king when he is victorious.

13. The purpose of the poet's rhetoric and reasoning is to
    (A) venerate the classics and suggest that Americans study them in greater depth.
    (B) help get George Washington elected to the American presidency.
    (C) convince Americans to support the British side in the American Revolution.
    (D) celebrate George Washington and the cause of American freedom.
    (E) persuade Americans to look to nature for solutions to their problems.

14. What does this poem suggest about the poet's feelings regarding her country?

    (A) The poet is violently anti-American.

    (B) The poet is deeply patriotic.

    (C) The poet is glad that she is British.

    (D) The poet recognizes America's flaws but is still happy to be an American.

    (E) The poet knows that America will improve with Washington at the helm.

Questions 15–28. Read the following selection carefully before you mark your answers. The passage below is from Winston Churchill's first speech as Prime Minister, delivered on May 19, 1940.

I speak to you for the first time as Prime Minister in a solemn hour for the life of our country, of our Empire, of our Allies, and, above all, of the cause of Freedom. A tremendous battle is raging in France and Flanders. The Germans, by a remarkable combination of air bombing and heavily armored tanks, have broken through the French defenses north of the Maginot Line, and strong columns of their armored vehicles are ravaging the open country, which for the first day or two was without defenders. They have penetrated deeply and spread alarm and confusion in their track. Behind them there are now appearing infantry in lorries, and behind them again, the large masses are moving forward. The regroupment of the French armies to make head against, and also to strike at, this intruding wedge has been proceeding for several days, largely assisted by the magnificent forces of the Royal Air Force.

We must not allow ourselves to be intimidated by the presence of these armored vehicles in unexpected places behind our lines. If they are behind our Front, the French are also at many points fighting actively behind theirs. Both sides are therefore in an extremely dangerous position. And if the French Army, and our own Army, are well handled, as I believe they will be; if the French retain that genius for recovery and counter-attack for which they have so long been famous; and if the British Army shows the dogged endurance and solid fighting power of which there have been so many examples in the past— then a sudden transformation of the scene might spring into being.

It would be foolish, however, to disguise the gravity of the hour. It would be still more foolish to lose heart and courage or to suppose that well-trained, well-equipped armies numbering three or four million men can be overcome in the space of a few weeks, or even a few months, by a scoop, or raid of mechanized vehicles, however formidable. We may look with confidence to the stabilization of the Front in France, and to the general engagement of the masses, which will enable the qualities of the French and British soldiers to be matched squarely against those of their adversaries. For myself, I have invincible confidence in the French Army and its leaders. Only a very small part of that splendid army has yet been heavily engaged; and only a very small part of France has yet been invaded. There is good evidence to show that practically the whole of the specialized and mechanized forces of the enemy have already been thrown into the battle; and we know that very heavy losses have been inflicted upon them. No officer or man, no brigade or division, which grapples at close quarters with the enemy, wherever encountered, can fail to make a worthy contribution to the general result. The Armies must cast away the idea of resisting behind concrete lines or natural obstacles, and must realize that mastery can only be regained by furious and unrelenting assault...

Our task is not only to win the battle—but to win the war. After this battle on France abates, there will come the battle for our island—for all that Britain is, and all that Britain means. That will be the struggle. In that supreme emergency we shall not hesitate to take every step, even the most drastic, to call forth from our people the last ounce and the last inch of effort of which they are capable. The interests of property, the hours of labor, are nothing compared with the struggle for life and honor, for right and freedom, to which we have vowed ourselves....

Today is Trinity Sunday. Centuries ago words were written to be a call and a spur to the faithful servants of Truth and Justice: "Arm yourselves, and be ye men of valor, and be in readiness for the conflict; for it is better for us to perish in battle than to look upon the outrage of our nation and our altar. And the Will of God is in Heaven, even so let it be."

15. The first paragraph of the speech serves to
    (A) compare and contrast the British and French armies.
    (B) correct a misconception about the progress of the war.
    (C) make the abstract ideal of war into a concrete reality.
    (D) assert Churchill's conviction that the Allies can definitely win the war.
    (E) describe the movement of the Germans through the French lines of defense.

16. What effect does Churchill create with his descriptive language in paragraph 1?
    (A) He creates an image of desperation to worry his listeners.
    (B) He introduces a metaphor that compares the Axis army to a rampaging beast
    (C) He creates an image of strength to show the importance of the Maginot Line.
    (D) He captures the world's political climate at the time.
    (E) He uses abstract language to make the war seem less terrifying.

17. Churchill uses the word *ravaging* in paragraph 1 to connote
    (A) violent anger.
    (B) rape and despoilment.
    (C) controlled looting.
    (D) hurried theft.
    (E) staggering deaths and injuries.

18. The phrase the "magnificent forces of the Royal Air Force" is an example of the speaker's use of which rhetorical device?

    (A) Verbal irony

    (B) Metaphorical allusions

    (C) Loaded language

    (D) Onomatopoeia

    (E) Hyperbole or exaggeration

19. As used here, *dogged* most nearly means (paragraph 2)

    (A) like a canine.

    (B) useless.

    (C) debasing.

    (D) determined.

    (E) humiliating.

20. Churchill praises the British and French armies to

    (A) suggest that no other help is needed.

    (B) convince the army to rush the enemy instead of fighting defensively.

    (C) illustrate how he is an effective leader.

    (D) contrast the Allied forces to their enemies, the Axis.

    (E) convey the impression of strong fighting forces that complement each other.

21. What purpose would Churchill have in addressing civilians rather than soldiers?

    (A) He wants to convince civilians to enlist as soon as possible.

    (B) Civilians are a vital part of the war effort, even though they do not serve on the front lines.

    (C) He suspects that the civilians do not back the war.

    (D) Civilians are feeling ignored, since all efforts are directed at the soldiers.

    (E) He wants to make his message more allusive and subtle.

22. As used here (in the third paragraph), *gravity* most nearly means

    (A) power.

    (B) pull.

    (C) force.

    (D) weight.

    (E) seriousness.

23. Why does Churchill use the words *supreme, drastic, last inch, right, freedom,* and *honor* in paragraph 4?

    (A) To invoke strong feelings of patriotism and the feeling that any effort to win the war will be worthwhile

    (B) To allude to past wars in which the British were victorious

    (C) To avoid using concrete language that could negatively affect his audience

    (D) To contrast the French and the English armies

    (E) To beseech his audience to not give up hope of victory

24. What illusion does Churchill foster in this speech?

    (A) That war is hell, even for the righteous

    (B) That peace is transitory and cannot be gained without sacrifice

    (C) That war is a noble, even sublime effort

    (D) That the Allies are superior because they have virtue on their side

    (E) That death with honor is unavoidable in a righteous war

25. Churchill's tone in this speech is best described as

    (A) exhilarating.

    (B) inspiring.

    (C) hotheaded.

    (D) inflammatory.

    (E) irresolute.

26. What types of arguments does Churchill use to achieve his aim?

    (A) Appeal to reason and emotions

    (B) Appeal to ethics and reason

    (C) Appeal to common sense

    (D) Appeal to emotion alone

    (E) Appeal to ethics and emotions

27. The final quote serves most directly to

    (A) imply wars that are conducted on holy days are fated for success.

    (B) contrast Truth and Justice.

    (C) characterize England as a religious nation on a holy quest.

    (D) suggest that the Allies' battle to win the war is divinely sanctioned.

    (E) temper England's enthusiasm for revenge with caution and cunning.

28. This speech is best characterized as
    (A) propaganda.
    (B) brainwashing.
    (C) unemotional.
    (D) poetic.
    (E) highly symbolic.

Questions 29–40. Read the poem carefully before you mark your answers.

A Song on the End of the World

(1) On the day the world ends
     A bee circles a clover,
     A fisherman mends a glimmering net.
     Happy porpoises jump in the sea,
(5) By the rainspout young sparrows are playing
     And the snake is gold-skinned as it should always be.
     On the day the world ends
     Women walk through the fields under their umbrellas,
     A drunkard grows sleepy at the edge of a lawn,
(10) Vegetable peddlers shout in the street
     And a yellow-sailed boat comes nearer the island,
     The voice of a violin lasts in the air
     And leads into a starry night.
     And those who expect lightning and thunder
(15) Are disappointed.
     And those who expected signs and archangels' trumps
     Do not believe it is happening now.
     As long as the sun and the moon are above,
     As long as the bumblebee visits a rose,
(20) As long as rosy infants are born
     No one believes it is happening now.
     Only a white-haired old man, who would be a prophet
     Yet is not a prophet, for he's much too busy,
     Repeats while he binds his tomatoes:
(25) There will be no other end of the world,
     There will be no other end of the world.

29. The images in the first two stanzas combine to form an impression of
    (A) panic and tension.
    (B) serenity laced with evil.
    (C) peace and tranquillity.
    (D) keen intelligence.
    (E) fear and loathing.

30. The rhetorical purpose of the first two stanzas can best be described as
    - (A) allusive.
    - (B) inductive.
    - (C) argumentative.
    - (D) expository.
    - (E) ironic.

31. Which of the following best describes the effect of the parallelism in lines 18–20 ("As long as...")?
    - (A) It implies that things are neither normal nor expected.
    - (B) It characterizes the people as well aware of their impending doom.
    - (C) It alerts the reader that the world really is coming to an end.
    - (D) It creates an incantatory effect that lulls the people into complacency.
    - (E) It reinforces the importance of everyday events in building a meaningful life.

32. What is ironic about lines 22–24?
    - (A) It shows that people espouse false prophets as easily as they do real ones.
    - (B) Prophecy is rejected in favor of tying up tomatoes.
    - (C) It shows that food is more important than truth.
    - (D) Tomatoes cannot grow without careful, close attention.
    - (E) Prophecy is eagerly embraced.

33. The old man's actions in lines 22–25 symbolize the
    - (A) assertion of individuality and normalcy in the face of disaster.
    - (B) human inability to accept reality.
    - (C) ability of everyday people to adhere to routine.
    - (D) difficulty of distinguishing false prophets from real ones.
    - (E) constant presence of disaster.

34. Which of the following ideas can be inferred from the first two stanzas?
    - (A) Contemporary people are too busy to take notice of the end of the world.
    - (B) Ancient people were hobbled by a reliance on prophets and other self-proclaimed truth-tellers.
    - (C) The human race will endure forever because people are eternally optimistic.
    - (D) Prophets can be easily recognized by their appearance and mannerisms.
    - (E) The world will end with a bang, not a whimper.

35. What rhetorical devices does the poet use in the last two stanzas to reinforce the poem's theme?

   (A) Onomatopoeia and personification

   (B) Alliteration and onomatopoeia

   (C) Metaphors and irony

   (D) Allusion and irony

   (E) Repetition and parallelism

36. In context, the last two lines suggest the poet's

   (A) recognition that the human race will long endure.

   (B) assurance in the supremacy of human forbearance.

   (C) view that appearance and reality are one and the same.

   (D) belief that the world really is coming to an end.

   (E) opinion that the end of the world will be heralded with great fanfare.

37. The tone of this poem is best described as

   (A) neutral.

   (B) hysterical.

   (C) soothing.

   (D) frenzied.

   (E) sullen.

38. The poem's rhythm is best characterized as a

   (A) rant against the unfairness in the universe.

   (B) song or song-like prayer.

   (C) dirge or requiem at the end of the world.

   (D) lament at human waste and ignorance.

   (E) threnody.

39. The poem's rhythm and mood therefore serve to

   (A) provide evidence that the poet's vision is valid.

   (B) contrast with the theme.

   (C) underscore the horror of the scene.

   (D) alert the reader to the truth underlying his assertions.

   (E) intimidate the reader into following the poet's edicts.

40. The poet's central rhetorical strategy in this poem can best be described as
    (A) developing an idyllic scene by using strong imagery.
    (B) arguing that people should pay attention to events around them.
    (C) making an ironic commentary on contemporary life.
    (D) providing specific examples to illustrate an abstract idea.
    (E) constructing an extended metaphor that describes the reality of modern life.

Questions 41–52. Read the following selection carefully before you mark your answers.

Letters to His Son (1747)

Pleasure is the rock which most young people split upon; they launch out with crowded sails in quest of, but without a compass to direct their course or reason sufficient to steer the vessel; for want of which, pain and shame, instead of Pleasure, are the returns of their voyage. Do not think that I mean to snarl at Pleasure, like a Stoic, or to preach against it, like a parson; no, I mean to point it out, and recommend it to you, like an Epicurean: I wish you a great deal; and my only view is to hinder you from mistaking it.

The character which most young men first aim at is that of a Man of Pleasure; but they generally take it upon trust; and, instead of consulting their own taste and inclinations, they blindly adopt whatever those, with whom they chiefly converse, are pleased to call by the name of Pleasure; and a *Man of Pleasure*, in the vulgar acceptation of that phrase, means only a beastly drunkard and a profligate swearer and curser. As it may be of use to you, I am not unwilling, though at the same time ashamed, to own, that the vices of my youth proceeded much more from my own inclinations. I always naturally hated drinking; and yet I have often drunk, with disgust at the time, attended by great sickness the next day, only because I then considered drinking a necessary qualification for a fine gentleman, and a Man of Pleasure.

The same as to gaming. I did not want money, and consequently had no occasion to play for it but I thought Play another necessary ingredient in the composition of a Man of Pleasure, and accordingly I plunged into it without desire, at first; sacrificed a thousand real pleasures to it; and made myself solidly uneasy by it, for thirty of the best years of my life.

I was even absurd enough, for a little while, to swear, by way of adorning and completing the shining character which I affected; but this folly I soon laid aside, upon finding both the guilt and indecency of it.

Thus seduced by fashion, and blindly adopting nominal pleasures, I lost real ones; and my fortune impaired, and my constitution shattered, are, I must confess, the just punishment of my errors.

Take warning then by them; choose your pleasures for yourself, and do not let them be imposed on you. Follow nature, not fashion; weigh the present enjoyment of your pleasures against the necessary consequences of them, and then follow your common sense.

Were I to begin the world again, with the experience which I now have of it, I would lead a life of real, not imaginary, pleasure. I would enjoy the pleasures of the table, and of wine; but stop short of the pains inseparably annexed to an excess of either. I would not, at twenty years, be a preaching missionary of abstemiousness and sobriety; and I should let other people do as they would, without formality and sententiously rebuking them for it: but I would be most firmly resolved not to destroy my own faculties and constitution, in compliance to those who have no regard to their own. I would play to give me pleasure, but not to give me pain; that is, I would play for trifles, in mixed companies, to amuse myself, and conform to custom: but I would take care not to venture for sums, which, if I won, I should not be the better for; but, if I lost, should be under a difficulty to pay; and, when paid, would oblige me to retrench in several other articles. Not to mention the quarrels which deep play commonly occasions.

I would pass some of my time in reading and the rest in the company of people of sense and learning, and chiefly those above me; and I would frequent the mixed companies of men and women of fashion, which, though often frivolous, yet they unbend and refresh the mind, not uselessly, because they certainly polish and soften the manners.

These would be my pleasures and amusements, if I were to live the last thirty years over again: they are rational ones; and moreover, I will tell you, they are really the fashionable ones: for the others are not, in truth, the pleasures of what I call people of fashion, but of those who only call themselves so. Does good company care to have a man reeling drunk among them? Or see another tearing his hair, and blaspheming, for having lost, at play, more than he is able to pay? No; these practices, and, much more, those who brag of them, make no part of good company, and are most unwillingly, if ever admitted into it. A real man of fashion and pleasure observes decency; at least, neither borrows nor affects vices; and, if he unfortunately, has any, he gratifies them with choice, delicacy, and secrecy.

I have not mentioned the pleasures of the mind (which are the solid and permanent ones), because they do not come under the head of what people commonly call pleasures, which they seem to confine to the senses. The pleasures of virtue, or charity, and of learning, is true and lasting pleasure; which I hope you will be well and long acquainted with. Adieu!

41. In the opening paragraph, the writer introduces his point that many young men go astray by
    (A) personifying pleasure as a rock upon which many unwary young men crash.
    (B) developing an extended metaphor comparing pleasure to a large rock in the ocean of life.
    (C) using understatement.
    (D) revealing his own personal experiences as a young Man of Pleasure.
    (E) paralleling his own experiences to those of other young men.

42. The writer achieves a balanced and reasonable tone in the first paragraph through the use of which rhetorical device?

   (A) Allusions to Stoics and Epicureans

   (B) Hyperbole

   (C) Parallel phrases

   (D) Deductive reasoning

   (E) Irony

43. As used here (in the second paragraph), *profligate* most nearly means

   (A) proficient.

   (B) unskilled.

   (C) maladroit.

   (D) embarrassing.

   (E) utterly immoral.

44. The rhetorical purpose of paragraphs 2–4 can best be described as

   (A) expository.

   (B) argumentative.

   (C) systematic.

   (D) narrative.

   (E) scientific.

45. The phrase "Thus seduced by fashion" shows that the writer makes the dangers of fashion more vivid through the use of

   (A) personification.

   (B) allusion.

   (C) simile.

   (D) onomatopoeia.

   (E) hyperbole.

46. What rhetorical device does the writer use to make the following sentences smooth and flowing?

   "... and constitution, in compliance to those who have no regard to their own. I would play to give me pleasure, but not to give me pain; that is, I would play for trifles, in mixed companies, to amuse myself, and conform to custom ..."

   (A) Hyperbole

   (B) Alliteration

   (C) Irony

   (D) Foreshadowing

   (E) Idiom

47. Overall, how is this essay organized?
    (A) Deductively
    (B) Chronological order
    (C) Comparison and contrast
    (D) Advantages and disadvantages
    (E) General descriptions to specific examples

48. What are the two distinct parts of this essay?
    (A) paragraphs 1–2; paragraphs 3–10
    (B) paragraphs 1–3; paragraphs 4–10
    (C) paragraphs 1–4; paragraphs 5–10
    (D) paragraphs 1–6; paragraphs 7–10
    (E) paragraphs 1–7; paragraphs 8–10

49. The speaker uses himself as an example to illustrate the idea that
    (A) people must be individuals, not blindly follow others.
    (B) all pleasure is transitory.
    (C) drinking, smoking, and gambling inevitably lead to a young man's ruin.
    (D) everyone needs some pleasure in their lives.
    (E) it is the responsibility of intelligent, cultured people to guide others on the true road to pleasure.

50. Which of the following ideas can be inferred from paragraph 7?
    (A) The speaker deeply regrets the mistakes of his youth.
    (B) The speaker was once a minister.
    (C) The speaker wants others to profit from his mistakes and experience.
    (D) The speaker enjoyed his youth more than he does his old age.
    (E) The speaker feels that people can never repair the mistakes of their youth.

51. The tone of this passage is
    (A) concerned and caring.
    (B) harsh and unyielding.
    (C) shrill and hectoring.
    (D) demanding and rigid.
    (E) bemused and ironic.

52. The writer's central rhetorical strategy in this passage can best be described as
    (A) strongly refuting the accepted viewpoint on the topic.
    (B) citing respected outside authorities to advance his argument.
    (C) highly metaphorical and allusive.
    (D) constructing an extended metaphor that describes the proper conduct of life.
    (E) developing his argument using experiences from his own life.

ENGLISH LANGUAGE AND COMPOSITION

SECTION II

Time—2 hours

Question 1:

Suggested Time: 40 minutes. Your response will count for one third of your total score on the essay portion of the exam.

> **Directions: Read the following poem carefully. Then write an essay in which you analyze how the poet uses rhetorical strategies and other stylistic devices to explain his feelings about his love.**

Sonnet 3

It was that very day on which the sun

in awe of his creator dimmed the ray,

when I was captured, with my guard astray,

for your fine eyes, my lady, bound me then.

It hardly seemed the time for me to plan

defense against Love's stroke; I went my way

secure, unwary; so upon that day

of general sorrow all my pain began.

Love found me with no armor for the fight,

my eyes an open highway to the heart,

eyes that are now a vent for tears to flow.

And yet he played no honorable part,

wounding me with his shaft in such a state;

he saw you armed and dared not lift the bow.

Question 2:

Suggested Time: 40 minutes. Your response will count for one third of your total score on the essay portion of the exam.

When the Peloponnesian War erupted in 431 B.C.E. between Athens and Sparta, the brilliant leader Pericles was called upon as head of state to honor the dead by delivering a funeral oration. Here is an excerpt from that oration.

Directions: Read the following passage closely. Then write an essay in which you analyze how the writer's rhetorical strategies and stylistic devices reveal the values of his time.

Such were the men who lie here and such the city that inspired them. We survivors may pray to be spared their bitter hour but must disdain to meet the foe with a spirit less triumphant. Fix your eyes on the greatness of Athens as you have it before you day by day, fall in love with her, and when you feel her great, remember that this greatness was won by men with courage, with knowledge of their duty, and with a sense of honor in action, who, if they failed in any ordeal, disdained to deprive the city of their services, but sacrificed their lives as the best offering on her behalf. So they gave their bodies to the commonwealth and received each for his own memory, praise that will never die, and with it the grandest of all sepulchers, not that in which their mortal bones are laid, but a home in the minds of men, where their glory remains fresh to stir speech or action as the occasion comes by. For the whole earth is the sepulcher of famous men; and their story is not graven only on stone over their native earth, but lives on far away, without visible symbol, woven into the stuff of other men's lives. For you know it remains to rival what they have done and, knowing the secret of happiness to be freedom and the secret of freedom a brave heart, not idly to stand aside from the enemy's onset. For it is not the poor and luckless, as having no hope of prosperity, who have the most cause to reckon death as little loss, but those for whom fortune may yet keep reversal in store and would feel the change most if trouble befell them. Moreover, weakly to decline the trial is more painful to a man of spirit than death coming sudden and unperceived in the hour of strength and enthusiasm.

Therefore I do not mourn with the parents of the dead who are here with us. I would rather comfort them. For they know that they have been born into a world of manifold chances and that he is to be accounted happy to whom the best lot befalls—the best sorrow, such as yours today, such as fell to these, for whom life and happiness were cut to the self-same measure.

Question 3:

Suggested Time: 40 minutes. Your response will count for one third of your total score on the essay portion of the exam. The following excerpt is part of an essay by contemporary novelist Barbara Kingsolver.

> **Directions: Read the following passage closely. Then write an essay in which you agree or disagree with Kingsolver's view of literature as a political act.**

Art has the power not only to soothe a savage breast, but to change a savage mind. A novel can make us weep over the same events that might hardly give us pause if we read them in a newspaper. Even though the tragedy in the newspapers happened to real people, while the one in the novel happened in an author's imagination.

A novel works its magic by putting a reader inside another person's life. The pace is as slow as life. It's as detailed as life. It required you, the reader, to fill in an outline of words with vivid pictures drawn subconsciously from your own life, so that the story feels more personal than the sets designed by someone else and handed over via TV or movies. Literature duplicates the experience of living in a way that nothing else can, drawing you so fully into another life that you temporarily forget you have one of your own. That is why you read it, and might even sit up in bed till early dawn, throwing your whole tomorrow out of whack, simply to find out what happens to some people who, you know perfectly well, are made up. That's why you might find yourself crying, even if you aren't the crying kind.

The power of fiction is to create empathy. It lifts you away from your chair and stuffs you gently down inside someone else's point of view. It differs drastically from a newspaper, which imparts information while allowing you to remain rooted in your own perspective.... Art is the antidote that can call us back from the edge of numbness, restoring the ability to feel for another. By virtue of that power, it is political, regardless of content.

Quick-Score Answers

1. D	14. B	27. D	40. C
2. B	15. E	28. A	41. B
3. E	16. A	29. C	42. C
4. A	17. B	30. E	43. E
5. C	18. C	31. D	44. D
6. D	19. D	32. B	45. A
7. C	20. E	33. A	46. B
8. A	21. B	34. A	47. C
9. E	22. E	35. E	48. D
10. C	23. A	36. E	49. A
11. B	24. C	37. C	50. C
12. E	25. B	38. B	51. A
13. D	26. E	39. C	52. E

Computing Your Score

You can use the following worksheet to compute an approximate score on the practice test. Since it is difficult to be objective about your own writing and since you are not a trained ETS scorer or English teacher, you may wish to ask a friend who has already taken the test (and earned a score of 4 or 5) to score your three essays.

Recognize that your score can only be an approximation (at best), as you are scoring yourself against yourself. In the actual AP English Language and Composition Exam, you will be scored against every other student who takes the test as well.

Section I: Multiple-Choice Questions

	_____	number of correct answers
-	_____	.25 x number of wrong answers
=	_____	raw score
	_____	raw score
x	_____	1.25
=	_____	scaled score (out of a possible 67.5)

Section II: Essays

	_____	essay 1 (0–9)
	_____	essay 2 (0–9)
	_____	essay 3 (0–9)
x	_____	3.055
=	_____	scaled score (out of a possible 82.5)

Scaled Score

	_____	multiple-choice scaled score
+	_____	essay scaled score
=	_____	final scaled score (out of a possible 150)

AP Score Conversion Chart

Scaled Score	Likely AP Score
150–100	5
99–86	4
85–67	3
66–0	1 or 2

Answers and Explanations

1. **The correct answer is (D).** The poet directly says "Columbia's scenes of glorious toils I write." Line 11 shows that she is a powerful and resplendent goddess: "Wherever shines this native of the skies." Eliminate choice (B) because the writer is not addressing the choir. You can eliminate choice (A) because Columbia is a goddess, not a drudge. Choice (C) cannot be correct because the poem has nothing to do with the university of the same name, Columbia. Choice (E) is clearly wrong.

2. **The correct answer is (B).** America is identified as Columbia, showing her beauty and strength. This is the opposite of choice (A). The other choices are off the topic.

3. **The correct answer is (E).** America is battling for her freedom from England, choice (E). This eliminates choice (C). Choice (D) is clearly off the topic, as is choice (B), which could result from a reading error. Choice (A) is the second-best choice, but choice (E) is far more precise.

4. **The correct answer is (A).** Use the context clues "See the bright beams of heaven's revolving light" (line 7) to infer that *refulgent* most nearly means "radiant and glowing."

5. **The correct answer is (C).** The olive is a symbol of peace; the laurel, a symbol of victory. Readers can infer this from the lines "Muse! bow propitious while my pen relates/How pour her armies through a thousand gates" (13–14). According to the poet, America will be victorious in her battle for victory and "first in peace and honors" (line 25) because of her leader George Washington and her virtuous cause.

6. **The correct answer is (D).** *Personification* is giving human characteristics to inanimate objects. Here, the god Eolus personifies the unbeatable American forces.

7. **The correct answer is (C).** The poet uses the metaphors in lines 13–20 to suggest that America's forces are as mighty, powerful, and valiant as the forces of nature. America's battles are compared to fierce storms— "tempest and a night of storms;/Astonish'd ocean feels the wild uproar,"—and fall foliage "thick as leaves in Autumn's golden reign."

8. **The correct answer is (A).** The personification developed in the poem is best understood to suggest that since the Americans are fighting for a worthy cause, they have God on their side. This is shown in the metaphors described in question 7 as well as directly stated in line 32: "The land of freedom's heaven-defended race!"

9. **The correct answer is (E).** In line 33, the poet refers to the scales of justice, which show that America will be victorious in her quest for freedom.

10. **The correct answer is (C).** The world believes that America is fighting for the cause of freedom and justice, so all eyes are fixed on the scales. People are optimist, so choice (D) isn't valid. The other choices have nothing to do with the poem's theme.

11. **The correct answer is (B).** The poet uses elevated diction to convey the solemn cause Americans are fighting against the British. Eliminate choices (A), (C), and (D) because the poet is firmly on America's side. Choice (D) is wrong because nothing is being satirized here.

12. **The correct answer is (E).** The last two lines suggest that the British monarchy has been so influential that the poet suggests that Washington be crowned king when he is victorious. This is a curious twist in a poem so devoted to the American cause.

13. **The correct answer is (D).** The purpose of the poet's rhetoric and reasoning is to celebrate George Washington and the cause of American freedom. The poem is concerned with the Revolutionary War, not classic literature, so choice (A) is incorrect. Question 12 reveals that choice (B) cannot be correct. Choice (C) is the exact opposite of the poet's theme. Nature is used as a metaphor, not a solution, so choice (E) is incorrect as well.

14. **The correct answer is (B).** The poet is deeply patriotic, celebrating America as a bastion of strength and right. This directly contradicts choices (A) and (C). She does not acknowledge that America has any flaws at all, so choice (D) cannot be correct; the same applies to choice (E).

15. **The correct answer is (E).** The first paragraph of the speech serves to describe the movement of the Germans through the French lines of defense. This is a reading comprehension question, not a matter of interpretation. The British and French armies are not being compared and contrasted, so choice (A) cannot be correct; choices (B) and (C) are off the topic. Churchill's conviction that the Allies can definitely win the war comes later and is not precise: Churchill is not "definite" that the Allies can win, only that everyone must pull together to have a chance at victory.

16. **The correct answer is (A).** Churchill creates an image of desperation to worry his listeners. This is shown in these images: "a remarkable combination of air bombing and heavily armored tanks," "strong columns of ..armored vehicles...ravaging the open country," and "penetrated deeply and spread alarm and confusion in their track."

17. **The correct answer is (B).** Churchill uses the word *ravaging* in paragraph 1 to connote rape and despoilment. His use of loaded language, words with emotional connotations, is designed to sway his readers to action.

18. **The correct answer is (C).** The phrase the "magnificent forces of the Royal Air Force" is an example of the speaker's use of loaded language. This is language with strong emotional overtones or connotations. There is nothing ironic about the phrase, so eliminate choice (A). It is not an *allusion,* choice (B); *onomatopoeia,* choice (C); or *hyperbole*, choice (D).

19. **The correct answer is (D).** As used here, *dogged* most nearly means "determined." The context makes this clear: "if the British Army shows the dogged endurance and solid fighting power of which there have been so many examples in the past." *Dogged* has nothing to do with dogs, so don't be tricked by choice (A). (*Dog-like* would describe canines.)

20. **The correct answer is (E).** Churchill praises the British and French armies to convey the impression of strong fighting forces that complement each other. He is cementing relationships between the two countries, united against a common enemy.

21. **The correct answer is (B).** Churchill addresses civilians rather than soldiers to convince the civilians to continue supporting the battles. Most of the people he is addressing cannot enlist, since they are women, children, or ineligible, so choice (A) is incorrect. We have no proof that he suspects that the civilians do not back the war, so choice (C) cannot be correct. The same is true of choice (D). Choice (E) is the direct opposite of the truth: Churchill wants to make his message obvious, not "allusive and subtle" at all.

22. **The correct answer is (E).** As used here (in the third paragraph), *gravity* most nearly means "seriousness." This is a difficult question because *gravity* has multiple meanings. Deduce the correct meaning from context clues: "It would be foolish, however, to disguise the gravity of the hour."

23. **The correct answer is (A).** Churchill uses the words *supreme, drastic, last inch, right, freedom,* and *honor* in paragraph 4 to invoke strong feelings of patriotism and the feeling that any effort to win the war will be worthwhile. Again, he is using loaded language, words with strong emotional overtones, to sway his listeners.

24. **The correct answer is (C).** Churchill fosters the illusion that war is a noble, even sublime effort. This is an illusion because people know that war is really "hell, even for the righteous," choice (A). None of the other choices are illusions.

25. **The correct answer is (B).** Churchill's tone in this speech is best described as *inspiring.* His purpose is to stir up patriotic fervor and thus support for the war effort.

26. **The correct answer is (E).** Churchill uses appeals to ethics and emotions to achieve his aim. The ethical appeals are shown in phrases

such as "It would be foolish, however, to disguise the gravity of the hour." Emotional appeals are shown in his use of loaded language and the highly emotional conclusion: "Arm yourselves, and be ye men of valor, and be in readiness for the conflict; for it is better for us to perish in battle than to look upon the outrage of our nation and our altar. And the Will of God is in Heaven, even so let it be."

27. **The correct answer is (D).** The final quote serves most directly to suggest that the Allies' battle to win the war is divinely sanctioned. This is shown in the last line: "And the Will of God is in Heaven, even so let it be."

28. **The correct answer is (A).** This speech is best characterized as *propaganda*. Don't be tricked by the negative connotation the word "propaganda" carries; propaganda can also be used to sway people to a righteous cause. Choice (B), *brainwashing*, is much too strong; choice (C), *unemotional;* choice (D), *poetic;* and choice (E), *highly symbolic,* are not accurate reflections of the content of the speech.

29. **The correct answer is (C).** The images in the first two stanzas combine to form an impression of peace and tranquillity. This is shown in the image of the bee circling a clover, of a fisherman mending a glimmering net, and happy porpoises jumping in the sea, for example.

30. **The correct answer is (E).** The rhetorical purpose of the first two stanzas can best be described as *ironic*. It is ironic—a reversal of the reader's expectations—that the world could end on such a peaceful day. We expect more drama and horror at the end of the world.

31. **The correct answer is (D).** The parallelism in lines 18–20 creates an incantatory effect that lulls the people into complacency. Note especially the repeated phrase "As long as..."

32. **The correct answer is (B).** Lines 22–24 are ironic because something of vital importance—prophecy—is rejected in favor of something mundane and even foolish—tying up tomatoes.

33. **The correct answer is (A).** The old man's actions in lines 22–25 can be interpreted as a positive symbol of the assertion of individuality and normalcy in the face of disaster. He refuses to panic; rather, he sticks to his routine. Do not assume that he cannot accept reality, choice (B): there is no proof of this in the poem.

34. **The correct answer is (A).** From the first two stanzas, readers can infer that contemporary people are too busy to take notice of the end of the world. We refuse to stop for death.

35. **The correct answer is (E).** In the last two stanzas, the poet uses repetition and parallelism to reinforce the theme. The other rhetorical

devices are not present in this part of the poem (and in several instances, not in the poem at all).

36. **The correct answer is (E).** In context, the last two lines suggest the poet's belief that the world really is coming to an end. This can be inferred from the repetition of the line "There will be no other end of the world."

37. **The correct answer is (C).** The tone of this poem is best described as *soothing*. Do not confuse the tone with the subject matter, choice (B) and choice (D). There is no support for the other choices.

38. **The correct answer is (B).** The poem's rhythm is best characterized as a song or song-like prayer. The poem has a gentle quality, like a child's lullaby. Again, do not confuse the rhythm with the subject matter.

39. **The correct answer is (C).** The poem's rhythm and mood therefore serve to underscore the horror of the scene. The contrast between the gentle rhythm and the horrific reality—the end of the world—serves to reinforce the speaker's point.

40. **The correct answer is (C).** The poet's central rhetorical strategy in this poem can best be described as making an ironic commentary on contemporary life. He is commenting on our inability to deal with unpleasant realities.

41. **The correct answer is (B).** In the opening paragraph, the writer develops an extended metaphor comparing pleasure to a large rock in the ocean of life to make the point that many young men go astray. You can see this in the lines "Pleasure is the rock which most young people split upon; they launch out with crowded sails in quest of, but without a compass to direct their course or reason sufficient to steer the vessel; for want of which, pain and shame, instead of Pleasure, are the returns of their voyage." Choice (A) is wrong because pleasure is not personified, made to come alive. It remains inanimate. The author does not reveal his own experiences until later in the essay, so choices (D) and (E) are incorrect. There is no understatement, eliminating choice (C).

42. **The correct answer is (C).** The writer achieves a balanced and reasonable tone in the first paragraph through the use of parallel phrases. This is most clearly shown in the following infinitive phrases:

- to snarl at Pleasure
- to preach against it
- to point it out

You can also see it in the following phrases:
- like a Stoic
- like a parson
- *like an Epicurean*

43. **The correct answer is (E).** *Profligate* most nearly means utterly immoral, as shown by the context clues "beastly drunkard" and "a profligate swearer and curser." The word "vices" also tips you off that *profligate* must refer to "immorality."

44. **The correct answer is (D).** The rhetorical purpose of paragraphs 2–4 can best be described as *narrative*, as the writer is telling a story. The writer is not *explaining*, choice (A), or *arguing,* choice (B). Choices (C) and (D) do not make sense in context, since there is nothing especially systematic or anything at all scientific in his discussion.

45. **The correct answer is (A).** The phrase "Thus seduced by fashion" shows that the writer makes the dangers of fashion more vivid through the use of *personification*. Remember that *personification* is giving life-like qualities to inanimate objects. Here, the writer is making fashion seem to come alive by suggesting that it can seduce someone. There is no *allusion* or reference, choice (B); *simile*, choice (C); or *onomatopoeia*, choice (D). Finally, there is no *hyperbole,* choice (E).

46. **The correct answer is (B).** The writer uses *alliteration* to make the highlighted sentences smooth and flowing. Recall that *alliteration* is the repetition of initial consonant sounds in several words in a sentence or line of poetry. Writers use alliteration to create musical effects, link related ideas, stress certain words, or mimic specific sounds. The words *constitution* and *compliance; play, pleasure,* and *pain*; and *conform* and *custom* are alliterative.

47. **The correct answer is (C).** Overall, this essay is organized through comparison and contrast. The writer compares and contrasts his experiences from the real (his youth) to the ideal (how he would relive his life if he could). He begins with chronological order, choice (B), but deviates from this in the second half of the essay, when he return to his youth again. There are specific examples throughout, so choice (E) is not correct. Choice (D) is wrong because there are no advantages to being a wastrel.

48. **The correct answer is (D).** The two distinct parts of this essay are paragraphs 1–6—his real life—and paragraphs 7–10—his model life, the life that he would live if he could go back and relive his life. This second half is also the model that he wishes to serve as an ideal for his son.

49. **The correct answer is (A).** The speaker uses himself as an example to illustrate the idea that people must be individuals, not blindly follow others. This is his theme. Choice (B) cannot be true, because he clearly states: "I have not mentioned the pleasures of the mind (which are the solid and permanent ones)." While drinking, smoking, and gambling *may* lead to a young man's ruin, this is not *inevitable,* as shown through his own experiences. Therefore, choice (C) cannot be correct. Choice (D) is too vague. He specifically argues against choice (E) when he says: "I would not, at twenty years, be a preaching missionary of

abstemiousness and sobriety; and I should let other people do as they would, without formality and sententiously rebuking them for it."

50. **The correct answer is (C).** Readers can infer from paragraph 7 that the speaker wants others to profit from his mistakes and experiences. That is his entire purpose in writing. He does not deeply regret the mistakes of his youth, choice (A), because he has learned from them. There is no textual support at all that the speaker was once a minister, choice (B). Since he seems very happy in middle age, choice (D) is incorrect. The speaker has himself repaired the mistakes of his youth, so choice (E) is wrong.

51. **The correct answer is (A).** The tone of this passage is concerned and caring. This is shown in passages such as this one: "A real man of fashion and pleasure observes decency; at least, neither borrows nor affects vices; and, if he unfortunately, has any, he gratifies them with choice, delicacy, and secrecy." This is the opposite of *harsh and unyielding,* choice (B); *shrill and hectoring,* choice (C); and *demanding and rigid,* choice (D). Since he is very serious, choice (E) cannot be correct.

52. **The correct answer is (E).** The writer's central rhetorical strategy in this passage can best be described as developing his argument using experiences from his own life. He is not strongly refuting the accepted viewpoint on the topic, choice (A), nor citing respected outside authorities to advance his argument, choice (B). Since he is quite specific and concrete, choice (C) is wrong. The metaphor ends in the first paragraph, so choice (D) has no textual support.

Question 1:

A well-written essay should analyze how the poet uses rhetorical strategies and other stylistic devices to explain his feelings about his love.

- The writer should describe how the speaker fell in love with a lady on the day the sun dimmed its ray. The speaker was not prepared to fall in love and has felt great heartache from the experience since his love has not been returned.

- Students should explain how the sonnet's form reinforces its meaning. The Petarchan sonnet has a rigid rhyme scheme: the *octave* rhymes abbaabba and presents the poem's subject; the concluding six lines, the *sestet,* rhyme cdecde and indicate the significance of the facts set forth or resolve the problem posed in the octave.

- Students should also discuss imagery ("when I was captured, with my guard astray") as it relates to the theme.

- In addition, students should analyze metaphors such as "my eyes an open highway to the heart" and "Love found me with no armor for the fight" (love compared to a battle or war) as they reinforce meaning.

- Finally, students can include a discussion of personification, as in "Love's stroke."

Question 2:

A well-written essay should analyze how the writer uses rhetorical strategies and stylistic devices to reveal the values of his time.

- In suggesting that his audience "Fix your eyes on the greatness of Athens as you have it before you day by day," Pericles promotes the values of patriotism and self-sacrifice to the state instead of personal consideration and gain.

- Pericles uses parallelism ("For you know it remains...," "For it is not...") to suggest the strength of his ideals of freedom through allegiance to the state.

- He also uses *oxymoron,* or seeming contradictions, especially as shown in the last paragraph: "Therefore I do not mourn with the parents of the dead who are here with us. I would rather comfort them. For they know that they have been born into a world of manifold chances and that he is to be accounted happy to whom the best lot befalls—the best sorrow, such as yours today, such as fell to these, for whom life and happiness were cut to the self-same measure." Phrases such as "Best sorrow" show this especially.

- The motifs of the sun and eyes (as the window to the soul) are also traditional conventions of the sonnet.

- The personification of love; love as a battle

Question 3:

A well-written essay should explore how literature does or does not have a political agenda. Writers should also comment on the writer's distinction between a real-life account of a disaster in a newspaper and a fictional account of a tragedy in a novel. Does one have more power than the other? If so why?

PRACTICE TEST 3

ENGLISH LANGUAGE AND COMPOSITION

SECTION 1

Time—1 hour

> **Directions: This section contains selections from two passages of prose and two poems with questions on their style, content, form, and purpose. Read each selection closely and carefully. Then choose the best answer from the five choices.**

Questions 1–12. Read the following selection carefully before you mark your answers. The passage below is from Herman Melville's novel What Redburn Saw in Launcelott's-Hey.

In the vicinity of the docks there are many very painful sights.

In going to our boarding house, I generally passed through a narrow street called Launcelott's-Hey, lined with dingy, prisonlike cotton warehouses. In this street, or rather alley, you seldom see anyone but a truckman, or some solitary old warehouse keeper, haunting his smoky den like a ghost.

Once, passing through this place, I heard a feeble wail, which seemed to come out of the earth. It was but a strip of crooked sidewalk where I stood; the dingy wall was on every side, converting the midday to twilight; and not a soul was in sight. I started, and could almost have run, when I heard that dismal sound. It seemed the low, hopeless, endless wail of someone forever lost. At last I advanced to an opening which communicated downward with deep tiers of cellars beneath a crumbling old warehouse; and there, some fifteen feet below the walk, crouched in nameless squalor, with her head bowed over, was the figure of what had been a woman. Her blue arms folded to her livid bosom two shrunken things like children, that leaned toward her, one on each side. At first, I knew not whether they were alive or dead. They made no sign; they did not move or stir; but from the vault came that soul-sickening wail.

I made a noise with my foot, which, in the silence, echoed far and near; but there was no response. Louder still; when one of the children lifted up its head, and cast upward a faint glance; then closed its eyes, and lay motionless. The woman also, now gazed up, and perceived me; but let her eye fall again. How they had crawled into that den, I could not tell; but there they had crawled to die…

But again I looked down into the vault, and in fancy beheld the pale, shrunken forms still crouching there. Ah! what are our creeds, and how do we hope to be saved? Tell me, oh Bible, that story of Lazarus again, that I may find comfort in my heart for the poor and forlorn. Surrounded as we are by the wants and woes of our fellow men, and yet given to follow our own pleasures, regardless of their pains, are we not like people sitting up with a corpse, and making merry in the house of the dead?

1. By using the word *prisonlike*, the narrator alludes to
    (A) the woman's former sins and subsequent imprisonment.
    (B) the literal dungeon in which she finds herself trapped by poor choices.
    (C) the constraints of poverty to emphasize the story's tragic dimension.
    (D) the prison in which we all find ourselves due to circumstances beyond our control.
    (E) writer's block and the terror it causes.

2. What rhetorical strategy does Melville use in these lines "...Or some solitary old warehouse keeper, haunting his smoky den like a ghost"?
    (A) Simile
    (B) Allusion
    (C) Alliteration
    (D) Onomatopoeia
    (E) Parallelism

3. The "deep tiers of cellars" can best be understood as a metaphor for
    (A) the warehouse.
    (B) the narrator's soul.
    (C) a funeral vault.
    (D) the woman's fate.
    (E) shoddy building and workmanship.

4. The narrator describes the children as "shrunken things like children" to
    (A) argue that people need to take better care of their children.
    (B) use a literary metaphor.
    (C) suggest they are not really children at all.
    (D) describe their appearance and convey their profound misery.
    (E) argue in favor of foster care for the abused and indigent.

5. What point of view does Melville use in this passage?
    (A) Third-person limited
    (B) Omniscient
    (C) Second person
    (D) First person
    (E) All-knowing

6. Melville uses this point of view to
   (A) help the reader feel closer to the narrator and therefore closer to the events of the story.
   (B) see events from every character's perspective.
   (C) experience events from only one character's perspective.
   (D) distance the reader from the narrator and thus achieve a more balanced and impartial tone.
   (E) establish the setting and theme.

7. From this excerpt, you can infer that Redburn is
   (A) the father of the two children.
   (B) the old warehouse keeper.
   (C) basically compassionate, decent, and caring.
   (D) personally responsible for the woman's fate.
   (E) deeply religious.

8. What rhetorical strategy forms the basis of the following line: "Are we not like people sitting up with a corpse, and making merry in the house of the dead?"
   (A) Extended metaphor
   (B) Analogy
   (C) Proof by extended example
   (D) Verbal understatement
   (E) Verbal irony

9. In the fourth paragraph, Melville makes an implicit comparison between the children and
   (A) devils.
   (B) corpses.
   (C) ghosts.
   (D) wild animals.
   (E) monsters.

10. The final lines of the story suggest that
    (A) the speaker does not believe that the situation will ever improve.
    (B) the situation will be relatively easy to ameliorate.
    (C) only religion can save the poor.
    (D) we are enjoying ourselves while ignoring those who have nothing and will surely die.
    (E) we should pursue pleasure because that is the only consolation left to us.

11. The mood of this excerpt is best described as
    (A) combative.
    (B) bleak and horrific.
    (C) resigned.
    (D) hopeful.
    (E) chilly.

12. The religious allusion at the end of the excerpt suggests that
    (A) rich people must help, for only they have the means to correct society's ills.
    (B) if we hope for our souls to be saved, we must care for each other.
    (C) we are already among the damned.
    (D) even religion cannot help in such despairing situations.
    (E) we are all doomed.

Questions 13–28. Read the following selection carefully before you mark your answers.

Now estimate how few of those who do work are occupied in essential trades. For, in a society where we make money the standard of everything, it is necessary to practice many crafts which are quite vain and superfluous, ministering only to luxury and licentiousness. Suppose the host of those who now toil were distributed only over as few crafts as the few needs and conveniences demanded by nature. In the great abundance of commodities which must then arise, the prices set on them would be too low for the craftsmen to earn their livelihood by their work. But suppose all those fellows who are not busied with unprofitable crafts, as well as all the lazy and idle throng, any one of whom now consumes as much of the fruits of other men's labors as any two of the workingmen, were all set to work and indeed to useful work. You can easily see how small an allowance of time would be enough and to spare for the production of all that is required by necessity or comfort (or even pleasure, provided it be genuine and natural)...

Now is not this an unjust and ungrateful commonwealth? It lavishes great regards on so-called gentlefolk and banking goldsmiths and the rest of that kind, who are either idle or mere parasites and purveyors of empty pleasures. On the contrary, it makes no benevolent provisions for farmers, colliers, common laborers, carters, and carpenters without whom there would be no commonwealth at all. After it has misused the labor of their prime and after they are weighted down with age and disease and are in utter want, it forgets all their sleepless nights and all the great benefits received at their hands and most ungratefully requites them with a most miserable death.

Yet when these evil men with insatiable greed have divided up among themselves all the goods which would have been enough for all the people, how far they are from the happiness of the Utopian commonwealth? In Utopia all greed for money was entirely removed with the use of money. What a mass of trouble was then cut away! What a crop of crimes was then pulled up by the roots! Who does not know that fraud, theft, rapine, quarrels, disorders, brawls, seditions, murders, treasons, poisonings, which are avenged rather than restrained by daily executions, die out with the destruction of money? Who does not know that fear, anxiety, worries, toils, and sleepless nights will also perish at the same time as money? What is more, poverty, which alone money seems to make poor, forthwith would itself dwindle and disappear if money were entirely done away with everywhere.

13. The first paragraph of this passage serves to
    (A) define the abstract ideal of "work."
    (B) cite a common misconception among the wealthy.
    (C) compare and contrast social classes.
    (D) argue that economic equality can be achieved by following his plan.
    (E) posit that the wealthy deserve their lofty position.

14. In the opening lines, the speaker is critical of
    (A) workingmen who do not suit their abilities to their jobs.
    (B) the indolent upper classes.
    (C) unnatural pleasures and diversions.
    (D) essential trades.
    (E) our contempt for trades and elevation of the aristocracy.

15. The phrase "any one of whom now consumes as much of the fruits of other men's labors as any two of the workingmen" refers to which of the following?
    (A) "the fruits of other men's labors"
    (B) "all those fellows"
    (C) "unprofitable crafts"
    (D) "useful work"
    (E) "the lazy and idle throng"

16. As used in the first paragraph, *licentiousness* most nearly means
    (A) a disregard for morals.
    (B) extravagance.
    (C) comfort.
    (D) delicacy.
    (E) self-denial.

17. The "unjust and ungrateful commonwealth" in the second paragraph refers to
    - (A) America.
    - (B) the workingmen.
    - (C) the vain and foolish upper classes.
    - (D) the current system of government.
    - (E) the author's proposed system of government.

18. In context, the phrase the "so-called gentlefolk" suggests the speaker's
    - (A) ironic stance toward people who disagree with him.
    - (B) awareness of the sharp distinctions among social classes in his day.
    - (C) contempt for the idle, titled rich.
    - (D) desire to curry favor with his social superiors.
    - (E) admiration for people who have succeeded in a cutthroat world.

19. What is the speaker's bias in the second paragraph?
    - (A) Toward the workingman
    - (B) Against the workingman
    - (C) Toward the commonwealth
    - (D) Toward banking goldsmiths
    - (E) Against age and disease

20. What is the antecedent of the word "it" in the following sentence: "After it has misused the labor of their prime and after they are weighted down with age and disease and are in utter want, it forgets all their sleepless nights and all the great benefits received at their hands and most ungratefully requites them with a most miserable death"?
    - (A) Fate
    - (B) The workingman
    - (C) The wealthy
    - (D) The commonwealth
    - (E) Reality

21. The phrase "Now is not this an unjust and ungrateful commonwealth?" is an example of a(n)
    - (A) inversion.
    - (B) paradox.
    - (C) metaphor.
    - (D) literary allusion.
    - (E) symbol.

22. The rhetorical questions in the last paragraph serve most directly to
    (A) signal a change in emphasis from the previous paragraphs.
    (B) built up to an angry and resolute climax.
    (C) comment ironically on the lenient way in which crime was regarded in the speaker's day.
    (D) comment on his previous assertions.
    (E) emphasize the difference between appearance and reality.

23. The tone of the last paragraph is best described as
    (A) calm and dispassionate.
    (B) relaxed and self-assured.
    (C) tentative.
    (D) passionate and critical.
    (E) violent.

24. What rhetorical device does the author use in the phrase "In Utopia all greed for money was entirely removed with the use of money"?
    (A) Dramatic irony
    (B) Parallelism
    (C) Paradox
    (D) Metaphor
    (E) Verbal irony

25. Which phrase would the author most likely agree with?
    (A) A penny saved is a penny earned.
    (B) Money is the root of all evil.
    (C) Money makes the world go 'round.
    (D) You can't win it if you're not in it.
    (E) Money is essential.

26. The metaphor "What a crop of crimes was then pulled up by the roots" serves to
    (A) make his abstract concept more specific and recognizable to his audience.
    (B) emphasize his main point about criminal activity.
    (C) refer to the recent outbreak of crime.
    (D) refute his critics.
    (E) compare and contrast his plan to his opponent's plan.

27. The author's style is best described as
    (A)   highly abstract.
    (B)   objective.
    (C)   highly allusive.
    (D)   informal and relaxed.
    (E)   formal and elevated.

28. Which is the best title for this except?
    (A)   The Collapse of the Commonwealth
    (B)   Utopia
    (C)   Economics and the Common Man
    (D)   The Rich vs. the Poor
    (E)   Work and Play

Questions 29–42. Read the selection carefully before you mark your answers.

The kitchen gave a special character to our lives; my mother's character. All my memories of that kitchen are dominated by the nearness of my mother sitting all day long at her sewing machine, by the clacking of the treadle against the linoleum floor, by the patient twist of her right shoulder as she automatically pushed at the wheel with one hand or lifted the foot to free the needle where it had stuck in a thick piece of material.

The kitchen was her life. Year by year, as I began to take in her fantastic capacity for labor and her anxious zeal, I realized it was ourselves she kept stitched together. I can never remember a time when she was not working. She worked because the law of her life was work, work and anxiety; she worked because she would have found life meaningless without work. She read almost no English; she could read the Yiddish paper, but never felt she had the time to. We were always talking of a time when I would teach her how to read, but somehow there was never time. When I awoke in the morning she was already at her machine, or in the great morning crowd of housewives at the grocery getting fresh rolls for breakfast. When I returned from school she was at her machine, or conferring over McCall's with some neighborhood woman who had come in pointing hopefully to an illustration—"Mrs. Kazin! Mrs. Kazin! Make me a dress like it shows her in the picture!" When my father came home from work she had somehow mysteriously interrupted herself to make supper for us, and the dishes cleared and washed, was back at her machine. When I went to bed at night, often she was still there, pounding away at the treadle, hunched over the wheel, her hands steering a piece of gauze under the needle with a finesse that always contrasted sharply with her swollen hands and broken nails. Her left hand had been pierced through when as a girl she had worked in the infamous Triangle Shirtwaist Factory[1] on the East Side. A needle had gone straight through the palm, severing a large vein. They had sewn it up for her so clumsily that a tuft of flesh always lay folded over the palm.

1. A New York sweatshop that was the site of a fire that killed many immigrant workers, mainly women, and brought demands for safer working conditions.

29. The first sentence is distinguished by
    (A) parallel prepositional phrases.
    (B) sentence fragments.
    (C) sentence run-ons.
    (D) elevated diction.
    (E) frequent literary allusions.

30. Which of the following ideas can be inferred from the first paragraph?
    (A) The speaker's mother is devoted to her family.
    (B) The speaker feels guilty about going to school while his mother worked so hard.
    (C) The speaker is embarrassed that his mother must take in sewing.
    (D) The speaker's mother is very proud of her son.
    (E) The family has not remained intact.

31. The lengthy opening sentence serves to
    (A) show the writer's understanding and compassion.
    (B) create a reflective, contemplative tone.
    (C) capture the rhythm of the mother's constant work.
    (D) signal a change of direction.
    (E) suggest the difference between appearance and reality.

32. Which of the following is shown in the second paragraph?
    I.   Metaphor
    II.   Irony
    III. Personification
    (A) III only
    (B) I and II
    (C) I and III
    (D) II and III
    (E) I only

33. The kitchen becomes a symbol of
    (A) the family's poverty.
    (B) the mother's strength.
    (C) grossly unfair social conditions.
    (D) the need for women's liberation.
    (E) oppression and pain.

34. The images in this passage combine to form an impression of
    (A) constant struggle and toil.
    (B) great joy in work and family.
    (C) suspicion and danger.
    (D) isolation and fear.
    (E) grudging gratitude tinged with resentment.

35. You can infer from this passage that Yiddish must be
    (A) a publication.
    (B) a religion.
    (C) a language.
    (D) a social movement.
    (E) a type of needlework.

36. The narrator used dialect to
    (A) allude to the difficulty he had communicating with his mother.
    (B) compare and contrast his mother to her customers.
    (C) show how people should talk rather than how they did talk.
    (D) mock his mother and her illiteracy.
    (E) more fully describe his mother and his world.

37. This selection is told from which point of view?
    (A) First person
    (B) Third-person limited
    (C) All-knowing
    (D) Omniscient
    (E) Second person

38. The author's attitude toward his mother is best described as
    (A) condescending.
    (B) admiring.
    (C) neutral.
    (D) pitying.
    (E) resentful.

39. The author's footnote refers to
    (A) reasons why the mother no longer works outside the home.
    (B) the need to work hard.
    (C) the family's past.
    (D) the historical milieu.
    (E) the need for social reforms.

40. Which of the following ideas can be inferred from the last sentence?
    (A) His mother cannot work to capacity because of her deformed hand.
    (B) His mother is stoical about any suffering she may experience.
    (C) The author bitterly resents that his mother did not get better medical care.
    (D) His mother was lucky not to have been killed in the fire.
    (E) Women bear the brunt of society's ills.

41. The speaker's central rhetorical strategy in this passage can best be described as
    (A) creating an extended metaphor that describes his mother as symbolic of a generation of immigrant women.
    (B) citing examples from his childhood to argue that women's lot has improved in the twenty-first century.
    (C) providing specific examples to celebrate his mother's hard work, determination, and forbearance.
    (D) showing the advantages and disadvantages of hard work.
    (E) arguing that no one should have to labor as hard as his mother did.

Questions 42–52. Read the following selection carefully before you mark your answers.

We know that the white man does not understand our ways. One portion of land is the same to him as the next, for he is a stranger who comes in the night and takes from the land whatever he needs. The earth is not his brother but his enemy, and when he has conquered it, he moves on. He leaves his father's graves, and his children's birthright is forgotten. He treats his mother, the earth, and brothers, the sky, as things to be bought, plundered, sold like sheep or bright beads. His appetite will devour the earth and leave behind only a desert.

I do not know. Our ways are different from your ways. The sight of your cities pains the eyes of the red man. But perhaps it is because the red man is a savage and does not understand.

There is no quiet place in the white man's cities. No place to hear the unfurling of leaves in spring, or the rustle of an insect's wings. But perhaps it is because I am a savage and do not understand. The clatter only seems to insult the ears. And what is there to life if a man cannot hear the lonely cry of the whippoorwill or the arguments of the frogs around a pond at night? I am a red man and do not understand. The Indian prefers the soft sound of the wind darting over the face of a pond, and the smell of the wind itself, cleansed by rain or scented with the pine cone.

42. Which of the following are evident in the first paragraph?
    I.   Alliteration
    II. Personification
    III. Similes
    (A) I and II
    (B) II
    (C) III
    (D) I and III
    (E) II and III

43. The statement "The earth is not his brother but his enemy, and when he has conquered it, he moves on" adds to the development of the passage by

    (A) contrasting the white and Native American view of the land.

    (B) aggressively insulting the white man.

    (C) showing that the Native Americans will not be conquered by the whites.

    (D) portraying the whites as barbarians.

    (E) focusing on a specific statement rather than vague generalities.

44. The speaker is most likely a

    (A) poet.

    (B) naturalist.

    (C) white man.

    (D) Native American.

    (E) contemporary social commentator.

45. Which of the following rhetorical strategies are evident in the last paragraph?

    I. Repetition

    II. Parallelism

    III. Alliteration

    (A) I only

    (B) I and II

    (C) II and III

    (D) III only

    (E) I, II, and III

46. This passage is primarily developed by

    (A) an extended metaphor.

    (B) comparison.

    (C) contrast.

    (D) inductive reasoning.

    (E) deductive reasoning.

47. The rhetorical purpose of paragraphs 2 and 3 can best be described as

    (A) argumentative.

    (B) academic.

    (C) expository.

    (D) narrative.

    (E) theoretical.

48. What primary effect does the speaker create through the repetition in the second and third paragraphs?

   (A)   Irony

   (B)   Pathos

   (C)   Sorrow

   (D)   Regret

   (E)   Exultation

49. How is this line ironic? "I am a red man and do not understand."

   (A)   The speaker claims that Native Americans are savages.

   (B)   The speaker argues that both whites and Native Americans are savages.

   (C)   The speaker claims that he is only a savage, incapable of understanding what is important, yet his argument suggests that the whites do not understand what matters.

   (D)   The writer admits his ignorance.

   (E)   The writer claims that he is only a savage, but he is far closer to nature than the whites are.

50. The images in the last paragraph combine to create an impression of

   (A)   conflict and misunderstanding.

   (B)   the joys of the wilderness.

   (C)   arrogant superiority.

   (D)   fear and hostility.

   (E)   life and death.

51. The author's style in this passage is marked by

   (A)   irony and parody.

   (B)   figurative language and imagery.

   (C)   allusions and personification.

   (D)   symbolism.

   (E)   regret and sorrow.

52. What is the author's purpose?

   (A)   To warn the white man against encroaching on Native American land

   (B)   To plea for the white man's understanding

   (C)   To inform the whites that the land is sacred and to persuade them to keep it sacred

   (D)   To persuade the whites to change their way of looking at nature before it is too late

   (E)   To tell a story about the glory of nature

ENGLISH LANGUAGE AND COMPOSITION

SECTION II

Time—2 hours

Question 1:

Suggested Time: 40 minutes. Your response will count for one third of your total score on the essay portion of the exam.

> **Directions: Read the following selection carefully. Then write an essay in which you analyze how the writer uses diction, figures of speech, and sensory images to convey the story's mood and tone.**

The following passage comes from Nathaniel Hawthorne's short story "Dr. Heidegger's Experiment."

If all my stories were true, Dr. Heidegger's study must have been a very curious place. It was a dim, old-fashioned chamber, festooned with cobwebs and besprinkled with antique dust. Around the walls stood several oaken bookcases, the lower shelves of which were filled with rows of gigantic folios and black-letter quartos, and the upper with little parchment-covered duodecimos. Over the central bookcase was a bronze bust of Hippocrates, with which, according to some authorities, Dr. Heidegger was accustomed to hold consultations in all different cases of his practice. In the obscurest corner of the room stood a tall and narrow oaken closet with its door ajar, within which doubtfully appeared a skeleton. Between two of the bookcases hung a looking glass, presenting its high and dusty plate within a tarnished gilt frame. Among many wonderful stories related to this mirror, it was fabled that the spirit of the doctor's deceased patients dwelt within its verge and would stare him in the face whenever he looked thitherward. The opposite side of the chamber was ornamented with the full-length portrait of a young lady, arrayed in the faded magnificence of silk, satin, and brocade, and with a visage as faded as her dress. Above half a century ago, Dr. Heidegger had been on the point of marriage with this young lady; but being affected with some slight disorder, she had swallowed one of her lover's prescriptions and died on the bridal evening.

Question 2:

Suggested Time: 40 minutes. Your response will count for one third of your total score on the essay portion of the exam.

Directions: Read the following selection carefully. Then write an essay in which you analyze how the writer uses rhetorical strategies and other stylistic devices to convey what he saw as the connection between God and humanity.

The following passage come from William Bradford's History of Plymouth Plantation.

In sundry of these storms the winds were so fierce and the seas so high, as they could not bear a knot of sail, but were forced to hull [drift] with the wind for divers days together. And in one of them, as they lay thus at hull in a mighty storm, a lusty young man called John Howland, coming upon some occasion above the gratings was, with a seele [pitch or roll] of the ship, thrown into the sea; but it pleased God that he caught hold of the topsail halyards which hung overboard and ran out at length. Yet he held his hold (though he was sundry fathoms under water) till he was hauled up by the same rope to the brim of the water, and then with a boat hook and other means got into the ship again and his life saved. And though he was something ill with it, yet he lived many years after and become a profitable member both in church and commonwealth. In this voyage there died but one of the passengers, which was William Butten, a youth, servant to Samuel Fuller, when they drew near the coast.

Question 3:

Suggested Time: 40 minutes. Your response will count for one third of your total score on the essay portion of the exam.

The selection is a diary entry penned by Governor John Endicott in 1645.

Directions: Read the following selection carefully. Then write an essay in which you defend, challenge, or qualify the speaker's view of women and education.

April 13. Mr. Hopkins, the governor of Hartford upon Connecticut, came to Boston, and brought his wife with him, (a godly young woman, and of special parts,) who was fallen into a sad infirmity, the loss of her understanding and reason, which had been growing on her diverse years, by occasion of her giving herself wholly to reading and writing, and had written many books. Her husband, being very loving and tender of her, was loath to grieve her; but he saw his error, when it was too late. For if she had attended to her household affairs, and such things as belong to women, and not gone out her way and calling to meddle in such things as are proper for men, whose minds are stronger, etc., she had kept her wits, and might have improved them usefully and honorably in the place God sent her. He brought her to Boston, and left her with her brother, one Mr. Yale, a merchant, to try what means might be had here for her. But no help could be had.

Quick-Score Answers

1. D	14. B	27. E	40. B
2. A	15. E	28. B	41. C
3. C	16. A	29. A	42. E
4. D	17. D	30. A	43. A
5. D	18. C	31. C	44. D
6. A	19. A	32. E	45. E
7. C	20. D	33. B	46. C
8. B	21. A	34. A	47. A
9. D	22. B	35. C	48. A
10. D	23. D	36. E	49. C
11. B	24. C	37. A	50. B
12. B	25. B	38. B	51. B
13. D	26. A	39. D	52. C

Computing Your Score

You can use the following worksheet to compute an approximate score on the practice test. Since it is difficult to be objective about your own writing and since you are not a trained ETS scorer or English teacher, you may wish to ask a friend who has already taken the test (and earned a score of 4 or 5) to score your three essays.

Recognize that your score can only be an approximation (at best), as you are scoring yourself against yourself. In the actual AP English Language and Composition Exam, you will be scored against every other student who takes the test as well.

Section I: Multiple-Choice Questions

	_____	number of correct answers
-	_____	.25 x number of wrong answers
=	_____	raw score
	_____	raw score
x	_____	1.25
=	_____	scaled score (out of a possible 67.5)

Section II: Essays

	_____	essay 1 (0–9)
	_____	essay 2 (0–9)
	_____	essay 3 (0–9)
x	_____	3.055
=	_____	scaled score (out of a possible 82.5)

Scaled Score

	_____	multiple-choice scaled score
+	_____	essay scaled score
=	_____	final scaled score (out of a possible 150)

AP Score Conversion Chart

Scaled Score	Likely AP Score
150–100	5
99–86	4
85–67	3
66–0	1 or 2

Answers and Explanations

1. **The correct answer is (D).** By using the word *prisonlike*, the narrator alludes to the constraints of poverty. The mother and her two children are free to leave the cellar anytime they wish, but in effect they can never leave, because they do not have anywhere to go or the means to support themselves. This realization gives the story its tragic dimension. There is no suggestion that the woman has in any way brought this fate upon herself or her children. As a result, choices (A) and (B) cannot be correct. The woman's case does not stand for the larger human condition, as it is caused by poverty and other social issues, so choice (C) is wrong. Finally, the story is literal rather than metaphorical: Melville is describing the horrible poverty he saw. Therefore, eliminate choice (E).

2. **The correct answer is (A).** A *simile* is a figure of speech that compares two unlike things. Similes use the words "like" or "as" to make the comparison. Here, Melville is comparing the warehouse keeper to a ghost. Eliminate choice (B), *allusion*, which is a reference to a well-known place, event, person, work of art, or other work of literature. Eliminate choice (C), *alliteration,* which is the repetition of initial consonant sounds in several words in a sentence or line of poetry. *Onomatopoeia* is the use of words to imitate the sounds they describe, such as *crack, hiss,* and *buzz.* Therefore, you can eliminate choice (D). *Parallelism* is matching words, phrases, or clauses to create logic. There are no parallel phrases here.

3. **The correct answer is (C).** The "deep tiers of cellars" can best be understood as a metaphor for a funeral vault. The woman and her children are so far gone that they cannot survive, no matter what help the narrator can get them. Choice (A) is wrong because it is a literal reading, not a metaphorical one. The same is true for choice (E). Choice (B) is an incorrect reading of the sentence. Choice (D) is not a precise reading of the sentence.

4. **The correct answer is (D).** The narrator describes the children as "shrunken things like children" to describe their appearance and convey their profound misery. They are children, yet they look so terrible that he describes them as *like* children. He does not dip into polemic, so choice (A) and choice (E) are wrong. Choice (B) is vague. They are children, so Choice (C) is wrong.

5. **The correct answer is (D).** *Point of view* is the position from which a story is told. In the *first-person point of view,* the narrator is one of the characters in the story. As a result, the narrator explains the events through his or her own eyes, using the pronouns *I* and *me.* The second line clearly shows the first-person point of view: "In going to our boarding house, I generally passed through a narrow street called Launcelott's-Hey, lined with dingy, prisonlike cotton warehouses." In the *third-person limited point of view,* the narrator tells the story through

the eyes of only one character, using the pronouns *he, she,* and *they.* This eliminates choice (A). In the *omniscient point of view,* the narrator is not a character in the story. Instead, the narrator looks through the eyes of all the characters. As a result, the narrator is all-knowing. Therefore, choices (B) and (E) are the same and both can be eliminated.

6. **The correct answer is (A).** Melville uses this point of view to help the reader feel closer to the narrator and therefore closer to the events of the story. The first-person point of view creates an intimacy absent from the other points of view. Therefore, you can eliminate choice (D). Choice (B) describes the omniscient point of view; choice (C) describes the third-person limited point of view. Therefore, neither can be correct. Since point of view rarely impacts the establishment of setting and theme, you can eliminate choice (E).

7. **The correct answer is (C).** From this excerpt, you can infer that Redburn is basically compassionate, decent, and caring. He is appalled by what he sees. Further, he suggests in the conclusion that we have a responsibility to those less fortunate than ourselves. He feels responsible for the woman's fate, choice (D), but he is not personally culpable. Therefore, choice (A) is wrong. There is no suggestion that he is anything other than a casual passerby, so you can eliminate choice (B). The religious allusion in the conclusion is not enough to support choice (E).

8. **The correct answer is (B).** An *analogy* is the rhetorical strategy that forms the basis of the following line: "Are we not like people sitting up with a corpse, and making merry in the house of the dead." He is comparing eyewitnesses to this social tragedy to mourners at a funeral. The metaphor is not extended, so eliminate choice (A); there is certainly no verbal *irony,* choice (E), or *verbal understatement,* choice (D). Choice (C) is wrong because there is no proof here.

9. **The correct answer is (D).** In the fourth paragraph, Melville makes an implicit comparison between the children and wild animals. This is shown by the phrase "crawled into the den." Eliminate choices (B) and (C) because those comparisons are explicit rather than implicit. There is no suggestion of evil, so you can eliminate choices (A) and (E).

10. **The correct answer is (D).** The final lines of the story suggest that we are enjoying ourselves while ignoring those who have nothing and will surely die. This is the opposite of choice (E). Since he is suggesting that we help those less fortunate, choices (A) and (C) are wrong. The misery he describes makes it plain that the situation will *not* be relatively easy to ameliorate. Therefore, you can cross out choice (B).

11. **The correct answer is (B).** The mood of this excerpt is best described as bleak and horrific, as he describes the extreme misery he sees. This is the opposite of choice (D), *hopeful.* His plea at the end shows that

choice (C), *resigned,* cannot be correct. He is trying to help but not be combative, choice (A). *Chilly,* choice (E), cannot be correct because he tries to intervene and muster support.

12. **The correct answer is (B).** The religious allusion at the end of the excerpt suggests that if we hope for our souls to be saved, we must care for each other. In the Biblical parable, Lazarus is a poor beggar whom a rich man refuses to help. When they die, Lazarus is taken to heaven and the rich man to hell. (Luke 16:19–31). Do not confuse this with a plea to the rich, choice (A). Melville suggests that *all* people must help. Choice (C) cannot be correct, given his plea for assistance. The same is true for choice (E). His plea is not religious in nature, only his allusion. Therefore, eliminate choice (D).

13. **The correct answer is (D).** The first paragraph of this passage serves to argue that economic equality can be achieved by following the speaker's plan. He does not attempt to define the abstract ideal of "work," choice (A); rather, he assumes that everyone knows what work is. He is not concerned with a common misconception among the wealthy, choice (B), whom he regards with contempt for their idleness. While he does compare and contrast social classes, choice (C), by implication, it is not his primary purpose here. Finally, he argues just the opposite of choice (E), that the wealthy deserve their lofty position.

14. **The correct answer is (B).** In the opening lines, the speaker is critical of the indolent upper classes. This is shown in the first two sentences, in his reference to "luxury and licentiousness." He does not mention whether or not workingmen are suited to their jobs, choice (A). While he does argue for "genuine and natural" pleasure, his primary purpose is not to criticize "unnatural pleasures and diversions." choice (C). This is subsumed in his specific criticism of the idle rich. He is in favor of essential trades, the opposite of choice (D), so that can be eliminated. Finally, we do not have contempt for trades, even though we may have elevated the aristocracy, choice (E). Remember that all parts of a choice must be correct for the choice to be correct.

15. **The correct answer is (E).** The phrase "any one of whom now consumes as much of the fruits of other men's labors as any two of the workingmen" refers to "the lazy and idle throng." Here is the complete sentence: "But suppose all those fellows who are not busied with unprofitable crafts, as well as all the lazy and idle throng, any one of whom now consumes as much of the fruits of other men's labors as any two of the workingmen, were all set to work and indeed to useful work."

16. **The correct answer is (A).** As used in the first paragraph, *licentiousness* most nearly means a disregard for morals. Choices (B) and (C) have very similar meanings, so they can be eliminated. Choice (D) would not fit with his fiery, critical tone toward the idle rich, nor would choice (E).

17. **The correct answer is (D).** The "unjust and ungrateful commonwealth" in the second paragraph refers to the current system of

government. The author argues that the current system of government is unfair, but his proposal will abolish inequalities and create a heaven on earth. Therefore, choice (E) cannot be correct because he is not (and would not) argue against himself. He is in favor of the common workingman, so choice (B) is wrong. While he does condemn "the vain and foolish upper classes," choice (C), they do not refer to the "commonwealth." Finally, there is no indication that the author is talking about America, choice (A). On the contrary, the rigid social structure and vast class of inherited wealthy, coupled with the old-fashioned style, suggests that the author is writing about England.

18. **The correct answer is (C).** In context, the phrase the "so-called gentlefolk" suggests the speaker's contempt for the idle, titled rich. His contempt is shown in the adjective "so-called." That the people are rich is shown in the word "gentlefolk." The speaker is being serious, not ironic, so you can eliminate choice (A). While he is aware of the sharp distinctions among social classes in his day, choice (B), the word "so-called" suggests condemnation. This tone would not curry favor with his social superiors, choice (D), or show his admiration for people who have succeeded in a cutthroat world, choice (E).

19. **The correct answer is (A).** In the second paragraph, the speaker is biased toward the workingman. He feels that the common working man is thrown on the trash heap after he can work no more. Therefore, choice (B) must be wrong because it is the opposite. He is biased *against* the commonwealth, the opposite of choice (C), and *against* banking goldsmiths, the opposite of choice (D). He is not against age and disease, choice (E); rather, he is biased against those who misuse workers who can no longer toil because of age and/or disease.

20. **The correct answer is (D).** The antecedent of the word "it" in the sentence is the *commonwealth*: "After it has misused the labor of their prime and after they are weighted down with age and disease and are in utter want, it forgets all their sleepless night and all the great benefits received at their hands and most ungratefully requites them with a most miserable death." You have to trace this back to the previous sentence.

21. **The correct answer is (A).** The phrase "Now is not this an unjust and ungrateful commonwealth?" is an example of an *inversion*. The uninverted phrase would read: "Now is this not..."

22. **The correct answer is (B).** The rhetorical questions in the last paragraph serve most directly to built up to an angry and resolute climax. This is shown in the increasing urgency of his words, especially his vivid nouns ("brawls, seditions, murders, treasons..."). Choice (A) is wrong because it is the exact opposite. He is being very serious, not at all ironic, so choice (C) cannot be correct. He is not commenting on his previous assertions, choice (D), but rather summing them up. Finally, this passage does not emphasize the difference between appearance and reality but rather attacks reality for its inhumanity.

23. The correct answer is (D). The tone of the last paragraph is best described as *passionate and critical* as the speaker drives home his point. This is the opposite of choice (A), *calm and dispassionate*, and choice (B), *relaxed and self-assured*. He is very definite, not at all tentative, choice (C). Finally, *violent,* choice (E), is too strong a description of his tone.

24. The correct answer is (C). The phrase "In Utopia all greed for money was entirely removed with the use of money" is a *paradox* because it is a seeming contradiction. There is nothing ironic about it, so you can eliminate Choices (A), *dramatic irony*, and E, *verbal irony*. It is parallel, but choice (C) is more precise. Finally, there is no comparison here, so there cannot be a *metaphor,* choice (D).

25. The correct answer is (B). The author would agree with the phrase "Money is the root of all evil" because he is arguing against the necessity of using money. Instead, he argues that economic inequality can be solved through a drastic restructuring of society.

26. The correct answer is (A). The metaphor "What a crop of crimes was then pulled up by the roots" serves to make the author's abstract concept more specific and recognizable to his audience. Drawing a comparison from agriculture is familiar to nearly everyone. His main point is *not* concerned with criminal activity, so choices (B) and (C) are wrong. He is neither refuting his critics, choice (D), nor comparing and contrasting his plan to his opponent's plan, choice (E), in this particular place.

27. The correct answer is (E). The author's style is best described as *formal and elevated*. This is shown in his long sentences, elevated diction, and formal (if fiery) tone.

28. The correct answer is (B). The best title for this except is *Utopia* because the author clearly believes that he can create a heaven on earth through his economic plans. He is describing an imaginary society in which all citizens live dignified, meaningful, and secure lives.

29. The correct answer is (A). The first sentence is distinguished by parallel prepositional phrases. Each phrase begins with the preposition "by." Here are the phrases isolated:

- by the nearness of my mother sitting all day long at her sewing machine
- by the clacking of the treadle against the linoleum floor
- by the patient twist of her right shoulder ...

30. The correct answer is (A). You can infer from the first paragraph that the speaker's mother is devoted to her family. This is shown in the following phrase: "I realized it was ourselves she kept stitched together." He is very proud of her efforts and more than a little in awe of her capacity for work and determination to provide a better life for her children. As a result, you can eliminate choice (C). Since the mother makes dinner for her husband and children every night, you know that the family has remained intact. Therefore, choice (E) cannot be right. Finally, there is not enough evidence in the passage to infer that the speaker's mother is very proud of her son, choice (D), although it is clear that he is proud of *her*.

31. **The correct answer is (C).** The lengthy opening sentence serves to capture the rhythm of the mother's constant work. This stylistic technique is a brilliant marrying of form and function. The *length* of the sentence in no way shows the writer's understanding and compassion, so choice (A) is wrong. Rather, it is the *content* that reveals his attitude. The tone is vigorous rather than reflective and contemplative, so choice (B) cannot be correct. There is no change in direction, so choice (D) is not accurate. Finally, appearance *is* reality here—the mother works as hard as she seems to—so choice (E) cannot be correct.

32. **The correct answer is (E).** The first paragraph contains a *metaphor:* The kitchen was her life. There is neither irony nor any personification.

33. **The correct answer is (B).** The kitchen becomes a symbol of the mother's strength. Although the family is certainly poor, the kitchen does not reflect any deprivation. Therefore, eliminate choice (A). *The kitchen does not have anything to do with grossly unfair social conditions,* choice (C); the mother seems quite content with her role in life. Therefore, you can eliminate choice (D). While the mother works very hard, there is neither oppression nor pain, so choice (E) is wrong. On the contrary, the family seems content, given their difficult economic conditions.

34. **The correct answer is (A).** The images in this passage combine to form an impression of constant struggle and toil. The mother toils too hard to take great joy in work and family, so choice (B) is wrong. There is no hint of *suspicion and danger,* choice (C); *isolation and fear,* choice (D); or the *resentment,* choice (E). On the contrary, the author is in awe of his mother's organizational abilities and capacity for work.

35. **The correct answer is (C).** You can infer from this passage that Yiddish must be a *language*. If she reads a Yiddish (news)paper, the (news)paper must be in a foreign language.

36. **The correct answer is (E).** The narrator uses *dialect* to more fully describe his mother and his world. We see how the customers speak and get a flavor for the world of Jewish immigrants. Be careful with choice (A): even though the mother could not read English, that does not suggest that the narrator had any difficulty communicating with her. Rather, we know from the passage that she spoke English. Since everyone speaks the same dialect, the author is not comparing and contrasting his mother to her customers, choice (B). Since he wants to teach his mother to read, he clearly does not want to encourage her to use Yiddish speech patterns, choice (C). The tone of the passage is worshipful, so choice (D) cannot be correct.

37. **The correct answer is (A).** This selection is told from the first-person point of view, in which the narrator is a participant in the story.

38. **The correct answer is (B).** The author's attitude toward his mother is best described as *admiring*. This is shown in the following sentence: "Year by year, as I began to take in her fantastic capacity for labor and her anxious zeal, I realized it was ourselves she kept stitched together."

39. **The correct answer is (D).** The author's footnote refers to the historical milieu. Choice (C) is the second-best choice, but choice (D) is more precise. He is not arguing *the need to work hard,* choice (B), or the *need for social reforms,* choice (E). We cannot infer from the footnote that the fire explains why the mother no longer works outside the home. She might just as easily prefer to work at home so she can watch her children.

40. **The correct answer is (B).** You can infer from the last sentence that the writer's mother is stoical about any suffering she may experience. She does not complain about the scar. Since she works so hard, choice (A) is a stretch. The neutral tone belies choice (C). While she was lucky not to have been killed in the fire, this cannot be inferred from the last sentence, so choice (D) is wrong. Choice (E) reflects an overly polemical reading.

41. **The correct answer is (C).** The speaker's central rhetorical strategy in this passage can best be described as providing specific examples to celebrate his mother's hard work, determination, and forbearance. The author describes his mother's hard work to celebrate her life. The story is not an extended metaphor, although she may be symbolic of a generation of immigrant women. Since both parts of the response are not correct, you can eliminate choice (A). He is not arguing that women's lot has improved in the twenty-first century—indeed, the present is not mentioned at all. Therefore, choice (B) is wrong. He is telling a story, not explaining pros and cons, so you can cross off choice (D). In the same vein, he is not arguing any point, much less that no one should have to labor as hard as his mother did. Therefore, choice (E) is wrong.

42. **The correct answer is (E).** The first paragraph contains both *personification* and *similes*. The writer personifies the earth and sky as having human traits. In addition, he uses a simile when he says "He treats his mother, the earth, and his brothers, the sky, *as things to be bought,* plundered, sold *like sheep or bright beads.*" The similes are in italics.

43. **The correct answer is (A).** The statement "The earth is not his brother but his enemy, and when he has conquered it, he moves on" adds to the development of the passage by contrasting the white and Native American view of the land. The speaker never aggressively insults the white man, choice (B). Rather, he uses irony to be subtle. As a result, you can eliminate choice (D) as well. Neither does he show that the Native Americans will not be conquered by the whites, choice (C). This is not a declaration of war. Choice (E) is meaningless.

44. **The correct answer is (D).** The speaker is most likely a Native American. This is directly revealed in the repeated ironic sentence: "But perhaps because I am a savage and do not understand."

45. **The correct answer is (E).** The poet uses *repetition, parallelism,* and *alliteration* in the last paragraph. The repetition is shown in the sentence: "But perhaps because I am a savage and do not understand." This is repeated twice, with slight variation. We see parallelism in the first two sentences: "...no quiet place" and " No place to hear..." Alliteration is shown in following the sentence: "The Indian prefers the soft sound of the wind darting over the face of a pond, and the smell of the wind itself, cleansed by rain or scented with the pine cone." We see repeated "*s*'s" in the words *soft, sound, smell,* and *scented.*

46. **The correct answer is (C).** This passage is primarily developed by comparison and contrast. The author shows how the Native Americans and the whites are different, which is *contrast.* Do not confuse this with *comparison,* choice (B), which shows how things are the same. Since there is no comparison, we cannot have an *extended metaphor,* choice (A).

47. **The correct answer is (A).** The rhetorical purpose of paragraphs 2 and 3 can best be described as *argumentative.* The writer is arguing that the white man does not understand or appreciate nature. The passage is colloquial rather than academic, choice (B), specific rather than theoretical, choice (E). He is explaining, choice (C), only to further his argument. The same is true of choice (D), *narrative.*

48. **The correct answer is (A).** The speaker creates irony through the repetition in the second and third paragraphs. He is mocking the white man's perception of the Native American as a "savage." He twists the white man's perception by showing that the Native American is actually very attuned to nature, while the white man is not.

49. **The correct answer is (C).** "I am a red man and do not understand" is ironic because the speaker claims that he is only a savage, incapable of understanding what is important, yet his argument suggests that the whites do not understand what matters. Choice (A) is not ironic since it does not reverse the reader's expectations. The same is true of choice (D). In the same way, choice (E) is straightforward rather than a reversal of the reader's stereotype: the writer claims that he is only a savage, but he is far closer to nature than the whites are. Finally, the speaker directly states that only the "red men" are savages, not the whites. This eliminates choice (B).

50. **The correct answer is (B).** The images in the last paragraph combine to create an impression of joy of the wilderness. He does not show *conflict and misunderstanding,* choice (A); *arrogant* superiority, choice (C); or *fear and hostility,* choice (D). Choice (E) does not make sense in context.

51. The correct answer is (B). The author's style in this passage is marked by *figurative language* and *imagery*. This is shown in his use of personification and similes. Choice (A) is wrong because he uses irony but not parody. Choice (C) is wrong because he uses personification but not allusions. Choice (D) is wrong because there are no symbols in this passage. Choice (E) is wrong because he has nothing to regret or feel sorrow for, since his people have the upper hand in appreciating nature.

52. The correct answer is (C). The author's purpose is to inform the whites that the land is sacred to persuade them to keep it sacred. Choice (A) is wrong because there is no warning here, nor does he plea for the white man's understanding, choice (B). Choice (D) is close, but he is not persuading. Rather, he accepts that the white man cannot or will not change. Choice (E) is wrong because he is not telling a story about the glory of nature.

Question 1:

A well-written essay will analyze how the writer uses diction, figures of speech, and sensory images to convey the story's mood and tone. Students should first identify the mood as creepy, spooky, or mysterious.

- Students can back up their assertion with phrases such as "festooned with cobwebs and besprinkled with antique dust."
- Figures of speech include the simile "....with a visage as faded as her dress." This adds to the mysterious mood.
- Sensory images appeal to touch (high and dusty plate within a tarnished gilt frame) and sight (dim, old-fashioned chamber), for example.

Question 2:

A well-written essay should analyze how the writer uses rhetorical strategies and other stylistic devices to convey the connection between God and humanity. The writer sees God's hand in everything, directing all human endeavor. This is shown in the writer's use of anecdote, especially the story of John Howland. It is also shown in word choice, such as "mighty storm" to show God's power over humankind. Students should be especially careful to leave off their own opinions in their analysis.

Question 3:

A well-written essay should defend, challenge, or qualify the speaker's view of women and education. It is apparent that the speaker's view of women is laughable, as he attributes the woman's mental collapse to too much learning. Clearly, he feels that women are unfit for the rigors of learning, especially reading and writing.

PRACTICE TEST 4

ENGLISH LANGUAGE AND COMPOSITION

SECTION 1

Time—1 hour

> **Directions:** This section contains selections from two passages of prose and two poems with questions on their style, content, form, and purpose. Read each selection closely and carefully. Then choose the best answer from the five choices.

Questions 1–14. Read the selection carefully before you mark your answers.

The passage below is from a speech that Sojourner Truth delivered at the women's rights convention in Akron, Ohio, in 1851.

Well, children, where there is so much racket there must be something out of kilter. I think that 'twixt the Negroes of the South and the women at the North, all talking about rights, the white men will be in a fix pretty soon. But what's all this here talking about?

That man over there says that women need to be helped into carriages, and lifted over ditches, and to have the best place everywhere. Nobody ever helps me into carriages, or over mud-puddles, or gives me any best place! And ain't I a woman? Look at me! Look at my arm! I have ploughed and planted, and gathered into barns, and no man could head me! And ain't I a woman? I could work as much and eat as much as a man—when I could get it—and bear the lash as well! And ain't I a woman? I have borne thirteen children, and see them all sold off to slavery, and when I cried out with my mother's grief, none but Jesus heard me! And ain't I a woman?

Then they talk about this thing in the head; what's that they call it? ["Intellect" someone whispers.] That's it, honey. What's that got to do with women's rights or Negro's rights? If my cup won't hold but a pint, and yours holds a quart, wouldn't you be mean not to let me have my little half-measure full?...

If the first woman God ever made was strong enough to turn the world upside down all alone, these women together ought to be able to turn it back, and get it right side up again! And now they is asking to do it, the men better let them.

Obliged to you for hearing me, and now old Sojourner ain't got nothing more to say.

1. By directly addressing the members of the audience as "children," Sojourner suggests that
   - (A) they are acting very immaturely.
   - (B) we are all equal in God's eyes.
   - (C) she is morally and intellectually superior to the members of her audience.
   - (D) the members of the audience should be ashamed of the way they are acting.
   - (E) the delegates at the assembly are young, but she is elderly and thus wiser.

2. As used in the first sentence, the idiom "something out of kilter" means that
   - (A) something is evil.
   - (B) something is dangerous.
   - (C) people are foolish.
   - (D) something is mysterious.
   - (E) something is wrong.

3. "Women being helped into carriages and lifted over ditches" can be understood
   - (A) in both a literal and metaphorical way.
   - (B) as an insult to women who do not work.
   - (C) as an acknowledgment of the wide social gulf between Sojourner Truth and wealthy white women.
   - (D) as an awareness of the social mores of the time.
   - (E) as Sojourner Truth's rage at the maltreatment she has received as a slave and as a woman.

4. "Look at my arm" suggests
   - (A) a threat.
   - (B) she has been injured and bears the scars.
   - (C) she is as strong as any man.
   - (D) the speaker's physical strength represents her psychological strength.
   - (E) she is physically superior to most men.

5. What rhetorical strategy or strategies does the speaker use with the phrase "And ain't I a woman?"

    I.   Hyperbole

    II.   Repetition

    III   Rhetorical questions

    (A)   I only

    (B)   I and II

    (C)   II and III

    (D)   II only

    (E)   I and III

6. The repeated refrain "And ain't I a woman?" serves to

    (A)   covey her ironic stance.

    (B)   stress the equality of *all* women while pointing out inequalities.

    (C)   alert the reader to the specific details to follow.

    (D)   intimidate the reader with the harsh question.

    (E)   provide evidence that the speaker is bitter at the treatment she has received.

7. The speaker is critical of

    (A)   upper-class women of leisure.

    (B)   men.

    (C)   the possibility that real social change can ever be effected.

    (D)   religion.

    (E)   male claims that women are the "weaker sex."

8. The statement "That's it, honey" serves most directly to

    (A)   provide an ironic counterpoint to her previous comments.

    (B)   signal the hopeless mood.

    (C)   remind the audience that the speaker is a woman.

    (D)   distance the audience from the speaker.

    (E)   draw the audience closer to the speaker.

9. The phrase "If the first woman God ever made was strong enough to turn the world upside down all alone…" is

    (A)   an allusion.

    (B)   alliteration.

    (C)   assonance.

    (D)   apostrophe.

    (E)   an aphorism.

10. The tone of this speech is best described as
    - (A) dignified.
    - (B) bitter.
    - (C) ironic.
    - (D) resigned.
    - (E) horrified.

11. What rhetorical device does Sojourner Truth use to make her closing more powerful?
    - (A) A direct command
    - (B) An allusion to a previous speech
    - (C) Parallelism
    - (D) Nonstandard usage, including "ain't" and the double negative "ain't got nothing"
    - (E) Sensory images

12. The speaker's rhetorical strategy in this speech is best described as
    - (A) telling the story of her life to illustrate the plight of all women.
    - (B) agreeing with the prevailing viewpoints to disarm her opponents.
    - (C) citing authorities and outside evidence to buttress her point.
    - (D) implying her direct experience.
    - (E) stating the point that was made and proving through examples that it is true.

13. The speaker's colloquial language and nonstandard usage serve to
    - (A) undercut her effectiveness as an expert.
    - (B) convey her sincerity and practical experience.
    - (C) widen the gulf between the educated and uneducated members of the audience.
    - (D) provide a humorous contrast to the "intellect" the speakers link to women's rights.
    - (E) reinforce the prevailing opinion.

14. Sojourner Truth uses rhetorical devices and persuasive techniques to prove that
    - (A) some women, but not all, can take up the mantle of autonomy.
    - (B) women are vastly superior to men.
    - (C) slavery must be abolished throughout the union.
    - (D) women will get the vote, regardless of what men say or do.
    - (E) women are as capable as men and deserve equal rights.

Questions 15–27. Read the following selection carefully before you mark your answers.

The passage below is from Captain John Smith's 1607 report to England concerning his exploration of America.

The winter [of 1607] approaching, the rivers became so covered with swans, geese, ducks, and cranes, that we daily feasted on good bread, Virginia peas, pumpkins, puchamins, fish, fowl, and diverse sorts of wild beasts as fat as we could eat them, so that none of our tuftaffety humorists desired to go to England.

But our comedies never endured long without a tragedy; some idle exceptions being muttered against Captain Smith for not discovering the head of the Chickahamania River, and vexed by the Council to be too slow in so worthy an attempt. The next voyage he proceeded so far that which much labor by cutting of trees asunder he made his passage; but when his barge could pass no farther, he left her in a broad bay out of danger of shot, commanding none should go ashore till his return: himself with two English and two savages went up higher in a canoe, but he was not long absent but his men went ashore, whose want of government gave both occasion and opportunity to the savages to surprise one George Cassen, whom they slew, and much failed not to have cut off the boat and all the rest.

Smith, little dreaming of that accident, being got to the marshes at the river's head, twenty miles in the desert, had his two men slain (as is supposed) sleeping by the canoe, whilst himself by fowling sought them victual; who, finding he was beset with two hundred savages, two of them he slew, still defending himself with the aid of a savage his guide, whom he bound to his arm with garters and used him as a buckler; yet he was shot in the thigh a little and had many arrows that stuck in his clothes but no great hurt, till at last they took him prisoner.

15. The first paragraph serves to
    (A) analyze the issue of food.
    (B) develop an argument by using a personal narrative.
    (C) provide specific examples to illustrate an abstract concept.
    (D) reflect on the author's good fortune in the New World.
    (E) convince people in England that Americans were not, in fact, starving.

16. In context, the line "so that none of our tuftaffety humorists desired to go to England" most nearly refers to
    (A) people who have come to America and then returned home.
    (B) colonists who stubbornly continue to live as they had in England.
    (C) misanthropic comedians whose jokes are at the expense of other's feelings.
    (D) critical, fashionable men who enjoyed living well.
    (E) well-fed colonists who nonetheless eat more than their fair share.

17. Which of the following rhetorical strategies does the writer use in this passage?

    I.   Hyperbole

    II.   Personification

    III. Allusions

    (A)   I only

    (B)   I and II

    (C)   I and III

    (D)   II only

    (E)   I, II, and III

18. What purpose does the third paragraph serve?

    (A)   It persuades people that the Native Americans were savages.

    (B)   It presents a subtle argument that Smith should be given more responsibility.

    (C)   It convinces readers that the New World is exciting and offers great adventures.

    (D)   It shows that Smith isn't quite as brave as he implies.

    (E)   It provides a specific example of the opening generality.

19. From what point of view is this account told?

    (A)   First person

    (B)   Omniscient

    (C)   Limited

    (D)   Analytical

    (E)   Third person

20. Smith selected this point of view to

    (A)   more closely identify with the events he describes.

    (B)   show the events from the widest possible viewpoint.

    (C)   present his own personal feelings about the subject.

    (D)   distance himself from his work to make it seem less subjective.

    (E)   make his work seem as analytical as possible.

21. Smith's adventures with the Native Americans are

    (A)   symbolic because they convey the British feeling of superiority.

    (B)   clearly an example of understatement.

    (C)   metaphorical because they represent all the encounters white men had with Native Americans.

    (D)   archetypal because they reveal the heroism of the Native American.

    (E)   evidence of the narrator's close identification with his new land.

22. As used in this passage, "victual" most nearly means
    (A) adventure.
    (B) a means of escape.
    (C) food.
    (D) water.
    (E) shelter.

23. Smith offers his readers
    (A) fame, fortune, and adventure.
    (B) a certain death.
    (C) ample food but little adventure.
    (D) a fair and good-humored leader.
    (E) a chance for literary immortality.

24. You can infer from Smith's rhetoric that his audience was
    (A) rich men and women.
    (B) Native Americans.
    (C) young women who were seeking husbands.
    (D) older men with well-established trades.
    (E) young men.

25. It is likely that
    (A) everything happened just as Smith described it.
    (B) Smith was not present at the events he described.
    (C) few people came to the New World after reading Smith's account of his adventures.
    (D) Smith greatly embellished his adventures.
    (E) Smith ended up getting killed by the Native Americans.

26. The writer's voice in this passage is best described as
    (A) whining.
    (B) vitriolic.
    (C) heroic and self-confident, even cocky.
    (D) resentful.
    (E) arrogant.

27. You can infer from Smith's rhetorical strategies that his main purpose in this passage was to
    (A) convince the Native Americans that the colonists were there to stay.
    (B) attract settlers to the New World.
    (C) attract money to the New World.
    (D) make peace with the Native Americans.
    (E) absolve himself from blame for the deaths of the men under his command.

Questions 28–41. Read the selection carefully before you mark your answers.

It was only when the whole ham was spoiled that it came into the department of Elzbieta. Cut up by the two-thousand-revolutions-a-minute flyers, and mixed with half a ton of other meat, no odor that was ever in a ham could make any difference. There was never the least attention paid to what was cut up for sausage; there would come all the way back from Europe old sausage that had been rejected, and that was moldy and white—it would be dosed with borax and glycerine, and dumped into the hoppers, and made over again for home consumption. There would be meat that had tumbled out on the floor, in the dirt and sawdust, where the workers had tramped and spit uncounted billions of consumption germs. There would be meat stored in great piles in rooms; and the water from leaky roofs would drip over it, and thousands of rats would race about on it. It was too dark in these storage places to see well, but a man could run his hand over these piles of meat and sweep off handfuls of the dried dung of rats. These rats were nuisances, and the packers would put poisoned bread out for them; they would die, and then rats, bread, and meat would go into the hoppers together. This is no fairy tale and no joke; the meat would be shoveled into carts, and the man who did the shoveling would not trouble to lift out a rat even when he saw one—there were things that went into sausage in comparison with which a poisoned rat was a tidbit. There was no place for the men to wash their hands before they ate dinner, and so they made a practice of washing them in the water that was to be ladled into the sausage...All of the sausage came out of the same bowl, but when they came to wrap it they would stamp some of it "special," and for this they would charge two cents more a pound.

28. The phrase "no odor that was ever in a ham could make any difference" is best described as
    (A) bitter.
    (B) sympathetic.
    (C) sarcastic.
    (D) vicious.
    (E) malicious.

29. For what purpose does the writer use the dash in this sentence: "...and that was moldy and white—it would be dosed with borax and glycerine, and dumped into the hoppers, and made over again for home consumption"?
    (A) To indicate cause and effect
    (B) To convey an ironic tone
    (C) To show a sudden change of thought
    (D) For emphasis
    (E) To undercut the opposition

30. The presentation of material in this selection is characterized by
    (A) generalizations followed by specific examples.
    (B) hard-hitting rebuttals of generally accepted public opinions.
    (C) the chronological analysis of a process.
    (D) analysis followed by opinions.
    (E) scientific data contradicted by personal observations.

31. The author's style in this passage is characterized by
    (A) sensory images.
    (B) literary allusions.
    (C) specific metaphors.
    (D) elegant figures of speech.
    (E) the juxtaposition of appearance and reality.

32. You can conclude that the author is primarily concerned with
    (A) creating a lyrical writing style.
    (B) driving home his point.
    (C) disarming his opponents.
    (D) describing what he has seen.
    (E) convincing people to become vegetarians.

33. The images in this selection combine to form an impression of
    (A) filth and deception.
    (B) desperation.
    (C) lack of sanitation.
    (D) modern manufacturing marvels.
    (E) power.

34. The author uses the phrase "This is no fairy tale and no joke" to
    (A) avoid being sued by the meat-packing industry.
    (B) lull the reader into a false set of expectations.
    (C) reinforce the truth of his narrative.
    (D) link his ideas with the horrors of make-believe.
    (E) lead into the fairy tale that follows.

35. As used in this passage, *consumptive* most nearly means
    (A) tuberculosis.
    (B) to eat.
    (C) bacteria.
    (D) filthy.
    (E) foreign.

36. From which point of view is this passage narrated?
    - (A) Second person
    - (B) Systematic
    - (C) First person
    - (D) Omniscient
    - (E) Scientific

37. The author selected this point of view to
    - (A) get closer to the subject.
    - (B) achieve a much-needed distance from the horror he describes.
    - (C) afford him the widest possible vantage point.
    - (D) identify with the people working in the meat-packing plant.
    - (E) recount events in a dispassionate manner.

38. In this sentence, the author uses which rhetorical technique(s)? "there were things that went into sausage in comparison with which a poisoned rat was a tidbit."
    - I. Irony
    - II. Personification
    - III. Allusion
    - (A) I only
    - (B) II only
    - (C) III only
    - (D) I and II
    - (E) I and III

39. The long sentences in this passage combine to suggest that
    - (A) the process of making sausage is long and difficult.
    - (B) the process of making sausage is continuous, as workers toil around the clock.
    - (C) the meatpackers regret the necessity of selling adulterated meats.
    - (D) the deception will continue for a long time.
    - (E) the meatpackers have gone to great lengths to deceive the public.

40. The tone of this passage is best described as
    - (A) neutral.
    - (B) hostile.
    - (C) venomous.
    - (D) outraged.
    - (E) malicious.

41. The rhetorical purpose of this selection is
    (A) analytical.
    (B) expository.
    (C) descriptive.
    (D) narrative.
    (E) persuasive.

Questions 42–52. Read the following selection carefully before you mark your answers.

Meanwhile, since 1862, Miss Dickinson had been writing poems, although there were very few of her friends who knew it...She wrote on sheets of notepaper, which she sewed together, rolling and tying the bundles with a thread or ribbon and tucking them away the drawers of her bureau; although sometimes the back of an envelope served her as well, or a scrap of the *Springfield Republican*. But, casual in this, she was anything but casual—she was a cunning workman—in her composition.

Poetry was her solitaire and, so to speak, her journal, for like Thoreau in Concord, she watched the motions of her mind, recording its ebbs and flows and the gleams that shot through it; and she labored over her phrases to make them right. Were they all her own? Were there echoes in them, or something of the conventional, the rhetorical, the fat? Were they clear, were they exact, were they compact? She liked the common hymn meters, and the meters of nursery jingles, which had been deeply ingrained in her mind as a child, and she seemed to take a rebellious joy in violating all their rules, fulfilling the traditional patterns while she broke them. She was always experimenting with her rhymes and her rhythms, sometimes adding extra syllables to break up their monotony, sometimes deliberately twisting a rhyme, as Emerson did, for the sake of harshness, to escape the mellifluous effect of conventional poems. Many of her pieces were like parodies of hymns, whose gentle glow in her mind had become heat lightning.

For Emily Dickinson's light was quick. It was sudden, sharp and evanescent, and this light was the dry light that was closest to the fire.

42. In the last sentence of paragraph 1, the writer sets off the clause *she was a cunning workman* with dashes to
    (A) show a sudden change in thought.
    (B) vary his sentence structure to create reader interest.
    (C) suggest that Dickinson was devious in her art.
    (D) make this clause stand out by contrast.
    (E) create irony.

43. Which of the following rhetorical technique(s) is evident in this sentence: "But, casual in this, she was anything but casual—she was a cunning workman—in her composition."
    I.   Apostrophe
    II.   Alliteration
    III. Allusion
    (A) I only
    (B) II only
    (C) III only
    (D) I and II
    (E) I and III

44. The phrase "Poetry was her solitaire" is
    (A) an allusion to a famous essay.
    (B) a simile.
    (C) a pun.
    (D) alliteration.
    (E) hyperbole.

45. The phrase "Poetry was her solitaire" adds to the development of the passage by
    (A) signaling a new point in his argument.
    (B) indicating that Dickinson had a rich life outside of her craft.
    (C) arguing that everyone needs to have an outlet besides work.
    (D) showing both Dickinson's devotion to her craft and her isolated lifestyle.
    (E) contrasting Dickinson's life to her art.

46. In the second paragraph, the writer uses which of the following elements?
    I.   Rhetorical questions
    II.   Metaphors
    III   Alliteration
    (A) I only
    (B) II only
    (C) III only
    (D) I and II
    (E) I, II, and III

47. What does "fat" mean, as used in this sentence: "Were there echoes in them, or something of the conventional, the rhetorical, the fat?"
    (A) Exaggeration
    (B) Abundance
    (C) Unnecessary embellishment
    (D) Luxurious imagery
    (E) Lush verbiage

48. The passage includes all the following rhetorical strategies and literary elements EXCEPT

    (A)   imaginative figures of speech.

    (B)   references to the rhythms in Dickinson's poems.

    (C)   an appreciation of Dickinson's poetic achievement.

    (D)   emphasis on Dickinson's knowledge of poetic techniques.

    (E)   the influence of contemporary poets on Dickinson's work.

49. The author's style in this passage is best described as

    (A)   highly descriptive, marked by vivid figures of speech.

    (B)   very abstract.

    (C)   metaphorical.

    (D)   analytical.

    (E)   dry but witty.

50. From this essay, Emily Dickinson emerges as

    (A)   disrespectful of religion and poetic convention.

    (B)   a conventional nineteenth-century poet.

    (C)   grasping for an individual style but never quite finding it.

    (D)   a literary maverick.

    (E)   a lonely recluse who never received the fame she deserved.

51. What does the writer mean in the last paragraph when he says that "...Emily Dickinson's light was quick. It was sudden, sharp and evanescent, and this light was the dry light that was closest to the fire"?

    (A)   There is a thin line between genius and madness.

    (B)   Poets of Dickinson's temperament run the risk of self-destruction.

    (C)   You must push yourself to the limit to create true, lasting art.

    (D)   Creativity is tragically brief and ephemeral.

    (E)   Dickinson had a short, disastrous life.

52. The narrative style of this passage is most accurately characterized as

    (A)   richly ornate.

    (B)   blunt and to-the-point.

    (C)   complex and confusing.

    (D)   superficial.

    (E)   direct and unadorned.

ENGLISH LANGUAGE AND COMPOSITION

SECTION II

Time—2 hours

Question 1:

Suggested Time: 40 minutes. Your response will count for one third of your total score on the essay portion of the exam.

> **Directions: Read the following essay carefully. Then write an essay in which you analyze how the writer uses rhetorical strategies and other stylistic devices to convey his views of the role of nature in our lives.**

Nature is a setting that fits equally well a comic or mourning piece. In good health, the air is a cordial of incredible virtue. Crossing a bare common, in snow puddles, at twilight, under a clouded sky, without having in my thoughts any occurrence of special good fortune, I have enjoyed a perfect exhilaration. I am glad to the brink of fear. In the woods, too, a man casts off his years, as the snake his slough, and at what period so ever of is always a child. In the woods is perpetual youth. Within these plantations of God, a decorum and sanctity reign, a perennial festival is dressed, and the guest sees not how he should tire of them in a thousand years. In the woods, we return to reason and faith. There I feel that nothing can befall me in life—no disgrace, no calamity (leaving me my eyes), which nature cannot repair. Standing on the bare ground—my head bathed by the blithe air and uplifted into infinite space— all mean egotism vanishes. I become a transparent eyeball; I am nothing: I see all; the currents of the Universal Being circulate through me: I am part or parcel of God. The name of the nearest friend sounds then foreign and accidental: to be brothers, to be acquaintances, master or servant, is then a trifle and a disturbance. I am the lover of uncontained and immortal beauty. In the wilderness, I find something more dear and connate than in the streets or villages. In the tranquil landscape, and especially in the distant line of the horizon, man beholds something as beautiful as his own nature.

Question 2:

Suggested Time: 40 minutes. Your response will count for one third of your total score on the essay portion of the exam.

> **Directions: Read the following two passages about Robinson Crusoe. Then write an essay in which you analyze how the distinctive style of each passage reveals its writer's purpose.**

Passage 1

This passage is part of Daniel Defoe's novel Robinson Crusoe, which describes the fictionalized adventures of a man shipwrecked on a far-off island.

September 30, 1659.   —I, poor miserable Robinson Crusoe, being shipwrecked, during a dreadful storm, in the offing, came on shore on this dismal unfortunate island, which I called the Island of Despair, all the rest of the ship's company being drowned, and myself almost dead.

All the rest of that day I spent in afflicting myself at the dismal circumstances I was brought to, viz., I had neither food, house, clothes, weapons, nor any place to fly to; and in despair of any relief, saw nothing but death before me; either that I should be devoured in wild beasts, murdered by savages, or starved to death for want of food. At the approach of night, I slept in a tree for fear of wild creatures, but slept soundly, though it rained all night...

I now began to consider seriously my condition, and the circumstances I was reduced to; and I drew up the state of my affairs in writing; not so much as to leave them to any that were to come after me, for I was like to have but few heirs, as to deliver my thoughts from daily pouring upon them, and afflicting my mind. And as my reason began now to master my despondency, I began to comfort myself as well as I could, and set the good against the evil, that I might have something to distinguish my case from the worse; and I stated it very impartially, like debtor and creditor, the comforts I enjoyed against the miseries I suffered.

Passage 2

This passage describes the writer's meeting with the model for Robinson Crusoe, Alexander Selkirk.

When I first saw him, I thought, if I had not been led into his character and story, I could have discerned that he had been much separated from company from his aspect and gesture; there was a strong but cheerful seriousness in his look, and a certain disregard to the ordinary things about him, as if he had been sunk in thought. When the ship which brought him off the island came in, he received them with the greatest indifference, with relation to the prospect of going off with them, but with great satisfaction in an opportunity to refresh and help them. The man frequently bewailed his return to the world which could not, he said, with all its enjoyments, restore him to the tranquillity of his solitude. Though I had frequently conversed with him, after a few months' absence he met me on the street, and though he spoke to me, I could not recollect that I had seen him; familiar converse in this town had taken off the loneliness of his aspect, and quite altered the air of his face.

This plain man's story is a memorable example, that he is happiest who confines his warmth to natural necessities; and he that goes further in his desires increases his wants in proportion to his acquisitions. *I am now worth eight hundred pounds, but shall never be as happy as when I was not worth a farthing.*

Question 3:

Suggested Time: 40 minutes. Your response will count for one third of your total score on the essay portion of the exam.

Directions: Read the following essay carefully. Then write an essay in which you identify the writer's views on love. Then agree, disagree, or qualify her opinion.

No girl should fall in love till the offer is actually made. The maxim is just. I will even extend and confirm it: No young lady should fall in love till the offer has been made, accepted, and the marriage ceremony performed, and the first half year of wedded life has passed away. A woman may then begin to love, but with great precaution, very coolly, very moderately, very rationally. If she ever loves so much that a harsh word or a cold look cuts her to the heart she is a fool. If she ever loves so much that her husband's will is her law, and that she has got into the habit of watching his looks in order that she may anticipate his wishes, she will soon be a neglected fool.

Quick-Score Answers

1. B	14. E	27. B	40. D
2. E	15. E	28. C	41. E
3. A	16. D	29. D	42. D
4. D	17. A	30. C	43. B
5. C	18. C	31. A	44. C
6. B	19. E	32. B	45. D
7. E	20. D	33. A	46. E
8. E	21. A	34. C	47. C
9. A	22. C	35. A	48. E
10. A	23. A	36. D	49. A
11. D	24. E	37. C	50. D
12. E	25. D	38. A	51. B
13. B	26. C	39. B	52. A

Computing Your Score

You can use the following worksheet to compute an approximate score on the practice test. Since it is difficult to be objective about your own writing and since you are not a trained ETS scorer or English teacher, you may wish to ask a friend who has already taken the test (and earned a score of 4 or 5) to score your three essays.

Recognize that your score can only be an approximation (at best), as you are scoring yourself against yourself. In the actual AP English Language and Composition Exam, you will be scored against every other student who takes the test as well.

Section I: Multiple-Choice Questions

	_____	number of correct answers
-	_____	.25 x number of wrong answers
=	_____	raw score
	_____	raw score
x	_____	1.25
=	_____	scaled score (out of a possible 67.5)

Section II: Essays

	_____	essay 1 (0–9)
	_____	essay 2 (0–9)
	_____	essay 3 (0–9)
x	_____	3.055
=	_____	scaled score (out of a possible 82.5)

Scaled Score

	_____	multiple-choice scaled score
+	_____	essay scaled score
=	_____	final scaled score (out of a possible 150)

AP Score Conversion Chart

Scaled Score	Likely AP Score
150–100	5
99–86	4
85–67	3
66–0	1 or 2

Answers and Explanations

1. **The correct answer is (B).** By directly addressing the members of the audience as "children," Sojourner Truth suggests that we are all equal in God's eyes. Her tone is sincere, so choice (A) and choice (D) cannot be correct. Choice (C) misses her point. Sojourner Truth's strength lies in her experience and her common sense; she makes no claim to intellectual achievements. Choice (E) cannot be correct because we do know neither Sojourner's age nor the ages of the people she is addressing. She may indeed be older than they are, but she could just as easily be younger. It is logical to assume that most of the people in the audience would be mature, given their leadership roles.

2. **The correct answer is (E).** As used in the first sentence, the idiom "something out of kilter" means that something is wrong. You can infer this from the "racket" [fuss] she notes. There is no suggestion that this is *evil,* choice (A); *dangerous,* choice (B); or *mysterious,* choice (D)—it is simply amiss. While people are indeed *foolish,* choice (C), that does not necessarily cause things to go wrong.

3. **The correct answer is (A).** *Women being helped into carriages and lifted over ditches* can be understood in both a literal and metaphorical way. Literally, women were helped into high carriages and carried over ditches. But Sojourner Truth's comments can also be understood in a metaphorical way: upper-class and middle-class women were shielded from life's harshness and mess. The cost? They were treated as children and denied a voice in their life. She is not *insulting women who do not work,* choice (B), for she is not even addressing the issue of working women. While this comment does acknowledge *the wide social gulf between her and wealthy white women,* choice (C), that is not her point. She is clearly *aware of the social mores of her time,* choice (D), but again that is not her point. Since her tone is level, you can eliminate choice (E).

4. **The correct answer is (D).** "Look at my arm" suggests that the speaker's physical strength represents her psychological strength. Not only can she toil as well as (or better than!) any man, but she has withstood the mental effects of brutal work. Eliminate choice (A) because she is not threatening anyone. You cannot assume from this comment that she has been injured and bears the scars, choice (B), for there is no evidence in the text of any scars. While she is indeed as strong as any man, choice (C), her point is wider. The same is true of choice (E).

5. **The correct answer is (C).** The phrase "And ain't I a woman?" is an example of both *repetition* and *rhetorical questions.* She repeats the phrase several times. Since she does not expect an answer to her question, it is rhetorical. She is not exaggerating at all, so this cannot be an example of *hyperbole* (exaggeration for literary effect).

6. **The correct answer is (B).** The repeated refrain "And ain't I a woman?" serves to stress the equality of *all* women while pointing out inequalities. She is being serious, not ironic, so you can eliminate choice (A). The phrase is not a lead-in to specific details, so you can cross out choice (C). She is not trying to frighten the reader, so choice (D) is out. Finally, "bitter" is too strong a word for her feelings, so choice (E) is wrong.

7. **The correct answer is (E).** The speaker is critical of male claims that women are the "weaker sex." This is shown through the examples she cites: "I have ploughed and planted, and gathered into barns, and no man could head me! ...I could work as much and eat as much as a man—when I could get it —and bear the lash as well! ...I have borne thirteen children, and see them all sold off to slavery, and when I cried out with my mother's grief, none but Jesus heard me!"

8. **The correct answer is (E).** The statement "That's it, honey" serves most directly to draw the audience closer to the speaker. This is accomplished by the familiar word "honey," which forges an intimacy between the speaker and her audience. Therefore, choice (D) cannot be correct. The mood is not *hopeless*, so you can eliminate choice (C) as well. There is nothing *ironic* about her statement, as it matches what has come before. Therefore, choice (A) is wrong.

9. **The correct answer is (A).** The phrase "If the first woman God ever made was strong enough to turn the world upside down all alone..." is an allusion. It is a reference to the Biblical story of Adam and Eve. It is not an example of *alliteration*, because the initial consonants are not repeated, so you can eliminate choice (B). *Assonance* repeats initial vowels, so choice (C) is wrong. *Apostrophe,* choice (D), is direct address, which is not the case here. *Aphorism,* choice (E), is a witty and memorable statement, such as "A penny saved is a penny earned." Sojourner Truth is not trying to be witty, so choice (E) is incorrect as well.

10. **The correct answer is (A).** The tone of this speech is best described as *dignified.* Sojourner Truth conveys her nobility in her plain speech, especially through her use of colloquialism and dialect. She has indeed had a tough life, but she is not *bitter,* choice (B). Neither is she *ironic*; rather, she is quite direct. This eliminates choice (C). If she were resigned, choice (D), she would not be giving this speech. Rather, she would agree to her fate. Finally, she is not at all *horrified,* choice (E); rather, she readily acknowledges the situation.

11. **The correct answer is (D).** To make her closing more powerful, Sojourner uses nonstandard usage, including "ain't" and the double negative "ain't got nothing." This provides an especially powerful close when added to her obvious knowledge and first-hand experience. It stands as an ironic counterpoint to the men's insistence on "intellect": she clearly has more "intellect" than most of the people in the room, despite her nonstandard speech. She is not making a *direct*

command, choice (A); an *allusion to a previous speech,* choice (B); or *drawing on any sensory images,* choice (E). The ending is parallel, but that does not make it as powerful as her diction does.

12. **The correct answer is (E).** The speaker's rhetorical strategy in this speech is best described as *stating the point that was made and proving through examples that it is so.* She states her point in the first paragraph—Well, children, where there is so much racket there must be something out of kilter—and follows it with specific examples. Here is one such example: "That man over there says that women need to be helped into carriages, and lifted over ditches, and to have the best place everywhere. Nobody ever helps me into carriages, or over mud-puddles, or gives me any best place! And ain't I a woman?" While she tells the story of her life, choice (A), it does not illustrate the plight of all women. Her experiences do not represent those of wealthy white women, for example. She does not agree with the prevailing viewpoints, so choice (B) is wrong. Neither does she cite authorities and outside evidence to buttress her point, choice (C). She directly states her experience rather than implying it, so choice (D) is wrong.

13. **The correct answer is (B).** The speaker's colloquial language and nonstandard usage serve to convey her sincerity and practical experience. She never claims to be an expert, so choice (A) is wrong. While her diction may serve to widen the gulf between the educated and uneducated members of the audience, choice (C), this is only true for those who would not listen to her anyway. There is no humor in her speech, so you can cross out choice (D). Finally, she is working *against* the prevailing opinion, not proving it, so choice (E) is incorrect.

14. **The correct answer is (E).** Sojourner Truth uses rhetorical devices and persuasive techniques to prove that women are as capable as men and deserve equal rights. She does not discriminate among women, so choice (A) is wrong. Neither is she trying to prove that women are vastly superior to men, simply that they are equal. Therefore, choice (B) is wrong. She is not talking about slavery, so you can cross out choice (C). If choice (D) were true, there would not be any reason for her to speak at the assembly. Therefore, it cannot be correct.

15. **The correct answer is (E).** The first paragraph serves to convince people in England that Americans were not, in fact, starving. Smith accomplishes this by listing an amazing abundance of food: "The winter [of 1607] approaching, the rivers became so covered with swans, geese, ducks, and cranes, that we daily feasted on good bread, Virginia peas, pumpkins, puchamins, fish, fowl, and diverse sorts of wild beasts as fat as we could eat them..." Even more telling, he sets this scene right before *winter,* to suggest that no one would be starving when winter finally comes. Rather, there would be ample food over the long, cold winter.

16. The correct answer is (D). In context, the line "so that none of our tuftaffety humorists desired to go to England" most nearly refers to critical, fashionable men who enjoyed living well. Even those people who are used to having ample food, he suggests, will find more than enough bounty in the New World. Choice (B) makes no sense, because according to Smith's catalog of food, *anyone* would be better off in the New World than anywhere else! Besides, why would a colonist be living in England? Likewise, choice (E) is illogical because there is so much food that people can eat as much as they desire without depriving others. Choice (A) is nonsensical, because people who had been in America would know that Smith was exaggerating. These might be the last people he would want to read his essay. Choice (C) cannot be inferred from the details in the passage.

17. The correct answer is (A). Smith uses *hyperbole,* exaggerating his adventures. For example, it is highly unlikely that he could escape an attack of 200 Indians with only a minor scratch!

18. The correct answer is (C). The third paragraph serves to convince readers that the New World is exciting and offers great adventures. Smith recounts exciting escapades with the Native Americans, filled with dramatic calamities and hair-breath escapes. While he calls the Native Americans "savages," he is not trying to persuade people that they were; rather, he presents the term so casually as to make it a given, considering his audience. Since Smith seems to be handling his responsibility rather poorly (he is not keeping up with his men, not knowing what was happening with them), he cannot be arguing that he should be given more responsibility, choice (B). Smith shows that he is very brave indeed, so choice (D) is wrong. Finally, the opening is specific, not general, so you can eliminate choice (E).

19. The correct answer is (E). This narrative is told from the third-person point of view. Remember that *point of view* is the position from which a story is told. In the *third-person point of view*, the narrator tells the story through the eyes of only one character, using the pronouns *he, she,* and *they*. Smith is telling this story through the eyes of a character he calls "Captain John Smith." Do not confuse this with the *first-person point of view.* Even though the narrator is both the author and one of the characters in the story, in the first-person point of view, the narrator explains the events through his or her own eyes, using the pronouns *I* and *me*. Smith uses third-person pronouns.

20. The correct answer is (D). Smith selected this point of view to distance himself from his work, to make it seem less subjective. This distance gives him far greater freedom to inflate his own role in events. This is the direct opposite of choice (A). If he wanted to show the events from the widest possible viewpoint, choice (B), he would use the omniscient (all-knowing) point of view. Likewise, if he wanted to present his own personal feelings about the subject, he would use the first-person point of view. Choice (E) would also have occasioned the omniscient point of view.

21. **The correct answer is (A).** Smith's adventures with the Native Americans are symbolic because they convey the British feeling of superiority. The Native Americans are "savages," yet Smith is able to conquer them with his bravery and intelligence. The narrative is clearly exaggerated rather than understated, so you can eliminate choice (B). Choice (C) is too large a leap from what is presented here. Choice (D) is clearly wrong because it is just the opposite of Smith's portrayal of the Native Americans. Smith does not show that he has closely identified with his new land, just that he is wholeheartedly enjoying the adventures it affords.

22. **The correct answer is (C).** As used in this passage, "victual" most nearly means *food*. You can infer this from the phrase "whilst himself by fowling sought them victual." The term "fowling" reveals that he was seeking fowl, birds.

23. **The correct answer is (A).** Smith offers his readers fame, fortune, and adventure. They have ample food and exciting encounters with Native Americans. Notice that Smith gets injured but only very slightly: "...yet he was shot in the thigh a little and had many arrows that stuck in his clothes but no great hurt." Obviously, this contradicts choices (B) and (C). Smith does not reveal himself to be either fair or good humored, so you can eliminate choice (D). Smith may have a shot at literary immortality, choice (E), but none of his followers will be offered this opportunity.

24. **The correct answer is (E).** You can infer from Smith's rhetoric that his audience was young men. He is trying to attract fighters and farmers in the prime of their life. If they were older, choice (D), they would not have the hunger for adventure. He doesn't need money, choice (A), as much as bodies to settle, clear the land, and set up homes and businesses.

25. **The correct answer is (D).** It is likely that Smith greatly embellished his adventures. For example, it is highly unlikely that he was attacked by 200 Indians and escaped with only a scratch. This is the opposite of choice (A). If he wasn't present at the events he described, choice (B), his account loses all effect. We can assume just the opposite of choice (C). It seems likely that many young men were attracted to America by his promises. Finally, Smith could not get killed by the Native Americans, choice (E), and live to recount it.

26. **The correct answer is (C).** The writer's voice is best described as *heroic and self-confident, even cocky*. Here is a typical passage: "... finding he was beset with two hundred savages, two of them he slew, still defending himself with the aid of a savage his guide, whom he

bound to his arm with garters and used him as a buckler..." He is not *whining,* choice (A), or *vitriolic,* choice (B). Neither is he *resentful,* choice (D); on the contrary, he is just the opposite of resentful—he welcomes the chance to have fun in nature. It is too strong a characterization to call him cocky but *arrogant,* choice (E).

27. **The correct answer is (B).** You can infer from Smith's rhetorical strategies that his main purpose was to attract settlement to the New World. This fits with his emphasis on food and adventure. His account is aimed at his peers, not the Native Americans, choices (A) and (D). *Money,* choice (C), would be useful only in the number of settlers it could buy; he does not seem concerned about the deaths of the men under his command, choice (E). Rather, he suggests that their deaths are their own fault for not paying attention.

28. **The correct answer is (C).** The phrase "no odor that was ever in a ham could make any difference" is best described as *sarcastic.* The writer is mocking any claims the meatpackers might have about producing "natural" products. Choices (A), (D), and (E) all miss the writer's ironic stance here. Choice (B) is way off target; the author is very much against the meatpackers and has no sympathy for them at all. On the contrary, he sees them as betrayers of the public trust.

29. **The correct answer is (D).** The writer uses the dash in this sentence for emphasis: "...and that was moldy and white—it would be dosed with borax and glycerine, and dumped into the hoppers, and made over again for home consumption." The dash serves to direct attention to the second half of the sentence. This directs readers to focus on the specific deception being highlighted here. A colon *does* show a sudden change of thought, choice (C), but choice (D) better reflects the author's purpose here and is thus a better choice. While the dash helps the writer indicate cause and effect, choice (A), he could have accomplished the same result with a colon (:). There is nothing ironic here, so choice (B) is wrong. The description may serve to undercut the opposition, choice (E), but he could have achieved this end with a colon rather than with a dash.

30. **The correct answer is (C).** The presentation of material in this selection is characterized by a chronological analysis of a process. The writer is analyzing the process of manufacturing commercial sausage. He traces the process from the arrival of the spoiled ham, through its dicing, and finally to its sale. Choice (A) is wrong because the writer does not begin with any generalization. He traces a process rather than offering a hard-hitting rebuttal of generally accepted public opinions, choice (B), even though the public may indeed believe that sausage is safe. The passage does not start with an analysis and is developed through facts, not opinions, choice (D). The passage does not open with scientific data and is developed through facts, not contradicted by personal observations, choice (E).

31. **The correct answer is (A).** The author's style in this passage is characterized by sensory images. He uses images that appeal to the five senses. For example "no odor that was ever in a ham could make any difference" appeals to the sense of smell, while "the water from leaky roofs would drip over it" appeals to touch and sight. "A man could run his hand over these piles of meat and sweep off handfuls of the dried dung" appeals to touch; "that was moldy and white" appeals to sight. There aren't any *literary allusions,* choice (B); *specific metaphors,* choice (C); or *elegant figures of speech,* choice (D). The author concentrates on reality, not appearance, choice (E).

32. **The correct answer is (B).** You can conclude that the author is primarily concerned with making his point about the corruption of the meat-packing industry. The piece is didactic, with a driving, strident pulse. He does describe what he has seen, choice (D), but this is not his point; rather, it is part of his technique. He is not trying to convince people to become vegetarians, choice (E); instead, he is trying to convince the government to regulate the meat-packing industry. His style is far more utilitarian than lyrical, choice (A). Finally, he is not concerned with disarming his opponents, choice (C), whom he does not even acknowledge.

33. **The correct answer is (A).** The images in this selection combine to form an impression of filth and deception. Images of the rat feces, dripping water, and spoiled meat create this impression. *Lack of sanitation,* choice (C), is part of this impression, but choice (A) is more inclusive and thus more precise. Since he is against the meat-packing industry, he cannot be describing modern manufacturing marvels, choice (D). He is not *desperate,* choice (B); rather, he is determined. He is describing the *abuse* of power rather than merely power, so choice (E) is wrong.

34. **The correct answer is (C).** The author uses the phrase "This is no fairy tale and no joke" to reinforce the truth of his narrative. Since the details are so extraordinary, the writer fears that people will believe that he is exaggerating the truth or even creating it. This disclaimer serves to establish the truth of what he has seen and heard about the abuses of the meat-packing industry. Choices (A) and (B) do not make sense. Telling the truth is a defense against being sued, and there is nothing false about what he is saying. He is telling the truth, not make-believe, so you can eliminate choice (D). Finally, we cannot assume that a fairy tale will follow, so cross off choice (E).

35. **The correct answer is (A).** As used in this passage, *consumptive* most nearly means "tuberculosis." The writer is using the word to describe a specific type of germ. Do not confuse this with a previous sentence: "over again for home consumption." The word is being used in that phrase to mean "eat."

36. **The correct answer is (D).** The passage is narrated from the omniscient point of view, in which the narrator is all-knowing. Recall that *point of view* is the position from which a story is told. In the *third-person point of view,* the narrator tells the story through the eyes of only one character, using the pronouns *he, she,* and *they.* Do not confuse this with the *first-person point of view,* in which the narrator explains the events through his or her own eyes, using the pronouns *I* and *me. Systematic,* choice (B), and *scientific,* choice (E), are not points of view.

37. **The correct answer is (C).** The author selected this point of view to afford him the widest possible vantage point. This allows him to see every aspect of the meat-packing industry. Choice (A) is the opposite of the omniscient point of view. Choice (B) is close, but choice (C) more accurately reflects his purpose here. The passionate tone argues against choice (E). The author is not concerned with identifying with the people working in the meat-packing plant, choice (D), just describing what he sees.

38. **The correct answer is (A).** "There were things that went into sausage in comparison with which a poisoned rat was a tidbit" is an example of irony. He is reversing our expectations, as a "tidbit" is a tasty morsel. He is not giving human qualities to an inanimate object (*personification*) or referring to a well-known place, event, person, work of art, or other work of literature (*allusion*). Therefore, you can eliminate choices II and III.

39. **The correct answer is (B).** The long sentences suggest that the process is continuous, as workers toil around the clock. In this way, the author mirrors form and function. *The process is long and difficult,* choice (A), but choice (B) is more precise. The other choices have nothing to do with the length of the sentences.

40. **The correct answer is (D).** The tone of this passage is best described as filled with moral outrage. He is not at all neutral, choice (A), as the sentence "This is no fairy tale and no joke" shows. He is angry but not *hostile,* choice (B); *venomous,* choice (C); or *malicious,* choice (E).

41. **The correct answer is (E).** The rhetorical purpose of this selection is *persuasive,* as the writer is trying to convince his readers to take steps against the abuses of the meat-packing industry. He is *explaining,* choice (B); *describing,* choice (C); and *telling a story,* choice (D), but these are techniques he uses to achieve his purpose. Choice (A), *analytical,* does not capture his tone of outrage.

42. **The correct answer is (D).** In the last sentence of paragraph 1, the writer sets off the clause *she was a cunning workman* with dashes to make this clause stand out by contrast. The essayist wants readers to be certain to focus on this aspect of his discussion. Choice (A) cannot

be correct because the embedded clause is central to his thesis. Choice (C) and choice (E) are misreadings of the passage. Choice (B) is too simplistic, as careful writers marry form and function so their sentences reinforce their points.

43. **The correct answer is (B).** The writer uses *alliteration* in the following sentence: "But, casual in this, she was anything but casual—she was a cunning workman—in her composition." The repeated letter "c" serves to unify the sentence and give it a lyric flow.

44. **The correct answer is (C).** The phrase "Poetry was her solitaire" is a pun. *Solitaire* is a play on *solitary,* the nature of a poet, especially Dickinson. The writer is not *exaggerating,* choice (E), or repeating the initial letters of *alliteration,* choice (D). Neither is the writer making an *allusion* to a famous essay, choice (A).

45. **The correct answer is (D).** The phrase "Poetry was her solitaire" adds to the development of the passage by showing both Dickinson's devotion to her craft and her isolated lifestyle. You can infer this from the pun. It does not signal a new point in his argument, choice (A), and does just the opposite of indicating that Dickinson had a rich life outside of her craft, choice (B). The writer is not arguing that everyone needs to have an outlet besides work, choice (C), although this may be true. Since her life matched her art, choice (E) cannot be true.

46. **The correct answer is (E).** In the second paragraph, the writer uses *rhetorical questions, metaphors,* and *alliteration.* Here are the rhetorical questions: "Were they all her own? Were there echoes in them, or something of the conventional, the rhetorical, the fat? Were they clear, were they exact, were they compact?" The metaphor is shown in this sentence: "she watched the motions of her mind, recording its ebbs and flows." The alliteration is shown here: " ... the common hymn meters, and the meters of nursery jingles" and "her rhymes and her rhythms."

47. **The correct answer is (C).** "Fat" means *unnecessary embellishment,* as used in this sentence: "Were there echoes in them, or something of the conventional, the rhetorical, the fat?" The writer is questioning whether Dickinson's writing needed further editing.

48. **The correct answer is (E).** The passage includes all the following rhetorical strategies and literary elements EXCEPT the influence of contemporary poets on Dickinson's work. All the other items can be found in the essay.

49. **The correct answer is (A).** The author's style is best described as highly descriptive, marked by vivid figures of speech. The writer used metaphors, similes, puns, and alliteration. It is precise, not abstract, so choice (B) cannot be true. It is much more than metaphorical, so choice

(C) is wrong. While it is analytical, choice (D), it is far more descriptive. So, choice (A) is more precise. He is not especially witty (except
for his pun on "solitaire/solitary"), so you can eliminate choice (E).

50. **The correct answer is (D).** From this essay, Emily Dickinson emerges
as a literary maverick. The writer describes how she used new rhythms
and rhymes and constantly experimented. This is the opposite of
choice (B), so that choice cannot be true. The writer makes it very clear
that Dickinson did indeed find her own style, so choice (C) is wrong.
Dickinson played with poetic convention but was not disrespectful
toward it, so choice (A) is wrong. While choice (E) is certainly true,
it is not the writer's point in this excerpt.

51. **The correct answer is (B).** When he says in the last paragraph that
"...Emily Dickinson's light was quick. It was sudden, sharp and
evanescent, and this light was the dry light that was closest to the fire,"
he means that poets of her temperament run the risk of self-destruction.
While choice (A) may be true, the writer does not touch on the theme
of madness. Neither does he advocate pushing yourself to the limit to
create true, lasting art; that choice was Dickinson's. As a result, choice
(C) is wrong. Choice (D) may be true but again is not the writer's point.
Finally, you can eliminate choice (E) because the writer does not
allude to it. In fact, her life was relatively long and not especially tragic
in the conventional meaning of the word.

52. **The correct answer is (A).** The narrative style of this passage is most
accurately characterized as *richly ornate:* the writer uses long sentences, many figures of speech, and elevated diction. This is the
opposite of choices (B) and (E). The writing was actually clear rather
than complex and confusing, choice (C). Since the analysis had great
depth and thought, you can eliminate choice (D).

Question 1:

A well-written essay will analyze how the writer uses rhetorical strategies
and other stylistic devices to convey his views of the role of nature in our
lives. The essay should

- show the writer's deep appreciation of nature
- show how nature refreshes the writer's soul
- provide specific examples of the spiritual comfort the writer gets from
  nature (For example: "I have enjoyed a perfect exhilaration.")
- conclude that the writer sees nature as essential, linking humankind

Question 2:

A well-written essay must analyze how the distinctive style of each passage reveals its writer's purpose. Here are some points to consider:

Passage 1

- This passage shows how the narrator passed from despair to acceptance of his fate, which is being marooned on a far-away island. He uses phrases such as "Island of Despair" to show his early feelings. Writers can note that the word "despair" comes up again: "All the rest of that day I spent in afflicting myself at the dismal circumstances I was brought to, viz., I had neither food, house, clothes, weapons, nor any place to fly to; and in despair of any relief, saw nothing but death before me..."

- The passage is filled with vivid images to convey the writer's emotions. It is narrated from the first-person point of view to give the closest possible link between writer and reader.

- In addition, the passage uses long sentences to mirror the long process of his acceptance of his fate.

Passage 2

- This passage describes the writer's first view of the real Robinson Crusoe, Alexander Selkirk. The narrator uses a familiar, relaxed tone to describe the meeting and the changes the character underwent as he became more acclimated to society.

- The writer uses sensory images to describe his subject and parallel structure to make his writing unified and graceful.

Question 3:

A well-written essay must identify the writer's views on love. Then you must take a stand by agreeing, disagreeing, or qualifying the writer's opinion.

- You can cite examples from novels, short stories, or articles on the subject. You can also draw from personal experience or popular culture to buttress your opinion.

- Regardless of source material used, all essays must contain specific references to the passage and relevant examples.

Glossary of Literary Terms

A

Accent   Emphasis or stress on certain words or parts of words.

Accentual Verse   A system of verse in which accents are used to determine the length of lines of poetry. The number of syllables per line is unimportant. Accentual verse is found mainly in the works of the earliest poets, dating from the eighth century.

Accentual-Syllabic Verse   A type of verse in which the counting of accents and syllables occurs within the same line. It is the type of poetry most people instantly recognize as "poetic," for it has a definite beat and often rhymes.

Aesthetic Movement   In the early nineteenth century, a devotion to beauty developed in France. The movement rejected the notion that the value of literature was related to morality—a sense of right and wrong—or some sort of usefulness. Instead, it put forth the idea that art was independent of any moral or didactic (instructive) end. The Aesthetics' slogan was "art for art's sake" (*"l'art pour l'art"*), and many of the writers involved actively attacked the idea that art should serve any "purpose" in the traditional sense. In the late 1900s in England, the movement was represented by Oscar Wilde and Walter Pater. The term *"fin de siècle"* ("end of the century"), which earlier stood for progress, came to imply decadence—great refinement of style but a marked tendency toward the abnormal or freakish in content. When used as a proper noun, *Decadence* refers to the Aesthetic Movement.

Allegory   *Allegory* occurs when one idea or object is represented in the shape of another. In medieval morality plays, abstract ideas such as virtues and vices appear as people to help readers understand the moral (lesson) more easily. In Emily Dickinson's poem "Because I Could Not Stop For Death," death appears as the allegorical figure of a coachman, kindly stopping to pick her up on the road to eternity.

Alliteration   The repetition of initial consonant sounds in several words in a sentence or line of poetry. Writers use alliteration to create musical effects, link related ideas, stress certain words, or mimic specific sounds. Here is an example:

> About the lilting house and happy as the grass was green

Note the repetition of *h* in "house" and "happy" and the *gr* in "grass" and "green." Alliteration is also called *initial rhyme*. In Macbeth's line, "after life's fitful fever," alliteration is found in the repeated *f*'s of "fitful fever" and hidden alliteration is found in the *f*'s of "after," "life," and "fitful."

Allusion   A reference to a well-known place, event, person, work of art, or other work of literature. Allusions enrich a story or poem by suggesting powerful and exciting comparisons.

Ambiguity   *Ambiguity* allows multiple meanings to coexist in a word or a metaphor. It does not mean that the word or term is unclear; rather, it means that the perceptive reader can see more than one possible interpretation at the same time. Puns, for example, offer ambiguity, as these lines from Wyatt's "They Flee From Me" show: "But since that I so kindely am served/I fain would know what she hath deserved." The word "kindely" means both "served by a group" and "courteously."

Anecdote   A brief story that gets the reader's interest and sheds light on the writer's main idea and theme. To accomplish the writer's aims, anecdotes often describe funny, interesting, and unusual events or people.

Antagonist   The force or person in conflict with the main character in a work of literature. An antagonist can be another character, a force of nature, society, or something within the character.

Apostrophe   A thing is addressed directly, as though it were a person listening to the conversation. For example, we have Wordsworth's "Milton! thou should'st be living at this hour," although Milton had been dead for a long time. Apostrophe and personification go hand in hand in Donne's "Busy old fool, unruly Sun," and Wyatt's "My lute, awake."

Article   A short work of nonfiction. You can find articles in magazines, newspapers, and books.

Assonance   A type of rhyme in which the vowels in the words are the same, but the consonants are not. For example, the words "seat" and "weak."

Atmosphere   See *Mood.*

Author's Purpose   The author's goal in writing a selection. Common purposes include to entertain, instruct, persuade, or describe. A selection may have more than one author's purpose, but one purpose is often the most important.

Autobiography   A person's story of his or her own life. An autobiography is nonfiction and describes key events from the person's life.

B

Ballad A story told in song form. Since ballads were passed down by word of mouth from person to person, the words are simple and have a strong beat. Ballads often tell stories about adventure and love. When professional poets write stanzas of this type, such as Auden's "I Walked Out One Evening," they are called *literary ballads*. Probably the most famous ballads are Coleridge's "Rime of the Ancient Mariner" and Keats's "La Belle Dame sans Merci."

The ballad stanza rhymes *abcb*. Ballads often contain *refrains,* musical repetitions of words or phrases. Some critics believe that ballads were originally two-line rhyming songs, thus explaining why there are only two rhymes in a four-line stanza. Because early ballads were nonliterary, half-rhymes and slant rhymes are often used. Ballads sometimes employ incremental repetition, the repetition of a previous line or lines but with a slight variation to advance the narrative, as in these lines from "The Cruel Brother":

> O what will you leave to your father dear?
>
> The silver-shode steed that brought me here.
>
> And what will you leave to your mother clear?
>
> My velvet pall and my silken gear.

Biography A true story about a person's life written by another person. Biographies are often written about well-known, important people, although any person can be the subject.

Blank Verse Unrhymed iambic pentameter. Blank verse was introduced into English poetry in the middle of the sixteenth century. By the end of the century, it had become the standard medium of English drama. Here is an example by William Shakespeare: "Time hath, my Lord, a wallet at his back,/Wherein he puts alms for oblivion."

Breve ∪ mark over a syllable to indicate that it is not accented.

Broadside ballad A poem of any sort printed on a large sheet—thus the "broadside"—and sold by street singers in the sixteenth century. Not until the eighteenth century was the word "ballad" limited to traditional narrative song.

Burlesque Any imitation of people or literary type that, by distortion, aims to amuse. Burlesque tends to ridicule faults, not serious vices. Thus, it is not to be confused with satire, for burlesque makes fun of a minor fault with the aim of arousing amusement rather than contempt or indignation. Also, it need not make us devalue the original. For example, T. S. Eliot's "The Hollow Men" is parodied in Myra Buttle's "Sweeniad." An excerpt from the original poem reads:

> Between the conception
>
> And the creation
>
> Between the emotion
>
> And the response
>
> Falls the shadow

while the burlesque is:

> Between the mustification
>
> And the deception
>
> Between the multiplication
>
> And the division
>
> Falls the Tower of London.

C

Character A person or an animal in a story. *Main characters* have important roles in the literary work; *minor characters* have smaller parts.

Characterization The different ways an author tells readers about characters. Writers can tell about characters directly or let readers reach their own decisions about a character indirectly by showing the comments, thoughts, and actions of the other characters.

Chronological Order The arrangement of the events of a story in time order from first to last.

Climax The highest point in the action. During the climax, the conflict is resolved and the end of the story becomes clear. The climax is also called the *turning point*.

Comedy A humorous play that has a happy ending.

Conceit A long, complex metaphor. In John Donne's "A Valediction Forbidding Mourning," the souls of two lovers become the same as the two legs of a draftsman's compass:

> If they be two, they are two so
>
> As stiff twin compasses are two;
>
> Thy soul, the fixed foot, makes no show
>
> To move, but doth, if th'other do.
>
> And through it in the center sit,
>
> Yet when the other far doth roam,
>
> It leans and harkens after it,
>
> And grows erect, as that comes home.

Conclusion The end of an article, play, poem, or book. The term can also refer to an opinion.

Concrete Poems Poems in which the shape, not the words, is what matters. George Herbert's "Easter Wings" is an example. Also called *emblematic poetry*.

Conflict A struggle or fight. Conflict makes a story interesting because readers want to find out the outcome. There are two kinds of conflict. In an *external conflict*, characters struggle against a force outside themselves. In an *internal conflict*, characters battle a force within themselves. Stories often contain both external and internal conflicts.

Connotation and Denotation *Connotation* is the generally accepted meaning(s) of a word, in contrast to the *denotation*, which is the dictionary meaning. Connotation adds additional richness to a word's meaning. In the line, "She was the sickle; I, poor I, the rake," the word "rake" has a clear denotation—a gardening tool designed to pick up clippings from a lawn or a garden that a sickle might have cut down. In the context of the entire poem, though, the word "rake" has the connotative meaning of a debauched man. The two meanings work together to give the poem greater depth and further the author's theme.

Context The part of a selection that contains a particular word or group of words. Effective readers use the context to help them define the meaning of a word.

Contrast Contrast shows the difference between two objects. Contrast is the opposite of *comparison*, which shows similarities. In the following example by William Shakespeare, we see his mistress contrasted to various accepted symbols of adoration:

> My mistress' eyes are nothing like the sun;
>
> Coral is far more red than her lips' red;
>
> If snow be white, why then her breasts are dun;
>
> If hairs be wires, black wires grow on her head.

Consonance A type of half-rhyme in which the consonants agree but the vowels do not, as in the words "luck" and "lick."

Couplet Two related lines of poetry. A couplet often rhymes.

D

Dead Metaphor A metaphor that has lost its figurative value through overuse. "Foot of a hill" or "eye of a needle" are examples.

Detail A small piece of information. In a paragraph, the main idea tells what the paragraph is about, and the details give information to support or explain the main idea.

Denouement The resolution of a story. At the denouement, all the loose ends of the plot are tied up to leave the reader feeling satisfied.

Description A word picture of what something or someone is like. Description is made up of sensory details that help readers form pictures in their minds.

Dialect The way people speak in a certain region or area. In a dialect, certain words are spelled and pronounced differently. Writers use dialects to describe their characters and setting more fully. Mark Twain's *The Adventures of Huckleberry Finn* used dialect extensively.

Dialogue The conversation in fiction or drama, the exact words a character says. In a story or novel, quotation marks are used to point out the dialogue. In a drama, quotation marks are usually not included.

Diary   A writer's record of his or her experiences, ideas, and feelings.

Didactic Literature   Literature that intends to instruct or teach rather than merely to delight and entertain. The term need not be pejorative, though many use it in this manner. A good case can be made that almost all of the world's finest poetry is didactic in some way. Satire makes fun of certain modes of behavior; Milton wrote his epic poem *Paradise Lost* to "justify the ways of God to men." The problem, then, is one of degree, as true didactic literature deals mainly with instruction. This does not make it any less "poetic." The following lines by John Gay, explaining how to clean worms, are an illustration of didactic literature:

> Cleanse them from filth, to give a tempting gloss,
>
> Cherish the sully'd reptile race with moss;
>
> Amid the verdant bed they twine, they toil,
>
> And from their bodies wipe the native soil.

Diphthong   Two syllables that are counted and pronounced as one, used in poetry to make the words fit the metrical requirements.

Doggerel   Verse made comic because irregular metrics are made regular by stressing normally unstressed syllables. In Butler's lines:

> More peevish, cross, and splenetic
>
> Than dog distract or monkey sick.

If the subject matter is mock heroic and the lines are iambic tetrameter couplets (as in the example quoted above), the poem is also referred to as *hudibrastic*, after Samuel Butler's "Hudibras."

Drama   A piece of literature written to be performed in front of an audience. The actors tell the story through their actions. Dramas can be read as well as acted.

Dramatic Monologue   The speaker in a dramatic monologue is usually a fictional character or a historical figure caught at a critical moment. His or her words are established by the situation and are usually directed at a silent audience. The speaker usually reveals aspects of his personality of which he or she is unaware. To some extent, every poem is a dramatic monologue, as an individual speaker is saying something to someone, even if only to himself, but in a true dramatic monologue, the above conventions are observed. A famous example of a dramatic monologue is Robert Browning's "My Last Duchess," in which a duke who has eliminated his last duchess reveals his cruelty to an emissary, who wants to arrange for the marriage to the latest duchess. T. S. Eliot's "The Love Song of J. Alfred Prufrock," in which the speaker's timid self addresses his aggressively amorous self, is another famous example.

Dramatic Poetry   A play written in poem form.

E

Elegy   A poem that deals solemnly with death. Gray's "Elegy Written in a Country Churchyard" is an example. If an elegy is a short funeral lament, it may be called a *dirge*, which in ancient times was a funeral song. Walt Whitman's elegy on Abraham Lincoln, "When Lilacs Last in the Dooryard Bloomed," and Milton's "Lycidas" are famous examples.

Elision   The elimination of a vowel, consonant, or syllable in pronunciation. It usually occurs in verse at the end of a word when the next word begins with a vowel and is used to shorten or lengthen a line to make it fit metrical requirements.

Emblematic Poems   A poem that takes the shape of the subject of the poem. An emblematic poem on a swan, for example, would be in the shape of a swan. George Herbert's "Easter Wings" is an example of an emblematic poem. Also called *concrete poetry*.

Epic   A long and serious narrative poem (a poem that tells a story) about a hero and his heroic companions, often set in a past that is pictured as greater than the present. The hero often possesses superhuman and/or divine traits. In Homer's *Iliad*, for example, the hero, Achilles, is the son of a goddess; in Milton's *Paradise Lost*, the characters are God the Father, Christ, angels, and Adam and Eve. The action is usually rather simple, Achilles' anger in the *Iliad* and the fall of man in *Paradise Lost*, but it is increased by figurative language and allusions that often give it cosmic importance. The style is elevated to reflect the greatness of the events, and certain traditional procedures are employed. For example, the poet usually calls to the muses for help, asks them what initiated the action (*the epic question*) and often begins his tale in the middle of the action (*in medias res*). At this point, the hero is at his lowest fortunes and later recounts the earlier part of the tale. Gods often participate in the tale, helping the heroes.

There are two types of epics: the *primary epic* (sometimes called a *folk epic*), which is a stately narrative about the noble class recited to the noble class; and the *literary epic,* a stately narrative about great events designed to be read. Primary epics include Homer's *Iliad* and *Odyssey* and the anonymous Old English *Beowulf.* Literary epics include Vergil's *Aeneid* and Milton's *Paradise Lost.* The poet of the primary epic speaks as the voice of the community, whereas the poet of the literary epic may show more individuality.

Modern epics include Hart Crane's "The Bridge," William Carlos Williams's "Paterson," and Ezra Pound's "Cantos." The first two are examples of American epics; the last is a case for Western civilization. Epics vary in structure. *Beowulf,* for example, uses alliteration and accentual stress rather than rhyme or stanza length to structure the poem.

Epigram   Originally meaning an "inscription," the epigram became for the Greeks a short poem, usually solemn. The Romans used the term to mean a short, witty poem, with the sting at the end. The term has come to mean any cleverly expressed thought in verse or prose. An example by John Wilmot:

We have a pretty witty King,

Whose word no man relies on,

Who never said a foolish thing,

Nor ever did a wise one.

Epitaph   A burial inscription, usually serious but sometimes humorous. John Gay's own serves as an example: "Life is a jest and all things show it:/ I thought so once, but now I know it."

Epithalamion (also spelled epithalamium)   A lyric poem in honor of a bride, bridegroom, or both. It is usually ceremonial and happy and is not simply in praise of marriage but of a particular marriage. Spenser's "Epithalamion" is the greatest epithalamion in English. It begins with an invocation, calls on young people to attend the bride, praises the bride, and welcomes the night. Spenser added deep Christian feeling and realistic description of landscape.

Essay   A brief prose writing on a particular subject or idea.

Eulogy   Frequently confused with *elegy*, a *eulogy* is a poem praising the memory of a living or dead person.

Exaggeration   Overstating an idea to achieve a specific literary effect.

Excerpt   A part of a literary work that is printed on its own, separate from the whole.

Existentialism   The writings of this literary movement stress the loneliness, insecurity, and irrevocability of human experience. It also focuses on people's anxious attempts to face these situations and their ultimately useless attempts to escape them. Our free choice asserts our actions as valid: in Jean-Paul Sartre's own words, "man makes himself." Existentialist criticism approached literature by asking how well a literary work depicts these complexities of the human situation.

Exposition   A kind of writing that explains, shows, or tells about a subject. The word "exposition" can also be used to mean the opening parts of a play or story. During the exposition, the characters, action, and setting are introduced.

Expressionism   This literary movement presents life as the author (or his character) passionately feels it to be, not as it appears on the surface. Thus, the Expressionist's work often consciously distorts the external appearance of an object in order to picture the object as the writer or artist feels it really is. Scenery in an Expressionist drama, for example, would not be photographically accurate but would be distorted so that, for instance, the wall of a courtroom may tilt at a weird angle to reveal the accused's state of mind. The movement was especially dominant in German painting during the decade following World War I.

Extended Metaphor   An extended metaphor results when a metaphor becomes long, elaborate, and complex.

Eye-rhyme   Words that are spelled the same and look alike but have a different sound. This is shown in the following lines from Sir Walter Raleigh's poem "The Nymph's Reply to the Shepherd":

> "These pretty pleasures might me move
>
> To live with thee and be thy love"

The words "move" and "love" have eye rhyme. These rhymes are also called *historical rhymes,* as their pronunciation has changed over the years. The word "tea," for example, once rhymed with "day," but today these two words are, at best, half-rhymes.

F

Fable   A short, easy-to-read story that teaches a lesson about people. Fables often feature animals that talk and act like people.

Fantasy   A kind of writing that describes events that could not take place in real life. Fantasy has unrealistic characters, settings, and events.

Farce   A humorous play that is based on a silly plot, ridiculous situations, and comic dialogue. The characters are usually one-dimensional stereotypical figures. They often find themselves in situations that start out normally but soon turn absurd. Often, humor is created through an identity switch and the other characters' reaction to it.

Feminine Ending   A line that ends on an accented syllable.

Fiction   Writing that tells about made-up events and characters. Novels and short stories are examples of fiction. Fiction that contains imaginary situations and characters that are very similar to real life is called *realistic fiction.*

Figurative Language   Words and expressions not meant to be taken literally. Figurative language uses words in fresh, new ways to appeal to the imagination. Figures of speech include *similes, metaphors, extended metaphors, hyperbole,* and *personification.* What is impossible or difficult to convey to a reader through the literal use of language may be highly possible through the use of figures of speech. When taken literally, "my love is a rose" is ridiculous, for few people love a plant with a prickly, thorny stem. But "rose" suggests many other possible interpretations—delicate beauty, soft, rare, costly, etc.—and so it can be implied in a figurative sense to mean "love" or "loved one."

Figure of Speech   See *Figurative Language.*

Flashback   A scene that breaks into the story to show an earlier part of the action. Flashbacks help fill in missing information, explain the characters' actions, and advance the plot.

Folk Tale   A story that has been handed down from generation to generation. Fables, fairy tales, legends, tall tales, and myths are different types of folktales. Many folktales contain unusual characters and a moral (a lesson).

Foot   A group of stressed and unstressed syllables combining to form a unit of verse. A foot is composed of either two or three syllables, such that the nature of the foot is determined by the placement of the accent. Every English sentence, no matter whether classified poetry or prose, is made up of these units. Their placement determines the rhythm of a line. One particular foot determines the poem's rhythm. There are four basic types of metrical feet in English verse:

iamb   ´∪

trochee   ∪´

anapest   ∪∪´

dactyl   ´∪∪

And two uncommon ones:

spondee   ´´

phyrrhic   ∪∪

The most common foot in English is the *iamb*, perhaps because the use of articles—*the, a,* and *an*—establishes that an unstressed syllable will occur before a stressed one. Children's verse, such as nursery rhymes, often has trochees dominating. This is also because children don't use as many articles as adults do in speech. The most common line in English poetry is the iambic pentameter line, in part because a line greater than ten syllables in length requires an intake of breath, which translates as requiring another line.

Poetic lines are usually not composed of only one type of metrical foot, for this would sound dull. Variations are constructed to give the line more exciting movement.

Foreshadowing   Clues that hint at what will happen later on in the story. Writers use foreshadowing to create suspense and link related details.

Frame story   A shorter story within a larger one. Often, the longer story introduces and closes the frame story.

Free Verse   Poetry composed of rhythmical lines varying in length, following no fixed metrical pattern, usually unrhymed. Often, the pattern is based on repetition and parallel grammatical structure. Although free verse may appear unrestrained, it does follow the rules outlined above. An example from Walt Whitman's "Song of Myself":

> I celebrate myself, and sing myself,
>
> And what I assume you shall assume,
>
> For every atom belonging to me as good belongs to you.

G

Genre   A major literary category. The three genres are prose, drama, and poetry.

H

Haiku   A type of Japanese verse form composed of seventeen syllables in three lines. The first and third lines have five syllables each; the second line has seven syllables. Most haiku describe images from nature. Haiku were greatly admired models for the Imagist school, an early twentieth-century movement that attempted to shed excess words to create poems of clear, concise details.

Half-rhyme (also called *slant rhyme, approximate rhyme, near rhyme,* or *off-rhyme*)   A type of rhyme in which only the final consonant sounds of the words are identical. The stressed vowel sounds as well as the initial consonant sounds (if any) differ. Examples include *soul: oil; firth: forth; trolley: bully.* The following lines from William Whitehead's "Je Ne Sais Quoi" exemplify half-rhyme:

> Tis not her face that love creates,
>
> For there no grace revel;
>
> 'Tis not her shape, for there the Fates
>
> Had rather been uncivil.

"Revel" and "uncivil" in lines 2 and 4 above illustrate half-rhyme because the vowel sound changes, but the "vl" sound has remained the same.

Hero/Heroine   Literary characters that we admire for their noble traits, such as bravery, selflessness, or cleverness. In the past, the term "hero" was used to refer to a male character; the term "heroine" for a female character. Today, "hero" is used for both male and female characters.

Hubris   A Greek word for a character's excessive pride, confidence, or arrogance. In tragedies, the hero's hubris usually causes his or her downfall. The word can also be spelled "hybris."

Humor   Parts of a story that are funny. Humor can be created through sarcasm, word play, irony, and exaggeration.

Hyperbole (also called *Overstatement*)   Exaggeration used for a literary effect such as emphasis, drama, or humor. Shakespeare's Sonnet 97 contains this example:

> How like a winter hath my absence been
>
> From thee, the pleasure of the fleeting year!
>
> What freezings have I felt, what dark days seen!
>
> What old December's bareness everywhere!

We realize that Shakespeare did not literally freeze with real cold when he was apart from his loved one. We also realize that the days did not turn dark, or June turn to December; however; Shakespeare is saying this to illustrate the depth of his despair at the separation from his beloved.

The same process is at work in Lovelace's "When I lie tangled in her hair/ And fetter'd to her eye." Obviously, he is not captured in her hair nor chained to her eye; what he is suggesting, however, is that he is a prisoner to her beauty and finds himself unable to escape its spell.

I

Ictus mark over a syllable to indicate that it is accented.

Idiom An expression whose meaning cannot be taken literally. "It's raining buckets" and "He hit the ceiling" are examples of idioms.

Idyll A short, picturesque piece, usually about shepherds. It presents an episode from the heroic past but stresses the pictorial rather than the heroic. The most famous English example is Tennyson's "Idylls of the King," with its detailed descriptions of several aspects of the Arthurian legends.

Image A word that appeals to one or more of our five senses: sight, hearing, taste, touch, or smell. Imagery can be found in all sorts of writing, but it is most common in poetry.

Imagery See *Image.*

Imagists/Imagism At their peak between 1912 and 1914, these poets sought to use common language, to regard all the world as possible subject matter, and to present in vivid and sharp detail a concentrated visual image. "There should be no ideas but things," said poet William Carlos Williams. Imagists usually wrote in free verse. The most frequently cited example of their aims is summed up in the following brief poem by Ezra Pound, the leader of the Imagist movement:

> The apparition of these faces in the crowd;
>
> Petals on a wet, black bough.

The title of this brief poem, "In a Station of the Metro," informs the reader that the poem is about a metro, a European subway, but the poem presents its statement without directly telling the reader what conclusions to draw. The images in the poem suggest that the colorful faces of people in the subway are like flower petals against dark branches. The poet selects his images and arranges them, but the reader must sense the relationships to experience the picture the poem presents.

Poems of all kinds contain imagery, carefully described objects of the world, but the Imagist movement went further than describing what was seen to create a theory of verse around the idea of the picture.

Implicit or Submerged Metaphor If both terms of the metaphor present ("My winged heart" instead of "My heart is a bird") are not present, we have a *submerged metaphor.*

Internal rhyme A type of rhyme that occurs *within* the line instead of at the end. Oscar Wilde's "Each narrow cell within which we dwell" is an example of internal rhyme because the words "cell" and "dwell" rhyme.

Inciting Moment The beginning of the conflict.

Invocation An address to a god or muse whose aid is sought. Invocation is commonly found at the beginning of an epic. For example, Milton's "Sing, Heavenly Muse" at the opening of his *Paradise Lost.*

Irony *Irony* occurs when something happens that is different from what was expected. In *verbal irony,* there is a contrast between what is stated and what is suggested. In *dramatic irony,* there is a contrast between what a character believes and what the audience knows is true. In *irony of situation*, an event reverses what the readers or characters expected.

Auden's "Unknown Citizen," for example, is ironic in that it condemns the State by using the State's own terms of praise: "Was he free? Was he happy? The question is absurd;/Had anything been wrong, we should certainly have heard."

L

Legend   A story handed down through time that explains how or why something in nature originated. Legends are sometimes based in historical facts, but they often contain exaggerated details and characters.

Light Verse   Playful poetry that often combines lightheartedness or whimsy with mild satire as in Suckling's "Why So Pale and Wan, Fond Lover?" that concludes, "If of herself she will not loved,/Nothing can make her;/The devil take her." The definition of light verse changed in the late nineteenth century, however, to include less polished pieces such as nursery songs with funny rhymes and distorted pronunciations.

Limerick   A form of light verse, a *limerick* is a jingling poem composed of three long and two short lines, the long lines (first, second, and fifth) rhyming with each other, and the short lines (third and fourth) rhyming with each other. The rhyming words in the first line can sometimes be misspelled to produce a humorous effect. The following limerick from an early sixteenth-century songbook is an example:

> Once a Frenchman who'd promptly said "oui"
>
> To some ladies who'd asked him if houi
>
> Cared to drink, threw a fit
>
> Upon finding that it
>
> Was a tipple no stronger than toui

Literature   A type of art expressed in writing. Literature includes poetry, fiction, nonfiction, and drama.

Litote   A special form of understatement. It affirms something by negating its opposite. For example, "He's no fool" means that he is very shrewd.

Lyric   Brief, musical poems that give a speaker's feelings. In the past, people sang lyrics as they played string-like instruments called "lyres." Lyrics have regular rhyme schemes and are brief, as in the fourteen-line sonnet. Burns' famous drinking song "Auld Lang Syne," Robert Frost's short poems, and George Herbert's religious meditations are lyrics. If the emotion is hate or contempt, and its expression is witty, the poem is usually called a *satire,* or if very brief, an *epigram.* A *complaint* is a lyric expressing dissatisfaction, usually to an unresponsive lover. Chaucer's humorous "Complaint to His Purse," for example, begins: "To you, my purse, and to noon other wight,/Complayne I, for ye be my lady dere!" For a brief period in the 1800s, nature as well as love became a major subject for lyrics, and poets such as William Wordsworth wrote more lyrics on clouds and daffodils than on love.

M

Macaronic Verse Verse containing words resembling a foreign language or a mixture of languages. For example:

> "Mademoiselle got the croix de guerre,
>
> For washing soldiers' underwear,
>
> Hinky-dinky, parley-vous."

Main Character The most important figure in a novel, short story, poem, or play.

Masculine Ending A line that ends on an unaccented syllable.

Masculine and Feminine Rhymes Types of rhymes that are the equivalents of masculine and feminine line endings. Rhymes that end on a stress, such as "van" and "span," are masculine, while those ending on an unstressed syllable, such as "falling" and "calling," are called feminine. Thus, "stark/mark" and "support/retort" would be masculine, while "revival/arrival" and "flatter/batter" are feminine. Feminine rhyme is also referred to as *double rhyme*.

Memoir A first-person prose selection about an event.

Metamorphosis A *metamorphosis* occurs when a person changes form or shape. For example, in ancient myths, different characters often change into stars, animals, and trees.

Metaphor A figure of speech that compares two unlike things. The more familiar thing helps describe the less familiar one. Metaphors do not use the words "like" or "as" to make the comparison. "My heart is a singing bird" is an example of a metaphor. In the following metaphor by John Donne, the poet's doctors become the map-makers of the heavens, while the poet's body becomes the map in which the ultimate destiny of his soul can be divined:

> Whilst my physicians by their love are grown
>
> Cosmographers, and I their map, who lie
>
> Flat on this bed.

Metaphysical Poets The most important Metaphysical poets include John Donne (1572–1631) and his seventeenth-century followers, Andrew Marvell, George Herbert, Abraham Cowley, Richard Crashaw, and Henry Vaughan. These poets reacted against the traditions and rules of Elizabethan love poetry to create a more witty and ironic poetry. Modern critics have also concluded that the verse was more passionately intense and psychologically probing than the Elizabethan poems. Instead of penning smooth lines comparing a woman's beauty to something traditional like a rose, these poets wrote colloquial and often metrically irregular lines, filled with difficult and more searching comparisons. These comparisons are called *conceits,* which came to refer to a striking parallel of two highly unlike objects, such as the sun partly hidden by a cloud to a lover's head reclining on a pillow. Certain Petrarchan conceits were often used in English poetry during this time. They included a lover as a ship tossed by a storm, shaken by his tears, frozen by the coldness of his love.

Meter The beat or rhythm in a poem. It is created by a pattern of stressed and unstressed syllables. The most common meter in English poetry is called *iambic pentameter*. It is a pattern of five *feet* (groups of syllables), each having one unstressed syllable and one stressed one. Here are the most common meters in English poetry:

Length	Name of Meter
one	monometer
two	dimeter
three	trimeter
four	tetrameter
five	pentameter
six	hexameter
seven	heptameter

Metonymy The substitution of one item for another item that it suggests or to which it is closely related. For example, if a letter is said to be in Milton's own *hand*, it means that the letter is in Milton's own *handwriting*. Sidney wrote in his sonnet "With How Sad Steps, O Moon," "What, may be that even in heav'nly place/That busy archer his sharp arrows tries?" "That busy archer" is a reference to Cupid, the god of love frequently depicted as a cherubic little boy with a quiver full of arrows. Thus, an archer, by relating to the god of love, describes love without specifically using the word "love."

Minor Character A less important figure in a literary work. A minor character serves as a contrast to the main character or to advance the plot.

Mixed Metaphor A combination of two metaphors, often with absurd results. For example, "Let's iron out the bottlenecks," would be silly, for it is obvious that it is an impossibility.

Mock Epic or Mock Heroic Also known as *high burlesque,* a mock epic pokes fun at low activities by treating them in the elevated style of the epic. The humor results from the difference between the low subject and the lofty treatment it is accorded. Alexander Pope's epic poem "The Rape of the Lock" is a famous mock epic. It deals with the cutting of a lock of hair. In the theatre, a burlesque may be a play that humorously criticizes another play by imitating aspects of it in a grotesque manner, as in John Gay's "Beggar's Opera," which make fun of serious operas.

Mood The strong feeling we get from a literary work. The mood is created by characterization, description, images, and dialogue. Some possible moods include terror, horror, tension, calmness, and suspense. Also called *atmosphere.*

Moral A lesson about right and wrong. Sometimes, the moral can be stated directly. Other times, readers have to infer the moral from the plot, characters, and setting.

Myth A story from ancient days that explains certain aspects of life and nature. The Greek and Roman myths, as with many other myths, are about gods and goddesses.

N

Narration Writing that tells a story. Narrations that tell about real events include biographies and autobiographies. Narrations that deal with fictional events include short stories, myths, narrative poems, and novels.

Narrative See *Narration.*

Narrative Poem A poem that tells a story in poetic form. As with a narrative story, a narrative poem has a plot, characters, and theme.

Narrator The person who tells a story. The narrator may also be a character in the work.

Naturalism This movement attempted to portray a scientifically accurate, detached picture of life, including everything and selecting nothing for particular emphasis. This is often called the "slice of life" technique when focused on a narrow bit of scientific realism. Many of the Naturalists were very much influenced by evolutionary thought and regarded people as devoid of free will and soul, creatures whose fate was determined by environment and heredity. The movement was represented in the works of Emile Zola, Theodore Dreiser, Frank Norris, Stephen Crane, and others to a lesser extent. The emphasis on scientific determinism, heredity, and environment—Social Darwinism—differentiates Naturalism from Realism.

Nonfiction A type of writing about real people and events. Essays, biographies, autobiographies, and articles are all examples of nonfiction.

Novel A long work of fiction. The elements of a novel—plot, characterizations, setting, and theme—are developed in detail. Novels usually have one main plot and several less important subplots.

O

Octets Eight-line stanzas

Ode A very long lyric poem characterized by elevated feelings. The Pindaric ode, named for the Greek poet Pindar (c. 522–443 B.C.E.), has two structurally identical stanzas, the *strophe* and *antistrophe* (Greek for "turn" and "counterturn"). These are followed by a stanza with a different structure, the epode (Greek for "stand"). The line length and rhyming patterns are determined by the individual poet. The odes were characterized by great passion. Notable English Pindaric odes are Gray's "The Progress of Poesy" and Wordsworth's "Ode: Intimations of Immortality." Horatian odes, named after the Latin poet Horace (65–8 B.C.E.), are composed of matched regular stanzas of four lines that usually celebrate love, patriotism, or simple Roman morality. Notable English Horatian odes include Marvell's "Horatian Ode Upon Cromwell's Return to Ireland" and Collins' "Ode to Evening." Keats' "Ode to a Grecian Urn" is probably the best known Horatian Ode. Although the ode is a serious poem expressing the speaker's passion, it may be passion about almost anything. Especially during the 1800s, the ode tended to become less public and more personal and introspective. Shelley's "Ode to the West Wind" and Keats' "Ode to a Nightingale" are examples of this introspection. The irregular ode, such as Wordworth's "Intimations on Immortality," has stanzas of various shapes, irregular rhyme schemes, and elaborate rhythms.

Onomatopoeia   The sound of word echoes or suggests the meaning of the word. "Hiss" and "buzz" are examples. There is a tendency for readers to see onomatopoeia in far too many instances, in words such as "thunder" and "horror." Many words that are thought to echo the sound they suggest merely contain some sound that seems to have a resemblance to the thing it suggests. Tennyson's lines from "Come Down, O Maid" are often cited to explain true onomatopoeia:

> "The moan of doves in immemorial elms
> And murmuring of innumerable bees."

Oral Tradition   Passing songs, poems, and stories down through the ages by word of mouth. Since these selections are spoken rather than written, their words get changed. As a result, there are many different versions of each work, and the original writers and tellers are no longer known.

Oxymoron   The combination of contradictory or incongruous terms. "Living death," "mute cry," and Milton's description of hell as "no light, but rather darkness visible" are all examples of this process. The two words that are brought together to form a description of this nature ought to cancel each other out by the nature of their contradictions; instead, they increase the sense of each word. Thus, "sweet pain" aptly describes certain experiences of love.

P

Parable   A short story that contains a moral or lesson. Parables are very similar to fables.

Pastoral   Any writing concerning itself with shepherds may be called *pastoral*. Often set in Arcadia, a mountainous area in Greece, known for its simple shepherds who live an uncomplicated and contented life, a pastoral can also be called a *bucolic, idyll,* or an *eclogue*. Rural life is usually shown as superior to tainted city life.

Pathetic fallacy   This is a specific kind of personification in which inanimate objects are given human emotions. John Ruskin originated the term in *Modern Painters* (1856). Ruskin uses the example of "the cruel crawling foam" of the ocean to discuss the pathetic fallacy: the ocean is not cruel, happy to inflict pain on others, as a person may be, although it may well seem cruel to those who have suffered because of it. Ruskin obviously disapproved of such misstatement and allowed it only in verse where the poet was so moved by passion that he could not be expected to speak with greater accuracy. But in all truly great poetry, Ruskin held, the speaker is able to contain his excess emotion to express himself accurately. The term is used today, however, without this negative implication.

Personification Giving human traits to nonhuman things. For example: "The book begged to be read."

Persuasion A type of writing or speech that tries to move an audience to thought or action. Newspaper editorials, advertisements, and letters to the editor are all examples of persuasive writing.

Play See *Drama*.

Playwright A person who writes a play.

Plot The arrangement of events in a work of literature. Plots have a beginning, middle, and end. The writer arranges the events of the plot to keep the reader's interest and convey the theme. In many stories and novels, the events of the plot can be divided as follows:

- *Exposition*: introduces the characters, setting, and conflict.
- *Rising Action*: builds the conflict and develops the characters.
- *Climax:* shows the highest point of the action.
- *Denouement: r*esolves the story and ties up all the loose ends.

Poetry A type of literature in which words are selected for their beauty, sound, and power to express feelings. Traditionally, poems had a specific rhythm and rhyme, but such modern poetry as *free verse* does not have regular beat, rhyme, or line length. Most poems are written in lines, which are arranged together in groups called *stanzas*.

Point of View The position from which a story is told. Here are the three different points of view you will encounter most often in literature.

- *First-person point of view:* The narrator is one of the characters in the story. The narrator explains the events through his or her own eyes, using the pronouns *I* and *me*.
- *Third-person omniscient point of view:* The narrator is not a character in the story. Instead, the narrator looks through the eyes of all the characters. As a result, the narrator is all-knowing. The narrator uses the pronouns *he, she,* and *they*.
- *Third-person limited point of view:* The narrator tells the story through the eyes of only one character, using the pronouns *he, she,* and *they*.

Prose All written work that is not poetry, drama, or song. Examples of prose include articles, autobiographies, biographies, novels, essays, and editorials.

Protagonist The most important character in a work of literature. The protagonist is at the center of the conflict and the focus of our attention.

Purpose See *Author's Purpose*.

Q

Quatrains   Four-line stanzas.

R

Realism   In contrast to Naturalism, Realism is the detailed presentation of appearances of everyday life. William Dean Howells, a notable Realist, said that the movement "sought to front the every-day world and catch the charm of its work-worn, care-worn, brave, kindly faces." This movement is closely linked to the Local Color school, which concentrated on picturesque details—scenery, customs, language—characteristic of a certain region. Though often sentimental, Local Color could go beyond externals and delve into character and thus is an important part of realism. In its humble, everyday subject matter, Realism has its roots in Romanticism, but Realism generally shuns the Romantic interest in the exotic and mysterious. After the Civil War, American Realism showed a note of disillusionment not present in Howells, painting little people who had their share of petty vices. This can be found in the work of Mark Twain, Stephen Crane, and Hamlin Garland. Realism is not the same as Naturalism, which usually paints a picture of life determined by the twin forces of heredity and environment.

Refrain   A line or a group of lines that are repeated at the end of a poem or song. Refrains serve to reinforce the main point and create musical effects.

Repetition   Using the same sound, word, phrase, line, or grammatical structure over and over. Authors use repetition to link related ideas and emphasize key points.

Resolution   The *resolution* of a plot occurs near the end when all the remaining strands of the story are woven together.

Rhyme   The repeated use of identical or nearly identical sounds. *End rhyme* occurs when words at the end of lines of poetry have the same sound. Lines that end with the words *bat, cat, sat*, or *rat* would have end rhyme. *Internal rhyme* occurs when words within a sentence share the same sound. Poets use rhyme to create a musical sound, meaning, and structure.

Rhyme Scheme   A regular pattern of words that end with the same sound.

Rhythm   A pattern of stressed and unstressed syllables that create a beat, as in music. The *meter* of a poem is its rhythm. When you read a poem, use the punctuation and capitalization in each line to help you decide where to pause and what words to stress to make the rhythm clear.

Romance   The Romance describes strange lands and wonderful adventures. It allows the writer greater latitude to "mingle the Marvelous as a slight, delicate, and evanescent favor," in Nathaniel Hawthorne's words (in his preface to *The House of the Seven Gables*). A novel, in contrast to a Romance, assumes the writer will aim at a very minute fidelity to facts, but here the writer may, as Hawthorne again remarks, "swerve aside from the truth of the human heart." The Romance may include the traditional hero with the white hat on the white horse, the evil villain with the long black mustache, the lovely young woman in need of rescue, and the hairbreadth rescue.

S

Sarcasm   Crude and heavy-handed verbal irony.

Scan/Scanning   To *scan* a poem is to figure out its meter (its pattern of stressed and unstressed syllables).

Scene   A part of a play. Each scene in a play takes place during a set time and in one place.

Science Fiction   Fantasy writing that tells about make-believe events that include science or technology. Often, science fiction is set in the future, on distant planets, or among alien races.

Sensory Language   Words that appeal to the five senses: sight, hearing, taste, touch, or smell.

Setting   The time and place where the events take place. The setting may be stated outright, or you may have to infer it from details in the story. To infer the setting, look for words that tell *when* and *where*. Also look for clues in the characters' speech, clothing, or means of transportation.

Sextets   Six-line stanzas.

Short Story   A narrative prose fiction shorter than a novel that focuses on a single character and a single event. Most short stories can be read in one sitting and convey a single overall impression.

Simile   A figure of speech that compares two unlike things. Similes use the words "like" or "as" to make the comparison. "A dream put off dries up like a raisin in the sun" is an example of a simile. Here are some additional examples:

> My heart is like a singing bird. (C. Rossetti)
>
> I am weaker than a woman's tear. (Shakespeare)
>
> Seems he a dove? His feathers are but borrowed. (Shakespeare)

Slash   A slash (/) is used as a divider to separate feet in a line. It is also used to separate lines of poetry written as straight text.

Socratic Irony   This form of irony is named for Socrates, who usually pretended to be ignorant when he was in fact cautious or tentative. People who state "I do not understand; please explain this to me" are Socratic ironists and their words are ironic, for they *do* understand.

Soliloquy   A speech one character speaks while alone on the stage. In the soliloquy, the character often voices his or her deepest thoughts or concerns. Hamlet's "To be or not to be" speech is a famous example.

Sonnet   A fourteen-line lyric poem, written in iambic pentameter (five accents per line). There are two main sonnet forms. Originally, both forms came into the language as love verses, but sonnets have been used for many different themes and subjects.

The first was originated by the Italian poets in the thirteenth century and reached its final form a century later in the work of Petrarch; thus, it came to be called the *Petrarchan* or *Italian sonnet*. The first eight lines, called the *octave*, rhyme abbaabba and present the subject of the poem; the final six lines, called the *sestet,* rhyme cdecde and resolve the problem or situation set forth in the first eight lines.

The English poets of the sixteenth century altered the rhyme scheme of the Italian sonnet, creating an abab/cdcd/efef/gg pattern, which has come to be called the *Shakespearean* or *English sonnet.*

Speaker   The personality the writer assumes when telling a story. For example, the writer can tell the story as a young girl, old man, or figure from history. It is important not to confuse the speaker with the author. Also called *personae.*

Sprung Rhythm   A reintroduction of accentual verse in the works of Gerard Manley Hopkins (1844–1889), in which strongly accented syllables are pushed up against unaccented ones to produce greater tension and emphasis within the verse.

Stage Directions   Instructions to the actors, producer, and director telling how to perform the play. Stage directions are included in the text of the play, written in parenthesis or *italics*. Stage directions can describe how actors should speak, what they should wear, and what scenery should be used, for example.

Stanza   A group of lines in a poem. Lines of poems are grouped into stanzas, just as sentences of prose are grouped into paragraphs. Each stanza presents one complete idea.

Stanzas may be classified as follows:

Couplets	Two-line stanzas
Quatrains	Four-line stanzas
Sextets	Six-line stanzas
Octets	Eight-line stanzas

Style   An author's distinctive way of writing. Style is made up of elements such as word choice, sentence length and structure, figures of speech, and tone. An author may change his or her style for different kinds of writing and to suit different audiences. In poetry, for example, authors might use more imagery than they would use in prose.

Surprise Ending   A conclusion that is different from what the reader expected. In most stories, the ending follows logically from the arrangement of events in the plot. In a surprise ending, however, final events take an unexpected twist. A surprise ending always makes sense in retrospect, however.

Surrealism   The Surrealist aims to go beyond what is usually considered "real" to the "super real," which would include the world of dreams and the unconscious. Surrealists especially shun middle-class ideals and artistic traditions, believing that all these deform the creations of the artist's unconscious. With its emphasis on spontaneity, feeling, and sincerity, Surrealism is linked to Romanticism. The movement was especially strong in France in the 1920s and 1930s.

Suspense   The feeling of tension or anticipation an author creates in a work. Authors create suspense by unexpected plot twists. This keeps readers interested in the story and makes them want to read on to find out what will happen.

Syllabic Verse   A system of verse in which syllables are used to determine the length of a line of poetry. This type of verse flourished mainly in the period between 1066–1400, although modern poets have experimented with it.

Symbol   A person, place, or object that represents an abstract idea. For example, a dove may symbolize peace or a rose may symbolize love.

Symbolism   Symbolism occurs when an image stands for something other than what was expected. The ocean, for example, may be said to symbolize "eternity," and the phrase "river to the sea" could stand for "life flowing into afterlife." In most instances, the symbol does not directly reveal what it stands for; rather, the meaning must be discovered through a close reading of the literary work and an understanding of conventional literary and cultural symbols. For example, we realize that the "stars and stripes" stands for the American flag. We know this because we are told it is so, for the flag itself in no way looks like the United States. Without cultural agreement, many of the symbols we commonly accept would be meaningless.

Symbolist Movement   The Symbolist movement arose in France in the second half of the nineteenth century and included writers Mallarmé and Valéry. W. B. Yeats, the Irish writer, was influenced by the movement. Some Symbolists believed in an invisible world beyond that of concrete events—Yeats, for example, experimented with automatic writing—but other Symbolists found the concrete world stimulated their writings. Symbolists believed that an object was neither a real thing nor the holder of divine essence; it simply called forth emotions, which were communicated by words whose sounds would be able, they thought, to call forth the same emotion in the reader. Extreme followers of the Symbolist movement believed that poetry was sound with associations rather than words with meanings.

Synecdoche   The substitution of a part of something for the whole, or the whole is used in place of one of the parts. "Ten sails" would thus stand for ten ships. In the stanza below by American poet Emily Dickinson, "morning" and "noon," parts of the day, are used to refer to the whole day. In the same manner, "Rafter of Satin" refers to a coffin, by describing its inner lining rather than the entire object:

> Safe in their Alabaster Chambers—
>
> Untouched by Morning—
>
> And untouched by Noon—
>
> Lie the meek members of the Resurrection—
>
> Rafter of Satin—and Roof of Stone!

Synesthesia   This figure of speech takes one of the five senses and creates a picture or image of sensation as perceived by another. For example, "the golden cry of the trumpet" combines "golden," a visual perception of color, with "cry," hearing. In the same manner, Emily Dickinson speaks of a fly's "blue, uncertain stumbling buzz."

T

Tall Tale   A folk tale that exaggerates the main events or the characters' abilities. Tall tales came from the oral tradition, as pioneers sitting around the campfires at night tried to top each other's outrageous stories. Twain's short story "The Celebrated Jumping Frog of Calaveras County" is a tall tale.

Theme   The main idea of a literary work, it's a general statement about life. The theme can be stated outright in the work, or readers will have to infer it from details about plot, characters, and setting.

Tone   The writer's attitude toward his or her subject matter. For example, the tone can be angry, bitter, sad, or frightening.

Transferred Epithet   A word or phrase shifted from the noun it would usually describe to one that has no logical connection with it, as in Gray's "drowsy tinklings," where "drowsy" literally describes the sheep who wear the bells, but here is figuratively applied to the bells. In current usage, the distinction between metonymy, synecdoche, and transferred epithet is so slight that the word *metonymy* is often used to cover them all.

Travesty   Also known as *low burlesque,* travesty takes a high theme and treats it in trivial terms, as in the Greek "Battle of the Frogs and Mice," which travesties Homer.

True, Exact, or Perfect Rhyme   When the first consonants change, but following consonants or vowels stay the same. These involve identity of sound, not spelling. "Fix" and "sticks," like "buffer" and "rougher," though spelled differently, are perfect rhymes. Anne Bradstreet's "Before the Birth of One of Her Children" (1678) illustrates true rhyme:

> All things within this fading world hath end,
>
> Adversity doth still our joys attend;
>
> No ties so strong, no friends so dear and sweet,
>
> But with death's parting blow is sure to meet.

   In the lines quoted, "end," which we shall call *a*, rhymes with "attend," also called *a*, while "sweet," called *b*, rhymes with "meet." The rhyme scheme, then, is *aabb,* etc.

Turning Point   See *Climax.*

U

Understatement   The opposite of *exaggeration,* a statement that states less than it indirectly suggests, as in Jonathan Swift's "Last week I saw a woman flayed, and you will hardly believe how much it altered her person for the worst." In the same way, Auden's ironic poem "The Unknown Citizen" has a great many examples of understatement that combine to show how numbers cannot evaluate the ultimate happiness of a person's life.

V

Verse   A stanza in a poem.

Villanelle   A poetic form that not only rhymes but also repeats lines in a predetermined manner, both as a refrain and as an important part of the poem itself. Five stanzas of three lines each are followed by a quatrain. The first and third lines of the first stanza are repeated in a prescribed alternating order as the last lines of the remaining tercets, becoming the last two lines of the final quatrain. Dylan Thomas's "Do Not Go Gentle Into That Good Night" is a modern villanelle.

Voice   The author's unique attitude toward the material.

Guide to Grammar and Usage

CRIB SHEET

Use the following section for a quick review of grammar and usage.

Adjectives are words that modify (describe or limit) nouns and pronouns.

Adjective clauses describe nouns and pronouns.

Adverb clause is a dependent clause that describes a verb, adjective, or other adverb.

Adverbial phrase is a prepositional phrase that modifies a verb, an adjective, or an adverb.

Agreement means that sentence parts match. Subjects must agree with verbs, and pronouns must agree with antecedents.

Appositive is a noun or a pronoun that renames another noun or pronoun.

Appositive phrases are nouns or pronouns with modifiers.

Bias-free language uses words and phrases that don't discriminate on the basis of gender, physical condition, age, race, or anything else.

Case is the form of a noun or pronoun that shows how it is used in a sentence. Case is the grammatical role a noun or pronoun plays in a sentence. English has three cases: *nominative, objective,* and *possessive.*

Clause is a group of words with its own subject and verb.

Collective nouns name a group of people or things. Collective nouns include the words *class, committee, flock, herd, team, audience, assembly, team, club,* and so on.

Complex sentences have one independent clause and at least one dependent clause.

Compound-complex sentences have at least two independent clauses and at least one dependent clause.

Conjugate a verb to list the singular and plural forms of the verb in a specific tense.

Conjunctions connect words or groups of words.

Conjunctive adverbs are used to connect other words. Conjunctive adverbs are also called *transitions* because they link ideas.

Connotation is a word's emotional overtones.

Dangling modifiers are words or phrases that describe something that has been left out of the sentence.

Denotation is a word's dictionary meaning.

Dependent (subordinate) clause is part of a sentence; it cannot stand alone.

Doublespeak is artificial, evasive language.

Diction is a writer's choice of words.

Compound sentences have two or more independent clauses.

Grammar is a branch of linguistics that deals with the form and structure of words.

Indefinite pronouns refer to people, places, objects, or things without pointing to a specific one.

Independent clause is a complete sentence; it can stand alone.

Indirect objects tell *to* or *for* whom something is done.

Infinitive is a verb form that comes after the word "to" and functions as a noun, adjective, or adverb.

Interjections show strong emotion. Often, interjections will be set off with an exclamation mark.

Linking verbs indicate a state of being (*am, is, are*, etc.), relate to the senses (*look, smell, taste*, etc.), or indicate a condition (*appear, seem, become*, etc.).

Mechanics include punctuation, numbers, quotation marks, capitalization, abbreviations, and italics.

Misplaced modifiers are a phrase, clause, or word placed too far from the word or words it modifies.

Mixed metaphors are a combination of images that do not work well together. They occur when writers string together clichés.

Mood shows the attitude expressed toward the action. It refers to the ability of verbs to convey a writer's attitude toward a subject.

Nouns name a person, place, or thing.

Noun clause is a dependent clause that functions as a noun.

Number refers to the two forms of a word: *singular* (one) or *plural* (more than one).

Parallel structure means putting ideas of the same rank in the same grammatical structure.

Participle is a form of a verb that functions as an adjective. There are two kinds of participles: *present participles* and *past participles.*

Phrase is a group of words, without a subject or a verb, that functions in a sentence as a single part of speech.

Predicate adjectives are adjectives separated from the noun or pronoun by a linking verb. Predicate adjectives describe the subject of the sentence.

Predicate nominatives are a noun or pronoun that follow a linking verb. A predicate nominative renames or identifies the subject.

Prepositions are words that link a noun or a pronoun to another word in the sentence.

Prepositional phrases are groups of words that begin with a preposition and end with a noun or a pronoun.

Pronouns are words used in place of a noun or another pronoun. An *antecedent* is the noun the pronoun stands for.

Redundancy is unnecessary repetition of words and ideas.

Relative clause is an adjective clause that begins with one of the relative pronouns.

Run-on sentences are two incorrectly joined independent clauses. A *comma splice* is a run-on with a comma where the two sentences run together.

Sentence is a group of words that express a complete thought.

Sentence coordination links ideas of equal importance.

Sentence fragments are a group of words that do not express a complete thought.

Sexist language assigns qualities to people on the basis of their gender. It reflects prejudiced attitudes and stereotypical thinking about the sex roles and traits of both men and women.

Simple sentence is a sentence with one independent clause.

Slang is coined words and phrases or new meanings for established terms.

Split infinitives occur when an adverb or adverbial phrase is placed between *to* and the verb.

Style is a writer's distinctive way of writing.

Subordination is connecting two unequal but related ideas with a subordinating conjunction to form a complex sentence.

Tense shows the time of a verb.

Tone is the writer's attitude toward his or her subject and audience.

Usage is the customary way we use language in speech and writing. The correct level of usage is the one that is appropriate for the occasion.

Verbal is a verb form used as another part of speech.

Verbs are words that name an action or describe a state of being.

Voice is the form of the verb that shows whether the subject performed the action or received the action.

GRAMMAR 101

Use this section to review grammar and usage in depth.

ADJECTIVES AND ADVERBS
Adjectives

Adjectives describe nouns and pronouns. Adjectives answer the questions *What kind? How much? Which one?* or *How many?*

There are four kinds of adjectives: *articles, common adjectives, compound adjectives,* and *proper adjectives.*

Articles: A, an, and *the* are "articles."

The is called the "definite article" because it refers to a specific thing.

Examples: The poem   The novel   The student

A and *an* are "indefinite articles" because they refer to general things.

Examples: A poem   A novel   An author

Use *an* in place of *a* when it precedes a vowel sound, not just a vowel.

Examples: an honor a UFO

Common adjectives: They describe nouns or pronouns.

Examples: big book   excellent poem superb style

Compound adjectives: These adjectives are comprised of more than one word.

Examples: nearsighted reader   first-time test taker
              hard-working student

Proper adjectives: These adjectives are formed from proper nouns.

Examples: <u>Mexican</u> poet   <u>French</u> bread

Here are two hints for using adjectives well:

* Use an adjective to describe a noun or a pronoun.
* Choose precise adjectives rather than piling them on. One perfect adjective is far more powerful than a string of inaccurate ones.

Predicate adjectives are adjectives separated from the noun or pronoun by a linking verb. Predicate adjectives describe the subject of the sentence.

Example: The weather was *cold* all week.

Adverbs

Adverbs describe verbs, adjectives, or other adverbs. Adverbs answer the following questions: *When? Where? How?* or *To What Extent?*

Most adverbs are formed by adding *-ly* to an adjective.

Examples: wrote <u>quickly</u>   edited <u>slowly</u> worked <u>carefully</u>

Here is a list of the most common adverbs that don't end in *-ly*:

Adverbs that Don't End in *-ly*

afterward	almost	already	also	back
even	far	fast	hard	here
how	late	long	low	more
never	next	now	often	rather
so soon	still	then	there	today
too	tomorrow	when	where	yesterday

Here are hints for using adverbs well:

* Use an adverb to describe a verb, an adjective, or another adverb.
* As with adjectives, choose the precise adverb to get just the meaning you want. You can use an online or print thesaurus to help you find the exact adjectives and adverbs you want.

Comparing with Adjectives and Adverbs

Adjectives and adverbs are often used to compare by showing that one thing is larger, smaller, bigger, or more important than something else. English makes this easy by giving us a special way to compare two things (the *comparative degree*) and a special way to compare more than two things (the *superlative degree*). Here's how to do it.

Use the *comparative degree* (*-er* or *more* form) to compare two things.

Examples: John is <u>taller</u> than Chris. Jess is <u>younger</u> than Nicole.

Use the *superlative form* (*-est* or *most* form) to compare more than two things.

Examples: This is the <u>finest</u> novel I have ever read!

Don't you think writing is the <u>nicest</u> way to spend a day?

Never use *-er* and *more* or *-est* and *most* together.

Examples: I have a <u>more slower</u> computer.   I have a <u>slower</u> computer.

I have the <u>most biggest</u> monitor.   I have the <u>biggest</u> monitor.

Good and *bad* do not follow these guidelines. They have irregular forms, as follows:

Part of Speech	Positive	Comparative	Superlative
adjective	good	better	best
adverb	well	better	best
adjective	bad	worse	worst
adverb	badly	worse	worst

AGREEMENT

Agreement means matching parts of a sentence. When sentence parts match, your writing sounds smooth. If they don't match, it sounds jarring or awkward.

Agreement of Pronoun and Antecedent

Pronouns and antecedents (the words to which they refer) must *agree* or match. Here's the basic guideline: a personal pronoun must agree with its antecedent in number, person, and gender.

<u>Number</u> is amount: singular or plural.

<u>Person</u> refers to first person, second person, or third person (the person speaking, the person spoken to, or the person spoken about).

<u>Gender</u> refers to masculine, feminine, or neuter references. *He* and *him* are masculine in gender, *she* and *her* are feminine, and *it* and *its* are neuter.

Examples:

Number: <u>Marla and Carol</u> wrote <u>their</u> essays.

Person: <u>Leigh</u> wrote in <u>her</u> journal every night.

Gender: <u>Jim</u> studies grammar, a subject <u>he</u> needs to do well on the AP Language exam.

In the past, the pronouns *he* and *his* were used to refer to both men and women. We would write or say: "A writer should try <u>his</u> hand at different kinds of poetry," or "Anyone can learn to write well if <u>he</u> applies <u>himself</u>."

Today, using the pronouns *he* and *his* to refer to both men and women is considered sexist language. As a result, avoid this usage. Try these ideas:

• Rewrite the sentence into the third-person *they* or *them*.

Example: <u>Writers</u> should try <u>their</u> hands at different kinds of poetry.

• Rewrite the sentence into the second person *you*.

Example: <u>You</u> should try <u>your</u> hand at different kinds of poetry.

• Eliminate the pronoun altogether.

Example: Try writing different kinds of poetry.

Agreement of Subject and Verb

To make your writing sound polished, be sure that subjects and verbs are in the same form. Here are some guidelines.

A singular subject takes a singular verb.

Example: <u>He edits</u> (not <u>edit</u>) everything he writes.

A plural subject takes a plural verb.

Example: <u>Luis and Marc edit</u> (not <u>edits</u>) everything they write.

Prepositional phrases that come between the subject and the verb don't affect agreement.

Example: Too many *mistakes* <u>in an essay</u> can *block* meaning.

(The plural subject *mistakes* requires the plural verb *block*. Ignore the

 prepositional phrase "in an essay.")

Subjects that are singular in meaning but plural in form take a singular verb. These subjects include words such as *measles, news,* and *economics*.

Example: The <u>news was</u> encouraging.

NOTE
A pronoun replaces a noun. To make sure that your writing is clear, always use the noun first before using the pronoun.
Example: <u>Justin</u> read his practice AP essay to his friends. <u>He</u> read with great emotion.

Singular subjects connected by *either/or, neither/nor,* and *not only/but also* take a singular verb.

Example: Either the student <u>or</u> the teacher <u>was</u> going to proofead the essay.

If the subject is made up of two or more nouns or pronouns connected by *or, nor, not only,* or *but also*, the verb agrees with the noun closest to the pronoun.

Examples: Neither Chris nor the <u>scorers are </u>done working.

Neither the scorers nor <u>Chris is </u>done working.

BIASED LANGUAGE

Avoid *biased language*, words and phrases that assign qualities to people on the basis of their gender, race, religion, or health. Here are some guidelines:

- Avoid using *he* to refer to both men and women.
- Avoid using *man* to refer to both men and women.
- Avoid language that denigrates people.

CAPITALIZATION

Capitalization is one of the writer's most useful tools, because it helps convey meaning. For example, when readers see a capital letter, they know they've reached the beginning of a sentence, a quotation, or a person's name. This helps your audience read your writing the way you intended it to be read! Below are the rules for using capital letters correctly.

Capitalize the first word of a sentence, the greeting of a letter, the

complimentary close of a letter, and each item in an outline.

Capitalize geographical places and sections of the country; the names of historical events, eras, and documents; and abbreviations that appear after a person's name.

Capitalize the names of languages, nationalities, races, and nationalities.

Capitalize proper nouns, proper adjectives, and brand names.

Capitalize the names of organizations, institutions, courses, and famous buildings.

Capitalize days, months, and holidays.

Capitalize abbreviations for time.

CONJUNCTIONS

Conjunctions are words or pairs of words that link ideas. Use them to help create meaning and logic in writing. As you draft, select the conjunctions that give you the precise shade of meaning you want. To make your job easier, you may wish to choose conjunctions from this list as you write:

Conjunctions

after	although	and	as
as if	because	before	both...and
but	either...or	even though	for
if	neither...nor	or	not only...but also
nor	since	so	so that
than	though	unless	until
when	where	wherever	while

CONTRACTIONS

Contractions are two words combined into one. When you contract words, add an apostrophe in the space where the letter or letters have been taken out.

Examples:

I + am	=	I'm		she + is	=	she's
you + are	=	you're		we + are	=	we're
he + is	=	he's		it + is	=	it's

Contractions are often confused with *possessive pronouns*. You may wish to use this chart to keep the two clear:

Contraction	Possessive Pronoun
it's (it is)	its
you're (you are)	your
they're (they are)	their
who's (who is)	whose

DOUBLE NEGATIVES

Use only one negative word to express a negative idea. Using two negative words cancels them both out.

Example: I do<u>n't</u> have <u>no</u> ideas.   I do<u>n't</u> have any ideas.

The most common negative words are *n't (don't, etc.), no, nobody, not, no one, nothing, nowhere, never,* and *neither.*

INTERJECTIONS

Interjections are words that show strong emotion. Often, interjections will be set off with an exclamation mark. For example: *Watch out!*, *Oh!*, *Wow!*

NONSTANDARD ENGLISH

Nonstandard English consists of words and phrases that are not considered standard written English.

Examples:	*Nonstandard:*	irregardless	being that	hisself
	Standard:	regardless	since	himself

Nonstandard English can work effectively in dialogue, as Mark Twain showed in *The Adventures of Huckleberry Finn,* however.

NOUNS

A *noun* is a word that names a person, place, or thing. There are different kinds of nouns, as follows:

Common nouns name a type of person, place, or thing.

Examples:	play	poem	movie

Proper nouns name a specific person, place, or thing

Examples:	*Hamlet*	"Trees"	*Citizen Kane*

Plural Nouns

Plural nouns name more than one person, place, or thing. Here are the guidelines for forming plural nouns.

Add *s* to form the plural of most nouns.

Examples:	book/books	play/plays	noun/nouns

Add *es* if the noun ends in *s, sh, ch,* or *x.*

Examples:	inch/inches	box/boxes

If the noun ends in *y* preceded by a *consonant,* change the *y* to *i* and add *es.*

Examples:	city/cities	baby/babies

If the noun ends in *y* preceded by a *vowel,* add *s.*

Examples:	essay/essays	journey/journeys

If the noun ends in *o* preceded by a *consonant,* some nouns take *es,* some take *s,* and some take either *s* or *es.*

Examples:	hero/heroes	piano/pianos	motto/mottos, mottoes

Some nouns ending in *f* take *s;* others change the *f* or *fe* to *v* and add *es*

Examples: belief/beliefs   life/lives

Some nouns change their spelling when they become plural.

Examples: child/children   foot/feet

Some nouns have the same form whether they are singular or plural.

Examples: series   moose

Possessive Nouns

Possession shows ownership. Here are the rules:

Add an apostrophe and an *s* to singular nouns.

Example: writer   writer's essay

With plural nouns ending is *s*, add an apostrophe after the *s*.

Example: writers   writers' essays

With plural nouns not ending in *s*, add an apostrophe and an *s*.

Example: children   children's story book

PREPOSITIONS

Prepositions are words that link a noun or a pronoun to another word in the sentence. Prepositions are handy because they allow you to show how parts of a sentence are related to each other.

Here are some of the most common prepositions:

Common Prepositions

about	against	around	behind
between	despite	for	into
off	out	since	under
upon	above	along	as
below	beyond	down	from
like	on	outside	through
underneath	with	across	amid
at	beneath	but	during
in	near	onto	over
to	until	within	after
around	before	beside	by
except	inside	opposite	of
opposite	past	toward	up

NOTE
Remember that possessive pronouns don't require an apostrophe. The possessive pronouns are *yours, hers, its, ours, theirs,* and *whose.*

A *prepositional phrase* is a preposition and its object.

Examples: on the wing   in the door

PRONOUNS

Pronouns are words used in place of a noun or another pronoun. There are several different kinds of pronouns. The most common ones are *personal pronouns, possessive pronouns, interrogative pronouns,* and *indefinite pronouns.*

Personal pronouns point out a specific person, place, object, or thing:

	Singular	*Plural*
first-person	I, me, mine, my	we, us, our, ours
second-person	you, your, yours	you, your, yours
third-person	he, him, his she, her, hers, it	they, them, their, theirs, its

Possessive pronouns show ownership.

Examples: mine   yours   his   hers
          its   ours   theirs whose

Interrogative pronouns begin a question.

Examples: who   what   which   whom whose

Indefinite pronouns refer to people, places, objects, or things without pointing to a specific one.

Examples: another   anybody everyone everything
          nobody   none   one   some

Pronoun Case

Pronouns often trouble us because they have different forms for different uses. *Case* is the form of a noun or pronoun that shows how it is used in a sentence. English has three cases: *nominative, objective,* and *possessive.* This means that the pronouns have one form as a subject, another as an object, and a third to show possession, as the following chart shows.

Pronoun Case

Nominative (as a subject)	Objective (as an object)	Possessive (to show ownership)
I	me	my, mine
you	you	you
he	him	his
she	her	hers
it	it	its
we	us	our, ours
they	them	their, theirs
who	whom	whose
whoever	whomever	whosoever

Here are some guidelines to make it easier for you to use pronouns with assurance.

Use the nominative case to show the subject of a verb.

Example: <u>We</u> took practice AP Language tests.

Use the objective case to show the noun or pronoun that receives the action.

Example: The book was helpful to <u>us</u>.

Use the possessive case to show ownership.

Example: The teacher gave us <u>her</u> advice about taking the AP Language test.

PUNCTUATION

Punctuation is an important writing tool because it helps determine meaning. Each mark of punctuation provides important visual clues to readers, showing where sentences begin and end, telling readers where to pause, and so on. Here are the basic rules.

Apostrophes (') are used three ways:

To show possession (ownership)

Examples: Morrison's novel   Shaw's play   Charles' letter

To show contractions (where a letter or number has been omitted)

Examples: can't   won't   didn't
              the '60s   the '90s

To show plural forms

Examples: three 8's or eight 3's   your n's look like h's

Brackets: Use [ ] to show words that interrupt a direct quotation.

Example: "Four score and seven years [87 years] ago, our fathers brought forth on this continent, a new nation, conceived in Liberty, and dedicated to the proposition that all men are created equal."

You probably won't be using brackets a lot, since it's not often that you'll have to interrupt a direct quotation to clarify it or add information.

Colons: Use a colon before a list. This is a colon :

Example: We proofread for the following issues: capitalization, punctuation, and spelling.

Commas: Use a comma after introductory words and expressions, to separate items in a series, to set off interrupting words and expressions, to separate parts of a compound sentence, and at the close of any letter.

Examples:

If you want to do well on the AP test, you must study hard.

You can study simulated test questions, write essays, and review novels.

This process, I know, will help you earn a high grade.

Dashes

Use a dash to show a sudden change of thought. A dash is a long hyphen, like this —

Example: Students can do very well on the AP Language and Composition test—if they prepare thoroughly.

Ellipses: Use these three spaced periods to show that something has been left out.

Example: (original quote) But in a larger sense, we cannot dedicate—we cannot consecrate—we cannot hallow—this ground.

(edited quote) But in a larger sense, we cannot dedicate. . . this ground.

Exclamation marks: Use an exclamation mark to show strong emotion.

Example: I can't believe I reviewed an entire novel last night!

Hyphen: Use a hyphen to show a word break at the end of a line, in some compound nouns, and in fractions and in compound numbers. A hyphen looks like this -

Example: mother-in-law   three-quarters   fifty-five

Parentheses: Use parentheses to enclose additional information.

TIP

Can't tell if you're using too many commas? When in doubt, leave it out!

NOTE

Unless you're writing comic books, use only one exclamation mark at the end of a sentence.

Example: Perhaps the best part about doing well on the AP test (despite the hard work) is the deep satisfaction it gives you to succeed at a difficult task.

Periods: Use a period after a complete sentence, most abbreviations, and initials.

Examples: Try to study for at least an hour a day.

I like to study before school or after 8:00 p.m.

Dr. Martin Luther King, Jr. was a superb writer.

Question Marks: Use a question mark after a question.

Example: Did you write that practice essay within 40 minutes?

Quotation Marks: Use quotation marks to set off a speaker's exact words.

Example: "This draft is astonishingly good," the teacher said.

The teacher said, "This is draft is astonishingly good."

"This draft," the teacher said, "is astonishingly good."

Semicolons: Use a semicolon between main clauses when the conjunction (*and, but, for, or, yet*) has been left out and to separate items in a series when the items contain commas.

Examples: I study on my own and I study in small groups.
I study on my own; I study in small groups.

SENTENCE ERRORS

A *sentence* is a group of words that expresses a complete thought. A sentence has two parts: a *subject* and a *predicate*. The subject includes the noun or pronoun that identifies the subject. The predicate contains the verb that describes what the subject is doing.

Example: Ernest Hemingway / wrote /   novels and short stories.
subject   verb   predicate

Sentence Fragments and Run-Ons

Sentence *fragments* and *run-ons* are often used in dialogue to show everyday speech, but they are considered sentence errors when used in straight text.

A *sentence fragment* is a group of words that does not express a complete thought. It may also be missing a subject, verb, or both.

Example: Studied all night.   **I** studied all night.

A *run-on sentence* consists of two incorrectly joined sentences.

Example: My teacher advised us not to study all night we will not absorb much.

There are three ways to correct a run-on sentence:

1. Separate the run-on into two sentences:

Example: My teacher advised us not to study all night. We will not absorb much.

2. Add a conjunction. You might add a coordinating conjunction (*and, but, or, for, yet, so):*

Example: My teacher advised us not to study all night, for we will not absorb much.

You might add a subordinating conjunction:

Example: My teacher advised us not to study all night because we will not absorb much.

3. Add a semicolon.

Example: My teacher advised us not to study all night; we will not absorb much.

Select the repair method depending on your audience, purpose, and unique writing style.

Dangling Modifiers

A *dangling modifier* is a word or phrase that describes something that has been left out of the sentence. As a result, the sentence does not convey the correct meaning. It may also unintentionally cause humor. Correct a dangling modifier by adding a noun or pronoun to which the dangling modifier can be attached.

Example: *Dangling*: Coming up the stairs, the clock struck midnight.
Correct: As he was coming up the stairs, the clock struck midnight.

Misplaced Modifiers

A *misplaced modifier* is a descriptive word or phrase that is placed too far away from the noun or the pronoun that it describes. As a result, the sentence is unclear. It may be confusing or unintentionally funny. To correct a misplaced modifier, move the modifier as close as possible to the word or phrase it is describing, as the following example shows:

Sam found a letter in the mailbox that didn't belong to her.

What the writer thinks this sentence says: Sam found a letter that didn't belong to her.

What this sentence really says: The mailbox doesn't belong to Sam.

Correction: Sam found a letter that doesn't belong to her in the mailbox.

SENTENCE TYPES

There are four types of sentences in English: *declarative, exclamatory, interrogative*, and *imperative*.

Declarative sentences state an idea. They end with a period.

Example: Good writers are made, not born.

Exclamatory sentences show strong emotions. They end with an exclamation mark.

Example: What a high score you will earn!

Interrogative sentences ask a question. They end with a question mark.

Example: When is the AP test given?

Imperative sentences give orders or directions. They end with a period or an exclamation mark.

Example: Do Practice Test 3, please.

SENTENCE VARIETY

Unless you are writing certain kinds of dialogue, all your sentences should be grammatically correct. In addition, craft your sentences to express your ideas in the best possible way. Strive for rhythm, pattern, and variety as well. Here are some ideas to try:

Expand short sentences by adding detail.

Short: The plane took off.

Expanded: The plane took off, a shrieking golden ribbon in the morning sky.

Combine short sentences.

Short: O. Henry wrote a short story called "The Gift of the Magi." A husband sells his watch to buy his wife combs. They are for her beautiful hair.

Combined: In O. Henry's short story "The Gift of the Magi," a husband sells his watch to buy his wife combs for her beautiful hair.

Change sentence openings to create emphasis and rhythm.

Sentence: I unlocked the attic door with great difficulty.

Revised: With great difficulty, I unlocked the attic door.

TRANSITIONS

Transitions—words and expressions that signal connections among ideas—can help you achieve coherence in your writing. Each transition signals to the reader how one idea is connected to the next. You'll want to choose the transitions that link your ideas just the way you want. You can use the following chart to help you make your choices:

Transitions	Relationship
Addition	also, and, besides, too, in addition to, further
Contrast	but, nevertheless, yet, in contrast, however, still
Comparison	likewise, in comparison, similarly
Example	for example, for instance, thus, namely
Place	in the front, in the back, here, there, nearby
Result	therefore, consequently, as a result, thus, due to this, accordingly
Summary	as a result, in brief, in conclusion, hence, in short, finally
Time	next, then, finally, first, second, third, fourth, afterwards, before, during, soon, later, meanwhile, subsequently

Use transitions to show how ideas are linked.

Without transition: Frank completed his research. He started his outline.

With transition: *After* Frank completed his research, he started his outline.

VERBS

Verbs are words that name an action or describe a state of being. There are three types of verbs: *action verbs, linking verbs,* and *helping verbs.*

Action verbs tell what the subject does.

Examples: write   draft   revise   edit

Linking verbs join the subject and the predicate and name and describe the subject.

Examples:	appear	become	feel	turn	grow	look
	remain	seem	smell	sound	stay	taste

Helping verbs are added to another verb to make the meaning clearer.

Examples:	am	can	could	does
	had	might	will	would

While all three types of verbs are necessary in writing, action verbs make your writing forceful, while linking verbs tend to make it wordy. As a result, you'll probably want to use action verbs whenever possible.

Verb Tense

Verbs can show time, called tense. Every verb has three parts:

Verb Part	Example
present tense	break
past tense	broke
past participle	broken

Some verbs are *regular*. This means they form the past tense by adding *-d* or *-ed* to the present form.

Other verbs are *irregular*. This means their form changes in the past tense. The following chart shows the most common irregular verbs.

Present Tense	Past Tense	Past Participle
arise	arose	arisen
bear	bore	born or borne
beat	beat	beaten
become	became	become
begin	began	begun
bend	bent	bent
bite	bit	bitten
blow	blew	blown
break	broke	broken
bring	brought	brought
burst	burst	burst
catch	caught	caught
choose	chose	chosen
come	came	come
creep	crept	crept
dig	dug	dug
dive	dived or dove	dived
do	did	done
draw	drew	drawn
drink	drank	drunk
drive	drove	driven
eat	ate	eaten
fall	fell	fallen
fight	fought	fought
fly	flew	flown
forget	forgot	forgotten
forgive	forgave	forgiven

freeze	froze	frozen
get	got	gotten or got
give	gave	given
go	went	gone
grow	grew	grown
hang	hung	hung
hang (execute)	hanged	hanged
hide	hid	hidden
hold	held	held
hurt	hurt	hurt
kneel	knelt	knelt
know	knew	known
lay	laid	laid
lead	led	led
lie (horizontal)	lay	lain
lie (falsehood)	lied	lied
lose	lost	lost
prove	proved	proved or proven
ride	rode	ridden
ring	rang	rung
rise	rose	risen
run	ran	run
say	said	said
see	saw	seen
shake	shook	shaken
show	showed	showed or shown
sing	sang	sung
speak	spoke	spoken
steal	stole	stolen
swim	swam	swum
take	took	taken
teach	taught	taught
throw	threw	thrown
wake	woke, waked	woken or waked
write	wrote	written

Verb Voice

In addition to showing time, most verbs also indicate whether the subject is performing an action or having an action performed on it. This is called verb *voice*. English has two verb voices: the *active voice* and the *passive voice*.

In the *active voice*, the subject performs the action.

Example: Angela took the practice AP Language exam.

In the *passive voice*, the action is performed upon the subject.

Example: The practice AP Language exam was taken by Angela.

The active voice is usually preferable to the passive because it is more vigorous and concise. For example, notice that there are six words in the second example but only four words in the first. Who needs that extra "was" or "by"? These words don't add anything to the meaning. Since they make the sentence wordy, they should be omitted.

Use the passive voice to avoid placing blame or when you don't know who performed the action.

Examples: A mistake was made.   A window was left open.

Tense

Avoid shifting tenses in the middle of a sentence or a paragraph.

Wrong: I *was walking* to class when a huge dog *jumps* up and *attacks* me.

Right: I *was walking* to class when a huge dog *jumped* up and *attacked* me.

Wordiness

Write simply and directly. Omit unnecessary details or ideas that you have already stated. Use a lot of important detail but no unnecessary words.

Omit unnecessary words.

Wordy: We watched the big, massive, black cloud rise up from the level prairie and cover over the sun.

Better: We watched the massive, black cloud rise from the prairie and cover the sun.

Rewrite sentences to eliminate unnecessary words.

Wordy: Sonnets, which are a beautiful poetic form, have fourteen lines and a set rhythm and rhyme.

Better: Sonnets are a beautiful poetic form with fourteen lines and a set rhythm and rhyme.

Study this chart:

Wordy	Concise	Wordy	Concise
honest truth	truth	revert back	revert
past history	history	partial stop	stop
foreign imports	imports	free gift	gift
true facts	facts	most unique	unique
proceed ahead	proceed	at this point in time	now
set a new record	set a record	at the present time	now
small in size	small	few in number	few
complete stop	stop	weather event	snow (rain, etc.)
due to the fact that	because	in order to	to

NOTE
Remember that an
independent clause is
a complete sentence.
A *dependent clause* is
a sentence fragment,
a sentence part.

Sentence Structure

There are four basic types of sentences: *simple sentences, compound sentences, complex sentences,* and *compound-complex sentences.* Let's look at each type of sentence a little more closely to see how you can use them to create your own personal style.

Words Often Confused

Some pairs of words are mixed up with each other. Sometimes, it's because the words sound alike; other times, it's because they're spelled alike. The following words are often confused, misused, and abused.

Word	Definition	Example
accept	take	Accept my thanks.
except	leave out	Everyone except him.
affect	influence	This affects your grade.
effect	result	The effect of the law.
already	before	Elvis already left the room.
all ready	prepared	He was all ready to go.
all together	everyone at once	They yell all together.
altogether	completely	It was altogether wrong.
altar	table of worship	Put the candles on the altar.
alter	to change	Alter the skirt.
ascent	rising	The rocket's ascent took an hour.
assent	agreement	Nod to show assent.
bare	uncovered	The window was bare.
bear	animal	The bear growled.
	endure	Can you bear the noise?
brake	stop	Use the car's brake.
break	destroy	Don't break the dish!
capital	government seat	Visit the capital.
Capitol	where the U.S. legislature meets	Congress meets in the Capitol.
conscience	morally right	Listen to your conscience.
conscious	awake	She was conscious during surgery.
desert	leave behind	Desert a sinking ship.
	arid region	Camels travel in the desert.
dessert	sweet food	I love a rich dessert.
emigrate	leave a country	She emigrated from France.
immigrate	enter a country	To immigrate means to enter a new homeland.

lay	put down	present: The cat lies down.
		past: The cat lay down.
		future: The cat will lie down.
		perfect: The cat has lain down.
lie	be flat	present: Lay your cards down.
		past: He laid the cards down.
		future: He will lay his cards down.
		perfect: She has laid her cards down.
lead	writing material	That's a lead pencil.
led	conducted	We were led to safety.
learn	receive facts	You learn grammar.
teach	give facts	I teach grammar.
loose	not fastened	The clasp is loose.
lose	misplace	I might lose the necklace.
passed	went by	Voters passed the law.
past	gone by	They helped in the past.
principal	main	The principal road is Woodward Parkway.
	head of a school	Murray Cantor is the principal.
principle	rule	You know the principles of grammar.
rise	get up	The cost of living will rise.
raise	lift	Raise your arms.
respectfully	with respect	The audience clapped respectfully.
respectively	in the stated order	The red, blue, and green books belong to John, Billie, and Lee, respectively.
stationary	staying in place	The car was stationary.
stationery	writing paper	Hotels have nice stationery.
than	comparison	Kansas is bigger than Rhode Island.
then	at that time	The state was then very dry.
their	belonging to them	It is their book.
there	place	Put it there.
they're	they are	They're good friends.
weather	atmospheric conditions	The weather is rainy.
whether	if	Whether or not you agree.

NOTES